ALL THE
JUSTICE
MONEY
CAN BUY

ALL THE JUSTICE MONEY CAN BUY

Corporate Greed on Trial

Snigdha Prakash

PUBLISHING

New York

© 2011 Snigdha Prakash

Published by Kaplan Publishing, a division of Kaplan, Inc.
395 Hudson Street
New York, NY 10014

Library of Congress Cataloging-in-Publication data has been applied for.

Printed in the United States of America

10 9 8 7 6 5 4 3 2 1

June 2011

ISBN-13: 978-1-60714-630-8

Kaplan Publishing books are available at special quantity discounts to use for sales promotions, employee premiums, or educational purposes. For more information or to purchase books, please call the Simon & Schuster special sales department at 866-506-1949.

TABLE OF CONTENTS

*For the thousands injured and killed by a medicine
that claimed to soothe, for their families,
and for Carlene Lewis (1954–2006) who had the
courage and imagination to fight back.*

"Hey babe, I have a pain in my chest and it won't go away."

PROLOGUE

Boise, Idaho, September 18, 2001

AT FIRST MIKE HUMESTON blamed the big, dead, heavy pain in the middle of his chest on the Chips Ahoy cookies. He'd grabbed a bag of the chocolate chip cookies and a glass of milk after supper and was eating them as he relaxed in his red leather recliner and watched the TV news in the family room at the back of the house. It was still all about the September 11 attack and very grim. Maybe he hadn't chewed the cookies enough, Mike thought, and he had heartburn. But he'd only eaten two. The pain wouldn't back off. It was a dull, hard pressure right under his rib cage—it felt like something was squeezing his heart.

Mike was 56 years old and he had lived with pain almost every minute of every day of his adult life. He had been a 20-year-old Marine in 1967, when an incoming mortar round on a hillside in Vietnam implanted so much shrapnel into his left knee that, even decades later, the jagged edges of metal fragments would pierce through his skin and catch on his Levis. When the Corps decided his injured knee wouldn't hold up on the front lines, Mike, who had won two Purple Hearts in just over a year of combat, took an honorable discharge.

Mostly Mike pretended the pain wasn't there. Pain is an old friend to me, he would say. The pain had worsened with time. Mike had brought home, buried deep inside his knee, a spray of dirt from the explosion, and over the years he lost most of the cartilage in that knee to infections set off by the dirt.

What cartilage the infections didn't take from Mike's knee, the post office did. For 18 years, Mike had spent his days unloading 70-pound bags stuffed with mail from post office trailers and lugging them across the Boise postal facility's hard concrete floors, to be loaded onto other trailers and sent to their final destinations. The cartilage in his left knee was so worn out that when Mike put the weight of his 6-foot 225-pound frame on it, the bones inside rubbed against each other. Some days Mike could see the bones grinding and his knee would be hot and swollen from pain. Mike blunted the pain's edges with ibuprofen pills every day. A few months earlier, he had torn a ligament in his *good* knee, and the pain was bad enough that the doctor had him on a prescription painkiller.

But Mike had never felt anything like the pain in his chest. It frightened him. He waited for it to go away. When it didn't, he started to think maybe he was having a heart attack.

It passed through Mike's mind that he should tell Mary. She was in the kitchen, cleaning up after supper. But he didn't want to get his wife excited for nothing. Maybe a shower would help. He remembered seeing on TV that if you take aspirin when you're having a heart attack, the heart attack isn't so bad. On his way to the bathroom, he grabbed three aspirins from a kitchen cabinet. He chewed hard and swallowed.

Mary thought it was strange that her husband was heading for the shower when the news was still on. She was almost done in the kitchen—just sweeping the crumbs into a dustpan—when Mike called for her. She could hear in his voice that something was wrong, and found him in their bedroom, putting on a clean undershirt.

"Hey babe, I have a pain in my chest and it won't go away," he said. "I think I'm having a heart attack."

"Get in the car!" Mary ordered, before she remembered the car wasn't there.

Seth had borrowed it to go to a friend's house. Mary called her son to tell him his father had to go to the hospital and to bring the car home. By the time she pulled on her Levis, Seth had pulled up outside the house.

People, mostly out East, would ask her later, "Why didn't you call an ambulance?" Western independence, she would say, and denial. Calling an ambulance would have meant admitting that Mike was having a heart attack. And though he'd said the words, he didn't believe them, and she didn't either.

Mary told herself to be careful as she sped down neighborhood streets. People were out walking their dogs, grabbing the last bit of light. She heard the high school band practicing in the distance. Mike was slouching in his seat with his hands on his knees. I can get him to St. Al's in 15 minutes, Mary thought, as long as we don't hit traffic.

As she drove, Mary went through all the reasons Mike couldn't be having a heart attack. He wasn't overweight or sedentary, he wasn't a smoker, and no one in his family had heart disease. But then there was a list of reasons on the other side, Mary thought: he's a man, and men have heart attacks more than women, and if this wasn't a heart attack, what was it?

Their route to the hospital took them within a few blocks of where Mike's doctor, Greg Lewer, lived, and Mike asked Mary to swing by Lewer's house. They were friends, and Mike was hoping Lewer would say the pain was just heartburn and Mike didn't have to go to the hospital after all. Mary balked at Mike's request, then relented, thinking Mike would get to a doctor sooner that way.

They found Lewer in his backyard, stargazing through his telescope. Mary explained that Mike was having chest pains. Lewer looked at Mike, standing doubled over, with his hands on his knees, trying to breathe. He took Mike's pulse, felt his clammy touch, and told Mary to rush Mike to the hospital.

There was a knot in Mary's stomach as she weaved her car through end-of-the-day neighborhood traffic along Boise's wide, clean streets. Her teeth were clenched so hard her jaw hurt. She pushed away the thought that Mike was having a heart attack, because it was followed by another one—people died from heart attacks. My task right now, she told herself, is to get him to the hospital. He's conscious, he's talking to me. He's not dying.

When they got to the hospital, she dropped Mike off at the entrance to the emergency room and prepared to park the car. As she watched her husband's graying head disappear behind the smoky glass doors of the emergency room, Mary was gripped by panic. I have just seen my husband alive for the last time, she thought. Mike was nine years older than she, and Mary had always thought he'd die before her. They had talked about it before they got married, and she'd made her peace with it. But the thought that he might die, alone, while she was parking the car was intolerable, and she ran out, leaving the key in the ignition. Somebody will move the car if it's in the way, she thought. Or else they'll steal it. She didn't much care what they did.

Mary caught up with Mike just as the nurses were wheeling him out of the triage area and onto the emergency ward for an EKG. When a doctor asked the nurses to give Mike a nitro pill, Mary heard her husband react with shock.

"What, am I having a heart attack?" he asked.

The doctor patted Mike's forearm.

"Yeah, man, you are," he said. "You're taking a heavy hit to the lower half of your heart."

Mary saw Mike sink into himself as he heard that. It was as if he'd had the air knocked out of him. The nurses were rushing to prepare Mike for the cath lab, where doctors would insert a catheter—a thin plastic tube—up his groin and into his coronary arteries in search of the blood clots that had caused the heart attack. Mike watched the bustle, consumed with anger. This was about the stupidest thing that had happened to him. He had four children—the youngest, Seth, was only 17. His own father had died of lung cancer when Mike was 16.

"I eat right. I've never smoked in my life. I don't drink," he thought. "This isn't right. I haven't brought this on."

He didn't understand why the doctors and nurses weren't talking to him. They were mostly talking to Mary.

"Am I going to die?" he thought.

He knew one thing, he wouldn't go easy.

"They'll have to drag me off the planet, one piece at a time," he thought.

Mary wasn't too sure herself if Mike would make it. The nurses were talking in low whispers.

One of them asked her, "Is there a minister or someone I can call?"

They're treating me like a widow, Mary thought, and began to call the children.

She thought of Seth first, who was home alone, waiting for word. But she didn't want him to hear of his father's heart attack over the phone. She called Dr. Lewer to ask if he would go break the news to Seth. Then she called her daughters Amanda, 24, and Olivia, 21, saving the call to her oldest, 27-year-old Rachel, for last. Rachel lived clear across the country in Boca Raton, Florida, with her husband.

Mary walked alongside Mike's gurney through the maze of corridors that connected the emergency room to the cath lab. He was only half conscious when she kissed him goodbye. Their friends, Helen and Duke Bersema, had arrived at the hospital in time to make the walk with her. All three got on their knees to pray out loud in the waiting room. They would accept God's will, they said, but asked that it be the outcome they wanted—that Mike would live.

Both of Mary's daughters brought their boyfriends to the hospital. Amanda's face, usually rosy, was white. How could her healthy, active, careful father have had a heart attack, she asked Mary. He wasn't overweight, he didn't smoke. Olivia was in shock and couldn't speak. She would open her mouth, but there were no words. All she could do was cry. Seth was too agitated to sit with them when he got there. He found the room where Mike was being catheterized and stood outside its doors, looking lonesome and brave in his cargo shorts, t-shirt, and sneakers.

"Is this all I am going to get with him? Twenty-seven years?" Mary thought bitterly, as she sat in silence with her family.

She had met Mike through a mutual friend in February 1973. She was 19, he was 28, and she had known quickly that she wanted to marry him. His clear green eyes had a depth and intensity she trusted. They married a few months later. The children had followed quickly: Rachel in Florida; then Rebecca, who died when she was a day old; Amanda, in North Dakota where Mike worked as a beekeeper; and finally Olivia and Seth, here in Idaho, where the family had moved in 1979. Mary was 47 now, not an age at which she'd expected to become a widow.

IT WAS SETH WHO ran into the waiting to tell them he'd seen Mike being brought out of the procedure room. Unbeknownst to him, his father had spied him too, as orderlies carried Mike in a gurney down the long hospital corridor to the intensive care unit. The sight of his son's running back filled Mike with emotion.

He said to the man in scrubs who was pushing his gurney, "When you are a man, daughters make you want to live, but sons make you want to live forever."

With Seth leading the way, the family hurried to the intensive care recovery room. This is surreal, Mary thought, when she saw her husband lying sedated and semiconscious. But Mike's made it this far, she thought. I think he's going to live.

Seth reached Mike's bedside first. He held his father's hand, and at last, he cried. Mary took Mike's other hand and kissed his forehead. Olivia was still too upset to speak. She just sobbed.

All the attention made Mike uncomfortable, and he searched, groggily, for a way to change the subject. He spotted Amanda's boyfriend, Tom, in the group, and remembering that Tom had just bought a new camera, he made an effort at small talk.

"Tom, did you get that camera working?" he said.

The cardiologist came into the room a few minutes later with a picture of Mike's heart. He showed Mary the clot that had caused Mike's heart attack. Then the cardiologist said something that confounded her.

"I really envy this guy's heart," he said. "He's got huge arteries. They're like garden hoses."

Mary stared at him, nonplussed. My husband's had a heart attack, she thought, and this guy's telling me he envies his heart?

The cardiologist told Mary he saw no reason for Mike's heart attack. He stood near her, his arms crossed, one index finger tapping his lips, and asked her matter-of-factly what drugs her husband was on.

"What are you talking about? My husband's a straight arrow," she thought, until she realized the doctor wasn't asking about street drugs.

"Nothing," she said, "He just takes aspirin, ibuprofen, and Vioxx."

Dr. Lewer had prescribed the Vioxx for pain after Mike tore a ligament in his good knee at work.

The cardiologist stopped tapping his lip and held up his index finger, as soon as Mary said, "Vioxx."

"Don't let him take that anymore," he told her.

Confused again, Mary asked why.

"There's a little-known study that shows Vioxx can cause heart attacks," he said.

Mike Humeston had taken 56 Vioxx pills over the course of five months before his heart attack.

Years later, Mary could still remember her shock.

"You could have knocked me over with a feather," she said.

She knew the government had to approve drugs before they could be sold. How could Vioxx be on the market if they knew it caused heart attacks? She came to believe the cardiologist had saved her husband's life by alerting her to Vioxx's potential risks long before they were generally known. Other doctors at the hospital were also apparently unaware of them, and continued Mike's daily Vioxx for two more days. When they got home, Mary made sure her husband never took a Vioxx again.

IT WAS A FEW MINUTES after noon, on Sunday, September 15, 2002 in Waupaca, Wisconsin, when 15-year-old Kyle Hermans knocked on the door of his father's second-floor apartment. The Green Bay Packers were about to start playing the New Orleans Saints, and Kyle and his father were diehard Packers fans. But his father didn't answer the door, and Kyle went back downstairs. He wasn't carrying his key. He only spent weekends at the apartment; his parents had been divorced since he was a baby, and he spent the week at his mother's.

His father's van was parked outside and it was unlocked. Kyle tuned the radio to the football game and waited. At half-time, when there was still no sign of his father, Kyle borrowed a neighbor's ladder. He made his way around the side of the house to where he had noticed an open window, and climbed up the ladder.

He saw his father through the window—lying face down on the floor in black warmup pants, a t-shirt, and white socks with the TV on. Kyle hoisted himself into the room, and knew as soon as he put his hand to his father's back. His father was dead.

"You have to come over right now," he told his mother on the phone, but he didn't say why.

He was sitting on the steps outside, shaking, when Kim Spoerl pulled up.

"Dad," he said, when she asked him what was wrong.

Spoerl found her ex-husband sprawled on his living room floor with a clear fluid oozing out of his mouth and nose. Brian Hermans was pronounced dead later that afternoon by the Waupaca County deputy coroner. In addition to his son, Hermans was survived by three siblings, Kathleen and Kevin, both of Green Bay, and Matthew of Saukville, Wisconsin; and by his parents, Vincent and Doris, also of Green Bay.

Many years later, Vincent Hermans recalled how he and his wife learned of their son's death on September 16, the day after Brian Hermans's body was found. The elder Hermanses had been away for the weekend and arrived home to find their children Kevin and Kathleen in the driveway. They had come to break the news to their parents.

"My wife went in the house first...and I heard her scream," Vincent Hermans recalled. "And then I went in, and they told me too."

An autopsy revealed that a "firm," "red-black" blood clot had lodged in one of Brian Hermans's arteries to cause an "acute myocardial infarction." Hermans, 44, had died of a massive heart attack.

The finding shocked his family.

Brian Hermans had been the fittest of his siblings. He had played racquetball competitively in college and had played a mean game until he died. He was an avid biker and an all-round athlete. His golf clubs were next to the couch when he died, ready for the early morning round he had hoped to squeeze in before the football game. The only health problem his family knew Brian to have was pain from a high-school knee injury, which had troubled him for many years.

The coroner's report noted that Brian Hermans was on two medications when he died: the antidepressant Fluoxetine, better known by its brand name, Prozac; and Vioxx, for the knee pain. His brother Matthew found the Vioxx prescription bottle next to the phone in Brian's kitchen with four pills remaining.

By the time Brian Hermans died, several large studies had shown that Vioxx could cause heart attacks. But it would be a long time before his family thought to ask if the pills played any part in Brian's death.

"This is a bad drug. We've got to do something about it."

CHAPTER I

The Beginning

THE LAWSUITS BEGAN WITH a phone call from a saleswoman at a Houston department store to a lawyer named Carlene Lewis. The saleswoman knew Lewis through Lewis's mother, who shopped at the department store. It was the fall of 2000, and Louise Bell, then 73, told Lewis of a car accident the year before in which she had banged up her knee. She was given a prescription painkiller, Bell said, and soon after she started taking it, her blood pressure shot up. It went so high that at the store's Estee Lauder counter, where she worked, the girls would say to her, "Louise, what's wrong with you? You're beet-red."

Eight months later, on her way to a formal dance, Bell had the worst headache of her life. She started babbling, and her date brought her home. Later that evening, Bell suffered a seizure. A cardiologist said it had been brought on by high blood pressure. He blamed the painkiller. Bell was forced to cut back her hours at the department store and was in debt. Could Lewis do anything to help, Bell asked. The painkiller, of course, was Vioxx.

Lewis, a soft-spoken woman who crackled with energy, promised to investigate. Vioxx was still a new drug, and in the United States, the most public controversies over its safety lay in the future. But

1

in Europe and Great Britain, scientists and regulators had begun to sound alarms.

Lewis's law partner, Shelly Sanford, remembers the day Lewis walked into Sanford's office with the fruits of her research—a stack of folders four inches thick. She threw them on Sanford's desk.

"This is a bad drug," Lewis said. "We've got to do something about it."

Lewis began by writing to manufacturer Merck & Company about Bell's adverse reaction and asking the company for compensation. The company's general counsel wrote back that there was no basis in Texas law for Bell's claim. She said Bell's medical records showed a history of high blood pressure, and that Merck had told doctors to use Vioxx cautiously with such patients. Eventually, Merck offered $7,500 to close the matter. Lewis hadn't thought of Bell's case as a big moneymaker. She'd taken it on mostly because Bell was friendly with her mother. But she thought Merck's offer was entirely inadequate.

She and Sanford decided to dig deeper and find out how big a problem Vioxx really was.

They did it discreetly, with an ad over the July 4 holiday in the Galveston County *Daily News*. Galveston was about 50 miles from Houston, far enough away that the ad was unlikely to tip off other plaintiffs' lawyers in Houston. "If you or your loved one has suffered heart attacks, strokes, high blood pressure, or seizures on Vioxx or Celebrex, call Shelly Sanford," the ad said, and listed an 800 number. The ad elicited responses mostly from people who'd had problems with Vioxx, and they got enough of those to know that bad things were happening to a lot more people than just Louise Bell. The two attorneys followed up with a month of TV and radio ads in Houston, this time focusing exclusively on finding potential plaintiffs with Vioxx injuries. By the end of the summer, Sanford and Lewis had collected 300 potential cases of heart attacks, strokes, and high blood pressure linked to Vioxx. Lewis sent another letter to Merck, asking if the company wanted to settle. This time the brush-off came from a big New York law firm, Hughes Hubbard & Reed, and it was a little more artful than the earlier one from Merck's general counsel. After several phone conversations with a midlevel partner at Hughes Hubbard, Lewis concluded that he was only interested in gathering information about the claims, and no settlement was in the offing. She had set up a meeting with him in New York. Over Sanford's objection, she cancelled it.

"We need to get serious about this litigation," Lewis told Sanford.

Thus began the two women's crusade against the most respected drug company in America. Sanford would say later that had Merck settled Louise Bell's claim, she and Lewis would never have taken on the fight.

"We would have moved on. I'm certain of it," she said.

LEWIS WAS AN UNLIKELY warrior. A product of Harvard College and the University of Virginia law school, Lewis had spent most of her 18-year legal career defending corporations against exactly the kind of product liability lawsuits she was now planning to bring. She did that first at the Houston firm of Sewell & Riggs, then five years later, in 1989, at the firm she formed with another Sewell & Riggs partner, Danny Goforth. By the time Sanford joined them in 2000, Lewis's heart was set on changing the focus of her practice, from fighting plaintiffs to representing them. Sanford was an old hand at that.

She had cut her teeth as a plaintiffs' lawyer, working for John O'Quinn, the legendary Texan who won billions in jury verdicts and settlements from tobacco, chemical, and drug companies. The two women met in the early 1990s, when O'Quinn brought in Goforth and Lewis to help on a case. Sanford was already assigned to the case, and wasn't too keen on the new arrangement until her first meeting with Lewis, at which Lewis arrived with a boxful of documents. Many lawyers would have shown up for such a meeting unprepared, Sanford thought, and she was impressed that Lewis had done her homework.

It turned out they were kindred spirits, smart and serious about their work, and a strong religious faith. Each had a stubborn streak. They were devoted mothers—Lewis had two young daughters, Sanford had one—and they were close in age. Lewis was on the cusp of turning 40; Sanford was in her early 30s when they met. As law partners, they often broke away from the office to walk the streets of downtown Houston, talking, always talking, about work, their families, and anything else that crossed their minds. Nothing was out of bounds. In the tight, mostly male club that was the plaintiffs' bar, the lean, blonde-haired Lewis and the big-boned, dark-haired Sanford were fast friends. Their friendship stood them in good stead in the long fight against Merck.

"We didn't know enough to know how tough the road would be," Sanford would say later. "We would get pounded. She would turn to me and ask 'Is this going to work? Are we right?'"

Sanford said she would tell Lewis they *were* right and they would prevail.

"Optimism was one of my gifts. Patience and being right were hers," Sanford said. "She was a real visionary about Vioxx," she said.

TWO THINGS WERE PERFECTLY clear to them from the start: First, being small fry, they needed some plaintiffs' lawyers with fearsome reputations to get Merck's attention. Second, they needed gobs of money, to hopscotch the country questioning Merck executives, hire expert witnesses who could make sense of the science, and fight Merck's stalling maneuvers before state judges from California to Florida.

The firm's third (and senior) partner, Danny Goforth, backed them, but warily, and Sanford and Lewis felt their relations with him grow strained. Both women were working full-time on Vioxx, and neither was bringing much money into the firm. They tried to make their dollars stretch—driving to meetings whenever they could, flying Southwest when they couldn't, taking day trips to avoid spending on hotels, and brown-bagging lunch or skipping it altogether. They worked until 9 or 10 every night, including Saturdays, Sundays, and holidays. There was so much to do, and they couldn't afford to hire other lawyers to help. Vioxx was either going to pay off big or be a financial catastrophe.

Though they hadn't gone into the Vioxx litigation intending to bet the farm, Sanford would say later, "You move forward one step at a time. Eventually, you're all in."

Lewis and Sanford went looking for allies to file additional cases against Merck and bring their firepower to the fight. Many people turned them away because Vioxx was a popular, heavily-marketed drug. Plaintiffs' lawyers liked to wait until problem drugs were taken off the market before filing product liability lawsuits.

"You're crazy! Call us, when Vioxx goes off the market," Lewis and Sanford were told again and again.

But the women persevered, and eventually they persuaded other lawyers to join forces with them. In Los Angeles, they enlisted the veteran plaintiffs' lawyer Tom Girardi. He had made his name and fortune suing companies for dumping toxic wastes, most famously in the case depicted in the movie *Erin Brockovich*. On the East Coast, they enlisted an up-and-coming New York lawyer named Chris Seeger, who had formed a firm with Stephen Weiss, the son of the famed securities class action lawyer Melvyn Weiss. Seeger flew to Houston to meet with Sanford and Lewis over breakfast on a Saturday morning in June 2001. He came prepared to turn them down.

Merck was, as he later put it, "a monster company with a great reputation." But something about Lewis caused him to change his mind.

"It was Carlene's passion. I remember being blown away by it," Seeger said.

Six months later, in early 2002, Seeger flew with Sanford to Vanderbilt University, where they met the author of a new paper published in the British medical journal *The Lancet* that had raised serious concerns about Vioxx's safety. Wayne Ray was well-respected in his field, and as far as Seeger could tell, his concerns about Vioxx were guided by the science. He harbored no grudge against the pharmaceutical industry.

"That's when we went all in," Seeger said.

Lewis and Sanford's hardest sell was in their own backyard, to a Houston lawyer named Mark Lanier, with whom they'd tried a few cases. They'd found him fun to work with, happy during trials, not a jerk, as many trial lawyers could be. And he was brilliant. They hounded Lanier for more than a year. "This will change your career. This is made for you," Lewis told Lanier over and over. But he was reluctant to jump in.

Walking in a spring rain from their downtown office to his in 2002, Sanford suggested Lewis give Lanier a polite ultimatum.

"Tell him, 'If you don't decide today, the case is going to John O'Quinn,'" she said to Lewis. She knew Lanier saw O'Quinn as both mentor and rival.

Sanford and Lewis didn't want the cases to go to O'Quinn. Sanford knew from working with O'Quinn for many years that he was no fun during trials, and she said "he took *all* the money afterwards."

Lewis did as Sanford had suggested. Turning to Lanier on her way out of the meeting, she said gently, "Well, if you don't want it, it's going to O'Quinn." That did the trick.

Lanier intercepted Lewis and Sanford as they were heading out to the elevator. "Come back, come back," he called. "We're doing this!" Sanford and Lewis walked back to his office, and now Lanier could barely contain his enthusiasm. He squatted with his feet on the couch, as they talked. Sanford and Lewis found his boyish enthusiasm endearing and treasured the memory for a long time.

Years later, Lanier remembered things differently. He said he took all of Lewis and Sanford's cases "almost immediately" after the two women approached him. And he said Lewis had never mentioned the possibility that John O'Quinn might get the cases.

"If I had thought John O'Quinn had been shopped the cases, I would have called John and talked to John about it," Lanier said. He had considered O'Quinn a friend and wouldn't have wanted the cases to come between them, he said. (O'Quinn died in 2009.)

By 2003, Sanford, Lewis, and their allies had all the pieces in place. They had a class action suit on behalf of injured users in Illinois, one on behalf of Merck investors in New Orleans, and a third on behalf of insurers in New Jersey. They also had a couple hundred personal injury cases in courts across the country, the first of which was inching its way towards trial. Merck had turned over millions of pages of internal documents, and there were more to come. In a business filled with sharp elbows and inflated self-regard, Lewis and Sanford had pulled together a diverse coalition of big talents and big egos to work for a common goal.

"There was something special about them as a team. They were these two little lawyers out of Houston, with no resources, no money. They were disarming. They weren't threatening to anyone's ego," Seeger said later, reflecting on how they did it.

Lewis and Sanford had a slightly different take. They said when two women put their mind to something, "Watch out!"

THEN, ON THE MORNING of September 30, 2004, came a bombshell. Shelly Sanford felt her BlackBerry's nonstop buzzing in her sleep. She knew it was somewhere on her bed. When she couldn't ignore the buzzing any longer, she roused herself to find it and see what all the fuss was about. It was lawyers on the East Coast, an hour ahead of Houston, sending stunning news. Merck was pulling Vioxx from the market because of a new study in which Vioxx subjects had heart attacks and strokes at twice the rate of those given sugar pills.

Sanford wrote Lewis right away. Lewis's response shot back through the ether, "Is this a joke?"

It was no joke. By the time the markets opened for trading, Merck's stock was in free fall. Vioxx was one of Merck's crown jewels. It had brought in one-eighth of Merck's total revenue, or roughly $2.7 billion in 2003, $2.6 billion in 2002, and $2.4 billion in 2001. Investors grappled all day with the news, and by day's end, the company had lost more than a fourth of its market value.

Sanford and Lewis felt sure that their lawsuits had played a role in bringing Merck to its costly decision. If nothing more ever happened with the Vioxx cases, they felt they had achieved something important. Vioxx could not hurt and kill any more.

When Sanford got to the office, the firm's senior partner, Danny Goforth, greeted her with his arms aloft in a V. "We're rich!" he shouted. The thought hadn't crossed Sanford's mind, and she found it ironic that it had occurred to Goforth, given his grudging support for the lawsuits up to then.

Chris Seeger learned about the withdrawal in the back of a crowded courtroom in downtown Philadelphia. He noticed lawyers all across the courtroom were turning away from the seven federal judges on the bench to bend their heads, almost prayerfully, over their BlackBerries. Something's going on, Seeger thought, and fished out his own BlackBerry. He was filled with the sweet thrill of vindication when he saw the Google news alert. As Seeger left the courtroom minutes later, lawyers were coming up to him to congratulate him on his prescience. "This is big," they said.

It had been three years since Lewis and Sanford had approached him for help with the Vioxx fight. Afterwards, he had put out the word that Seeger Weiss was looking for Vioxx cases. The cases began to trickle in from smaller firms. Now that trickle would become a flood. The newest front in the tort wars had just opened, and Seeger had the inside track.

A tort (derived from the Latin "torquere," meaning "to twist") is literally "a twisting—an injuring of another that the law empowers the injured person to straighten out by way of a lawsuit," to use the words of the legal scholar Richard Nagareda. Tort law came into its own as a branch of the law in the late 19th century as industrialization gave rise to new injuries, among them, factory accidents. By the mid-20th century, American courts had revolutionized product liability law, first by enabling consumers to sue not only those with whom they had a direct contractual relationship, such as the person from whom they purchased a product, but also the product's manufacturers and designers; and second, by extending the concept of a "defective product" to include "systematic design errors and inadequacies in the provision of risk information to the ultimate consumer." Mass tort litigation took off in the late 20th century as mass production and mass marketing became the norm. With millions of people exposed to a mass-produced product, the number of injuries could run into the tens and even hundreds of thousands, even if the injuries occurred only rarely. Hence, mass torts.

"Vioxx had all the makings of a mega-mass tort. Pain, after all, was a common condition, and almost 20 million Americans had used Vioxx since its introduction in 1999. Changes to federal law around that time had freed drug companies to market prescription drugs directly to consumers, and Merck had blanketed the country with upbeat television commercials. The commercials showed older men and women walking the dog, gardening, bathing a grandchild—in short, enjoying their golden years with the help of a daily Vioxx.

"Ask your doctor about Vioxx," the ads said. "And find out what Vioxx can do for *you*." Millions did. In an article published in *The Lancet* shortly after Vioxx was withdrawn, a senior FDA scientist estimated that Vioxx had caused between 88,000 and 140,000 cases of serious heart disease in the United States over its five-and-a-half-year life on the market. Roughly half were likely fatal.

Within days of pulling Vioxx from the market, Merck moved to get its arms around the anticipated crush of Vioxx cases, filing a motion to have all cases transferred to a single federal court for pretrial proceedings. The transfer procedure has increasingly become the judiciary's primary tool to keep the tens of thousands of individual lawsuits that make up a product liability mass tort from clogging up courts nationwide. The thinking is that it's more efficient for one judge (rather than multiple judges in courts across the country) to supervise those proceedings and make decisions on such important matters as what evidence each side is entitled to demand from the other, which witnesses must be produced to testify under oath in advance of a trial, or whether a scientific expert's testimony is admissible. The bundled cases are known colloquially as an "MDL," short for multidistrict litigation, because the cases are drawn from courts throughout the country. The federal judge in charge of them is called the "MDL judge."

The MDL system's ultimate aim is to bring about negotiated settlements to mass torts with as few trials and as speedily as possible. If a mass tort does not settle, the individual cases are sent back to the courts where they were filed to await trial. (Class actions, in which a plaintiff sues as a representative on behalf of everyone with the same claim, usually cannot be used in mass tort cases because of the variations in individual injuries, a point the Supreme Court drove home in the 1990s when it rejected two asbestos class actions.)

Corporate defendants like multidistrict litigation because it reduces the burden and expense of fighting in multiple courts around the country, and because the massive proceedings tend to slow down the litigation process. Also, multidistrict litigation puts the litigation's center of gravity squarely in federal court, which corporate defendants tend to favor over state courts. (That is so even when many cases in the mass tort remain in state court.)

Lewis and Sanford didn't know all this about multidistrict litigations. But they were about to find out.

SIX WEEKS AFTER MERCK'S stunning announcement, at the "Mass Torts Made Perfect" conference in Las Vegas's Venetian Resort, Sanford and Lewis found the long, darkened hallway outside the conference rooms packed with lawyers by 7:30 in the morning. Many appeared to have put in a full night at the Venetian's casinos. Their faces were tired and their eyes were bloodshot. But they were humming with purpose.

"How many Vioxx cases do you have? How are we going to get more?" they asked each other, as they stood in tight clusters that took up every inch of available space. "Wouldn't it be great if we got 1,000 cases?" Sanford heard one say.

These were the profession's marketing experts, who had mastered the art of building "inventories" of plaintiffs and cases. They ran television ads, set up phone banks, and sifted through the thousands of callers to find plaintiffs with viable claims. Then they referred the cases to larger law firms and waited for what they hoped would be a quick and generous settlement. In Vioxx, they smelled an easy kill.

"It feels like a poster for tort reform," Lewis remarked wryly to Sanford.

Among trial lawyers, "tort reform" was an epithet. It was the term pro-business interests used to describe the wave of laws in the mid-1980s and after, which were passed to make it harder for people to sue businesses for any kind of personal injury. Lewis was speaking with her tongue planted firmly in cheek, and yet... her sleepy little tort was growing up, and Lewis didn't like all that it was becoming.

In the era of multidistrict litigation, mass torts offer one prize even richer than the large inventories of cases that the marketers at the conference hoped to assemble. The richest prize is a seat on a small committee, called the plaintiffs' steering committee, whose members get a cut of the winnings from each and every case in the tort in which plaintiffs prevail. The MDL judge appoints the committee to supervise the pretrial work and to represent the interests of all lawyers with cases in the MDL "bundle." Members of the committee also finance the work, often through large monthly assessments. After a handful of trials, when the MDL judge pressures the two sides to settle, the plaintiffs' steering committee members play a lead role in negotiating an agreement with the defendants.

For top plaintiffs' lawyers, therefore, the game now was to win a seat on the Vioxx steering committee, and they were using the Las Vegas conference to lobby their peers. Sanford and Lewis learned that two of their early allies, Chris Seeger and Andy Birchfield, were vying to be co-leaders of the plaintiffs' steering committee. (Birchfield, a partner at Beasley, Allen, Methvin, Portis & Miles in Montgomery, Alabama, had been investigating Vioxx independently at about the same time as Lewis and Sanford, and filed his first Vioxx case soon after they did.) Chris Seeger had swung by the conference the night before to float the idea and lobby key lawyers. (The MDL judge appoints the committee, but peer support is vital to securing the top positions.)

A flamboyant Louisiana lawyer named Danny Becnel was campaigning as well. Becnel handed Sanford his card at the conference, with a note on the back, "I'm forming a PSC [plaintiffs' steering committee]. You are invited. Danny." Becnel sounded as if he had invented the Vioxx tort himself, Sanford thought. It was just comical. She didn't take him seriously.

But one week later Sanford found herself heading to New Orleans for a dinner meeting of plaintiffs' lawyers, organized by Becnel. Lewis couldn't go—Sanford promised to take notes and deliver a full report on the evening. Becnel had reserved the famed back room of Antoine's in the French Quarter. Plaintiffs' lawyers had met there almost exactly a decade earlier to launch a joint offensive against Big Tobacco, and he appeared to have chosen the venue for its symbolism.

Sanford found the narrow street in front of Antoine's clogged with limousines; Becnel's guests were arriving in style. The hallway leading to the back room rang with male laughter. A few men were accompanied by women who did not appear to be their wives. In her notes, Sanford described them as "arm candy," all dolled-up New Orleans style, in party dresses and high heels. Sanford was wearing business clothes, as was the one other woman lawyer present.

Becnel greeted Sanford with his arms spread wide, as if to encompass the whole scene. "Am I good, huh? Am I good or what?" he laughed, "This is how it happens, baby!" There was something seductive, and scary, in the way Becnel had taken charge, Sanford thought, and she still wasn't sure what to make of him.

They gathered around a long rectangular table, and Becnel got right to the business at hand. "We owe this meeting to a few people I want to recognize—Chris Seeger and Andy Birchfield," he said. "I move to appoint these two men as our leaders in the MDL. Do I have a second?"

Someone in the group yelled out, "Second!"

"Any nays?" Becnel asked.

There were no dissenters.

"The ayes have it, and we all agree. A toast to our leaders!" he said.

Sanford and Lewis supported their friends as co-leaders, but Sanford was stunned at how quickly that vote happened.

"Wow, this is a weird process," she thought.

Don Barrett, a veteran of the fight against Big Tobacco, spoke up and slowed things down. Hang on, he said, we all need to discuss this with the people who aren't here too. He had the room's unspoken assent, and the moment passed without the toast. Before long, white-coated waiters appeared with platters of fried oysters, fish with jumbo lump crab meat piled on top, and beignets. It was time to eat.

In a speech afterwards, Seeger made a point of singling out Lewis and Sanford's contributions, and Sanford returned the compliment when Seeger invited her to speak. She said Seeger hadn't hesitated for a moment when she and Lewis had approached him for help years earlier. Before she left, Sanford made a point of congratulating Seeger and Birchfield individually. We want you in leadership positions, she said.

Three months later, in February 2005, the Vioxx cases were consolidated under Judge Eldon E. Fallon of the Eastern District of Louisiana in New Orleans. Fallon appointed Seeger and Birchfield as co-leaders of the plaintiffs' steering committee. They had no competition for the positions, which was unusual for a large mass tort. Fallon also named Carlene Lewis to the committee; a proud moment for her. Mark Lanier applied but was not chosen, and put a good face on the snub later.

"There's a real camaraderie" among MDL lawyers, Lanier said. "I had never been in the MDL club," he said.

Still, it was an inauspicious beginning to relations between Lanier and the MDL.

AS IT HAPPENED, LANIER tried the first Vioxx case in the country. It was a Texas state case that had not been consolidated into the federal MDL because one of the named defendants was a Texas doctor who had conducted research for Merck. Lewis and Sanford had filed the case and later turned it over to Lanier. The plaintiff, Carol Ernst, was a widow whose 59-year-old marathoner-husband had died suddenly in 2001, after taking Vioxx for six months. The official cause of death was arrhythmia, or an irregular heartbeat, a condition that Merck said had never been linked to Vioxx. (Merck's defense ignored the fact that heart attacks, which *had* been linked to Vioxx, were known to cause arrhythmia.)

The trial was held in July 2005, about 40 miles south of downtown Houston, in the small town of Angleton, and it was covered by media from around the world.

I remember my first glimpse of Lanier across the packed courtroom a few moments before he was to give his opening statement. (I was covering the trial for National Public Radio.) Lanier was dressed in the sober blue uniform that lawyers favor, but his demeanor was distinctly casual. He sat near the edge of his chair at the plaintiff's counsel table, looking as if he might leap out of it without warning. He grinned irrepressibly. His face was boyish, his glasses nerdy. I thought he looked like a kid in a candy store on allowance day. When he stood up, his 6 foot 1 inch frame looked almost gangly. I gazed at him with disbelief. *This* was the man charged with opening the fight against Merck?

It turned out that Lanier's playfulness concealed an uncommon mix of gifts. He was unafraid to delve into the complicated science underlying the case, he knew how to go toe to toe with Merck's lawyers, *and* he had a strong connection with juries. Funny, self-deprecating, unapologetically idiosyncratic, and *very* well prepared, Lanier was an athlete at the top of his game. After a five-week trial, the jury awarded Carol Ernst a quarter of a billion dollars in damages. Under Texas law, Ernst's damages would be capped at $26 million, but the jury was sending a message.

"Respect us. That's the message," said one juror afterwards. "Respect us."

Theodore Mayer, a partner at the firm of Hughes Hubbard & Reed and the man in charge of coordinating Merck's national defense strategy, had flown in to Angleton for the verdict. Mayer was a slight, soft-spoken man with graying hair. In the months leading up to that trial, he often worked late into the evening at his Manhattan office and, at least sometimes, answered his own telephone. We had spoken a few times on the phone, so when I learned he was in the courtroom I asked his public relations person to introduce us. We shook hands and made small talk as we waited for the jury, and I noted that the man who had been so self-assured over the phone was suffering a case of nerves. His hands on that steamy afternoon in August 2005 were cold and clammy. I caught sight of Mayer after the verdict, looking shaken, almost white.

Outside the courthouse, Lanier was crowing about the victory to a gaggle of reporters and television cameras.

"My message to Merck is: You want to go again?" he said. "We're just getting warmed up."

Lanier had been a big name in Texas even before the Ernst verdict. Now he had won the kind of outsized award that drives companies to settle, and he was a star on the national stage.

THE SECOND VIOXX TRIAL took place a month later, in September 2005, in Atlantic City, New Jersey. Mike Humeston was the plaintiff.

Mike had not expected to sue Merck. But a couple of months after his heart attack in September 2001, he started getting letters from lawyers. First, one, then, another; pretty soon he had four. They all said the same thing—you've had a Vioxx heart attack, and we want to represent you. Mike never did figure out how law firms up and down the East Coast found out about his heart attack. But the letters got him thinking, "I got a wife and kids. I got to protect myself." He worried that the Vioxx still in his body could give him another heart attack, that he'd have to go to the cardiologist for the rest of his life, and where would regular people like him and Mary find the money for that?

Mike figured he didn't need out-of-town lawyers to take care of this. In the phone book, under "Product Liability Lawyers," he found a lawyer in Boise, and Mike mailed him a video of the procedure that doctors at the hospital had done to find where his arteries were blocked. The lawyer called back the day after he got the video. "I called in a doctor," the lawyer said, "and he said there's no reason for you to have a heart attack." It looks like you've got a good case, the lawyer said, but it was too big for him to handle. Three referrals later, Mike finally found a firm that was big enough to take on Merck. His lawyer was Chris Seeger.

Mike and Mary went to meet Seeger in New York, and Mary was surprised at how young he was—he looked to be in his 40s. Still, she liked the way he looked you in the eye when he talked to you. He brought in the other lawyers on his Vioxx team to meet them. "This is Mike Humeston. He's the man who is going to bring Merck to justice," Seeger said. "Wow!" Mary thought.

Mike expected he would win his case at trial. It was cut and dried. He didn't have heart disease or high cholesterol. He had no reason to have a heart attack except for the Vioxx. All the facts would come out at the trial, Mike thought, and before the end, Merck would say, "We're willing to take care of Mr. Humeston's medical bills for the rest of his life." They'd make him whole for the time he'd spent away from work, and he and Mary would go home to Idaho.

Mary was just as confident. She hadn't been too impressed by Lanier's big win in Texas. "Duh," Mary had thought when she heard about it. Of course Merck lost. She believed Merck's guilt was glaringly obvious. "They knew damn well what Vioxx did," she thought, but they gambled with their patients' hearts. "How *dare* they?" she thought.

On opening day, Mary and Mike found a wall of TV cameras, satellite trucks, and reporters outside the courthouse in Atlantic City. Mary held onto Mike's hand and concentrated on following the paralegal who escorted them to a courtroom packed with plaintiffs' lawyers and more reporters from around the country. This trial is much bigger than us, she thought again, and the crowd buoyed Mary's resolve.

Mike's case was the first to be tried on Merck's home turf of New Jersey.

"You're going to be the point man," Seeger told Mike.

Mike had taken a lot of fire as a Marine in Vietnam, and he thought he was ready. But he felt sick to his stomach when Merck's lawyers attacked. They insinuated he hadn't taken all the Vioxx he said he had and was trying to scam the system.

"That's not true," Mike protested to his lawyers.

They told him to calm down. This is worse than Vietnam, Mike thought. At least he had been able to defend himself there. In the courtroom, he felt helpless.

Mary also grew disillusioned as the trial progressed. She had grown up poor in the swamps of Northern Florida, the daughter of the town drunk. She had used her mind and her determination to leave that life behind, and it hurt her to be treated like she and Mike were using his heart attack as a way to live on Easy Street. It made her feel dirty. They're talking about us like we aren't even in the room, she thought, like we're invisible nobodies. A couple of times Mary found herself in the cramped ladies room with Merck lawyers. They didn't speak to her, but their steely gazes unnerved her. Mary began taking a paralegal with her to the bathroom.

Their lawyers had told them the trial would last a week or ten days. It dragged on for seven weeks, and Mike and Mary settled into a dreary routine at the dark, dingy, and smoke-filled Trump Marina Hotel Casino. They woke up, ordered oatmeal for breakfast, ate it in their room, and took a cab to the courthouse, where they waited in a tiny back room until the judge called court into session. The lawyers had sandwiches brought in for lunch. Dinner was in the hotel cafeteria. A couple of times, Mike thought he got food poisoning from something he ate there. Everywhere they went they were escorted by a paralegal, and they were under strict instructions not to talk to anyone outside the trial team. Though surrounded by people, they felt alone. The lawyers returned to their homes on the weekends, but Mike and Mary stayed in Atlantic City. (Idaho was too far to fly to and back in a weekend.) One of the paralegals stayed with them; Mike thought it was to make sure they didn't mingle with outsiders, and he felt like a rat in a box.

As the weeks went on, Mike noticed that some of the jurors had stopped looking at him and Mary. That was a bad sign. Still, he was stunned when the jury came back against them, 8–1.

Mike had been concerned about Seeger's performance in the courtroom since early in the trial. "You need to tell Chris to quit apologizing to the jury," he told a member of Seeger's team at one point. Like many plaintiffs' lawyers, 45-year-old Chris Seeger had attained his position and considerable wealth by settling cases rather than by trying them. He was a schmoozer and a deal-maker. Mike's case was only the second he had tried in his 18-year career, and Seeger thought he had it in the bag. While the jury deliberated, the lawyers celebrated at a festive dinner. Mike and Mary went too.

"I don't see the reason for the euphoria before the jury comes back," Mike told Mary.

Mike and Mary didn't see Seeger after the jury delivered its verdict that November afternoon in 2005. The next morning they left Atlantic City for the airport in Philadelphia and their journey home. In the United Airlines boarding lounge, Mary sat next to a man who was reading about the verdict in the newspaper. "Holy cow," she heard him say. "I can't believe Merck won. That's too bad." Mike said something in response and the man looked up from his paper. He looked at Mike. Then he looked at Mike's picture in the paper. "It's you," the man said. "I'm very, very sorry."

Mary was numb on the long flight home. But she sobbed when her friends held her in their arms at Boise airport. They said they were proud of her and of Mike for standing up to Merck. When she went back to work, co-workers said, "You thought you were going to get rich. Here you are, back at work." People can be so cruel, Mary thought.

LANIER HAD PREDICTED SEEGER would lose his case. On the trial's opening day, Seeger happened to turn on the TV in his hotel room to find Lanier, the media's new Vioxx darling, holding forth on CNBC's "Squawk Box" business program. Lanier said he had turned down Seeger's request for help in trying it. Seeger, who hadn't asked for help, seethed as he listened. (Lanier said later the lawyer who referred the Humeston case to Seeger had made the request.)

Lanier's remarks may have been born partly of pique. After his big victory in the Texas case, the plaintiffs' steering committee of the federal MDL, which Seeger co-chaired, had come calling to stake its claim to roughly $1 million of the $253 million jury award. The matter was moot until Merck paid up. But Lanier registered a protest in the press. He said he didn't want to pay, because the PSC had not done any work on his case.

Toward the end of the Humeston trial, Lanier lobbed another grenade Seeger's way. He announced he had formed a new coalition of lawyers to wage war against Merck in state court. (California, Texas, and New Jersey had mass tort consolidation regimes of their own, and state court cases were not part of the federal MDL.) He said he wanted nothing more to do with the federal MDL process.

"Merck would like to keep everything bottled up in one judge's courtroom and buy time and pick the worst cases and lower the value of an ultimate settlement," Perry Weitz, another prominent member of the new coalition, told the *Wall Street Journal*. "We want to be able to pick our own cases in the places we want them to be tried."

Judge Fallon took note of the rebellion at a monthly status conference a few days after the *Journal* story ran. Without mentioning Lanier by name, Fallon made it clear that he would exercise his influence in "formal and informal" ways to prevent the breakaway coalition from derailing the work of the federal MDL. Fallon said he would try five representative cases so that each side could evaluate its strengths and weaknesses. After the trials were completed, he said, he would meet with both sides to see if the entire mass tort could be resolved.

The breakaway coalition did not amount to much, but in the spring of 2006, Lanier and Weitz's firm did join forces to try two cases in a single trial in New Jersey state court. Lanier took the lead role. It was his second Vioxx trial, and remarkably, he won again. The damages included a $9 million punitive award—which, while puny compared to the quarter billion the Texas jury had awarded, was hefty by New Jersey standards. Pharmaceuticals were New Jersey's leading industry, and it was the first time ever that a jury in the state had awarded punitive damages to someone suing a drug company.

"I've got a big grin on my face from ear to ear," Lanier told National Public Radio as he drove to the airfield where his private plane awaited. "Merck said they couldn't be beat in their backyard. Merck said the punitive finding in Ernst was a fluke, a runaway jury, an uneducated jury…I'm smiling." Ernst, of course, was Lanier's first case against Merck.

IT WAS AROUND THAT time that Carlene Lewis learned she was dying. The first signs of trouble had surfaced during the Ernst trial when Lewis, an avid athlete, was often inexplicably exhausted.

"I don't know what's going on," she confessed to Sanford.

On October 16, 2005, Sanford drove to Lewis's house to pick her up for another Vioxx meeting. She found Lewis tired, out of breath, and in so much pain she could barely get into the car. Lewis's general practitioner had prescribed vitamins after the Ernst trial for her fatigue, which hadn't helped, but Lewis was soldiering on.

"I don't care what you say. We're going to the hospital," Sanford told Lewis that morning, and they did.

At the hospital, an ultrasound revealed a row of blood clots—clot after clot after clot—running along the length of each of Lewis's legs. A massive tumor in Lewis's ovary was pressing against the blood vessels leading to her legs. The doctors said the good news was that the cancer was Stage 2 and treatable. Lewis's friends and family rejoiced. But by spring the cancer had spread to her liver, and Lewis was given three months to live.

"I need to get my kids through high school. Please help," Lewis begged her doctor. Were there any experimental treatments she could try? She had been too stunned to ask those questions minutes earlier when he was breaking the news. Sanford, who had accompanied Lewis to the appointment, watched Lewis scribble the note on a pad of yellow Post-its® in the doctor's front office.

Lanier called from the New Jersey trial when he heard the grim prognosis. "This one's for you," he told Lewis. He offered her his private plane. Was there any place in the world she wanted to visit with her two teenage daughters, he asked. There wasn't.

It was just after Mother's Day when Lewis entered the hospital. She didn't want to die at home, lest it fall to her teenage daughters to discover her lifeless body. In the final weeks, Lewis's mother and brother kept her company in the hospital's intensive care unit during the day. Her husband shuttled the girls to their mother after school.

After her first night by herself in the ICU, Lewis told Sanford, "It's horrible. You have to stay." Sanford promised she would, and kept watch by Lewis's bed every night.

Lewis's parting words were to Sanford. Stirring briefly from a fitful rest, Lewis, who was oozing copious amounts of fluid by the end (a side effect of her chemotherapy), called out for Sanford. Sanford patted Lewis dry and rearranged her pillow the way she liked it.

"Good night," Lewis said when Sanford was done.

"Good night," Sanford replied.

Twenty minutes later, Lewis suffered a stroke. She lingered for a few days. On June 6, 2006, at around 6:30 P.M., she died. Several hours went by before an orderly came to disconnect Lewis from the equipment that had sustained her at the end. Sanford watched him wheel Lewis into the elevator. She could go no further with her friend. The elevator was headed to the morgue.

Years later, Lewis's mother, Alene Rhodes, recalled her daughter's grace, determination, and modesty. She said Lewis talked often of her work on the Vioxx cases.

"She talked about how she believed in the cause, and she was going to keep fighting," Rhodes said.

And Seeger said, "There *would* be no Vioxx litigation if it weren't for Carlene [Lewis] and Shelly [Sanford]... We probably wouldn't have had the time to develop the case." As it was, Lewis and Sanford had recognized Vioxx's dangers three years before Merck tacitly acknowledged them and pulled it from the market.

Lanier gave the eulogy at Lewis's funeral. "In fifty-one short years, Carlene came and left a mark [and] truly changed our world for good in ways that will be felt for the history of our civilization," he said.

But the fight Lewis began still had a very long way to go.

PLAINTIFFS' LAWYERS HAD BEEN filing Vioxx cases at a feverish pace since its withdrawal in 2004, adding first hundreds, and then thousands of new cases each month to federal and state dockets around the country. By the end of 2005, there were 10,000 cases against Merck. By the end of 2006, there were 27,000.

In the years leading up to the Vioxx withdrawal, more than one company had offered quick settlements when confronted with a similar onslaught of mass tort claims and large punitive verdicts in initial trials. But those settlements had not bought the defendants what they most craved—an end to the lawsuits and certainty about the size of their liability. Instead, they had spurred plaintiffs' lawyers to file tens of thousands of new claims. Among the best-known examples of failed settlements was the fen-phen litigation. In 1997, drug maker Wyeth withdrew two diet drugs in response to concerns of heart valve injuries. Early trials brought out evidence that Wyeth may have known of the risks well before it stopped selling the drugs. In 1999, faced with 18,000 claims and indications that it may face a large number of punitive jury awards, Wyeth offered plaintiffs roughly $4 billion to settle all existing and future claims. It was anticipated the total number of claims would top out at roughly 36,000. By 2006, Wyeth had spent over $20 billion, and thousands of lawsuits were still pending. It was the defendant's ultimate nightmare—an endless tort.

In the Vioxx litigation, Merck had maintained from the start that it had done nothing wrong and would defend itself vigorously in court.

"We'll fight every case," Kenneth C. Frazier, Merck's general counsel, vowed after the company's first victory, against Mike Humeston in New Jersey state court.

Opinion was divided on what Frazier's words signified. Some thought they signaled that Merck would follow in the footsteps of the tobacco companies, which for 40 years had fought every plaintiff who dared to take them on, giving ground only in the 1990s to concerted attack by the state attorneys general and a consortium of plaintiffs' lawyers. Others thought Merck's tough talk would eventually yield to a settlement. The plaintiffs' lawyers leaned towards that view. An estimated 20 million Americans had used Vioxx, and heart attacks—the injury associated with Vioxx—are the leading cause of death in the United States (along with other forms of heart disease). The plaintiff's lawyers reasoned Merck *had* to mount a serious defense even if it planned to settle or it would be overrun by litigants.

Merck was exceptionally well placed to fight the plaintiffs. Its business generated enough cash to finance the research, development, and marketing of its drugs; pay a healthy dividend to shareholders; *and* maintain billions of dollars in cash reserves. Drawing liberally from those reserves, the company created a legal fund of $675 million in 2004, replenishing it as the money was spent. By the end of 2006, Merck had spent all that money (plus an additional $110 million) *and* bolstered its legal reserves with an additional $858 million for expenses in 2007 and beyond. (These sums included the cost of defending itself in thousands of personal injury cases, and in shareholder lawsuits and government investigations.) Top-flight law firms in Houston; Chicago; Baltimore; Washington, D.C.; Philadelphia; Princeton, N.J.; Ridgeland, Miss.; and Los Angeles represented Merck's interests in courts around the country, while a prominent New York law firm, Hughes Hubbard & Reed, coordinated the company's overall legal strategy.

Merck had more than money on its side. It had luck. The general prevalence of heart attacks, which made settling quickly a high-risk proposition, was also an invaluable asset in Merck's defense. No tell-tale mark distinguished a heart attack caused by Vioxx from those in which Vioxx played no role. And many plaintiffs suffered from conditions, such as high blood pressure and diabetes, which caused heart attacks even in the absence of Vioxx use. Merck lawyers were able to argue at trial that the plaintiffs' heart attacks were caused not by Vioxx but by the usual culprits, such as bad diet and a sedentary lifestyle. The strategy worked.

As Andy Birchfield, co-chairman of the plaintiffs' steering committee in the federal MDL, explained, "You go to trial, and you have someone who is morbidly obese, a smoker, they have hypertension, high cholesterol, diabetes, they don't take their medicine...and it's much harder for a jury to say Vioxx was a motivating cause for the heart attack. [Jurors think] 'Did Vioxx make you have the heart attack that you were going to have anyway, just a year earlier?'" Birchfield spoke from bitter experience, having lost two of the three Vioxx cases he tried in federal court in 2006.

But those jurors were glossing over a crucial point. Every heart attack can be traced back to multiple factors. Indeed, the law, in most states, required plaintiffs to show that Vioxx was *a* cause of the plaintiffs' heart attack, not that it was *the* (only) cause. And people *already* at high risk of heart attack because of high cholesterol or high blood pressure, for example (those who were, in Lanier's words, "one pork chop away from a heart attack"), were precisely the ones who could least afford to amplify their high risk by taking Vioxx and they were most likely to be injured by Merck's failure to give a clear warning of Vioxx's risks. Of course jury decisions don't always follow the law or science, and Merck's lawyers proved adept at directing jurors' attention away from the company's conduct to the plaintiffs' lifestyle.

Of the 13 cases tried in 2006, Merck won eight, the plaintiffs won three, and two ended in a mistrial. (2005 had ended in a tie, with one victory apiece for the plaintiffs and Merck, and one mistrial.) Wall Street analysts revised their estimates of how much Merck would eventually have to pay to settle the lawsuits, from their early estimates of $30–$50 billion to a single-digit sum in the billions. Investors, who had driven Merck's stock down to a nine-year low in the aftermath of Lanier's first victory in Texas state court, pushed it back up, and the stock steadily regained its prewithdrawal value over the course of 2006.

"The fact remains that heart attacks are a major cause of death in the United States and have multiple causes. It will be difficult for plaintiffs to prove that Vioxx was the cause of any individual's heart attack," Merck's general counsel, Kenneth Frazier, said after one Merck victory. The company said it would continue to defend the cases one by one.

MORE THAN TWO YEARS after Merck's dramatic withdrawal of Vioxx from the market, the plaintiffs' lawyers still didn't know when, or even if, Merck would settle. Lucrative litigation against asbestos, tobacco, and other industries in the 1980s and 1990s had transformed plaintiffs' firms into large businesses with diverse income streams and access to bank lines of credit. While they had the capital to continue the fight against Merck, the plaintiffs' lawyers were anxious for returns on the millions they had already invested—they wanted a settlement. Because they worked on a contingent basis, they would not even recoup their expenses until Merck settled.

Their best shot at speeding things up was to try some more cases, and on favorable turf. That meant some place other than Judge Fallon's federal courtroom in New Orleans, where Merck had won three out of the four cases tried and the odds of a plaintiffs' victory were poor. There were many reasons why. Among them: Merck's very skilled lead lawyer, Phil Beck, who had been part of George W. Bush's legal team in Bush v. Gore in 2004 and whom Fallon treated with admiring deference; demographic changes in New Orleans since Katrina and a near absence of working-class residents from the city's jury pool; and the requirement in federal court for unanimity in jury verdicts. But while Merck executives liked to *say* they wanted to fight every Vioxx case in court, more trials are just about the last thing corporate defendants typically want. By the end of 2006, juries had found for the plaintiffs in four of the 15 cases that had been tried. And, according to experts in mass torts, such as Howard Erichson of the Fordham Law School, the losses loomed large for Merck.

"If you're Merck, the salient fact of all these trials is 'we can win many of these trials. On the other hand there are many juries that *will* find against us,'" Erichson said.

Those juries hit the company hard. The most dramatic instance of that, of course, was the quarter of a billion dollars awarded by a Texas jury in the first Vioxx trial. But the other jury awards were also impressive—$13.5 million in a New Jersey state case, $32 million in a second Texas state case, and $51 million in federal court. Two of the awards had already been slashed by judges, a third would be drastically reduced under state law, and Merck was appealing them all. The company hadn't paid a penny, and probably wouldn't for many more years. Still, every time the plaintiffs won a case they proved Merck was vulnerable in court, and they drove up the value of an eventual settlement.

THE PLAINTIFFS' LAWYERS FOUND an ally in, of all places, Merck's home state of New Jersey, where Superior Court Judge Carol E. Higbee presided over the country's largest docket of Vioxx cases. Plaintiffs from all over the country had filed their cases in New Jersey, because under the rules that govern civil lawsuits, Merck could not have them transferred to federal court. By the end of 2006, Higbee had 16,800 cases on her Vioxx docket, compared to 5,700 in the federal MDL under Judge Fallon. She and Fallon enjoyed a cordial relationship, but Higbee had made it clear from the start that she would not defer to Fallon in her efforts to resolve the cases and proposed an aggressive plan of representative trials, as a prelude to settlement talks. With Merck still insisting it had no plans to settle, Higbee said she needed to try more cases and faster and was eager to experiment with different trial formats.

She had already conducted one experiment in the spring of 2006, trying two cases in the same trial. That summer, she proposed a more ambitious experiment—trying seven or eight cases at a time and conducting the trial in two phases using a procedure called "bifurcation." Many judges used it during the peak of the asbestos mass tort to streamline trials. Higbee proposed that Phase I of the trial deal with the issue common to all the cases, namely, whether Merck had failed to warn that Vioxx posed cardiovascular risks, or in the jargon of tort law, whether Merck had "general liability" for the plaintiffs' alleged cardiovascular injuries. If the jury found for the plaintiffs, the trial would proceed to Phase II, in which the plaintiffs would be asked to show that Merck had "specific liability" for each plaintiff's injuries. Higbee said if the experiment worked, she might expand it to consolidate up to 20 separate cases into a single trial, and enlist other judges in the state to do such trials as well.

The plaintiffs embraced the proposal. Trying several cases together would give them multiple opportunities to beat Merck in a single trial. And they believed the trial's bifurcated structure would play to their strengths because Merck's deceptive marketing practices and scientific misconduct would take center stage first. Merck would have to wait until the second half of the trial to call the jury's attention to what had proven to be the strongest part of *its* case—how each plaintiff's lifestyle and preexisting risk factors may have contributed to the alleged injuries.

"Look, the plaintiffs are older men. Everyone has risk factors. It's just a question of how many and how bad," said Ellen Relkin, a partner at the plaintiffs' firm Weitz Luxenberg, explaining the plaintiffs' thinking on bifurcation. "The general liability story was so strong. Why dilute it with the devilish details?"

Merck fought the idea for many months. Its lawyers said trying many cases simultaneously would be confusing for the jury. They said the jury would be exhausted by the time it got to hear evidence of the third or fourth or fifth plaintiff's specific injuries. They said it was irrelevant to ask the jury at the end of Phase I whether Vioxx posed a generic risk. "To whom? When? How long?" they asked. The jury needed answers to specific questions such as those to answer the relevant question—whether Vioxx had harmed the plaintiffs in each case. Finally, and this was perhaps their greatest concern, they said the structure would prejudice the jury against Merck. If jurors found in Phase I of the trial that Merck failed to warn of Vioxx's risks, they would be predisposed to find against Merck in the second phase.

The plaintiffs countered by reminding Higbee at each turn that it was Merck's intransigence on settling the mass tort that made it necessary to try several cases at the same time and in a bifurcated trial. Lanier told Higbee that she was at risk of running out of jurors in Atlantic City if she had to try every Vioxx case, one at a time. Another lawyer alluded to Merck's "500-year plan" for the Vioxx mass tort.

Higbee scheduled a bifurcated trial of four cases (down from seven, in concession to Merck) for January 2007. Lanier, who had taken the lead in the previous two-case trial in Higbee's court, would take the lead again and present the general liability case against Merck in the first phase. Shortly before the trial was to begin, Merck raised a new concern, this time about the order in which the individual plaintiffs' cases would be presented to the jury if the trial progressed to Phase II. The plaintiffs' lawyers said they had always assumed they would get to decide the order (an assumption Higbee said she shared) because they had the burden of proof. Lanier, who had a daughter graduating from high school a few months later, said he didn't want to be away from home more than he had to be, and that the plaintiffs' lawyers had agreed among themselves he would go first.

His remarks drew a disbelieving and acerbic response from Hope Freiwald, a partner at Dechert, who represented Merck.

"Frankly, Your Honor, I hope there comes a time when a woman feels comfortable saying that she has three daughters at home who are going to miss her very much and who have their own personal issues," Freiwald said. (She had three young daughters.) "That's not the driver here."

The real reason Lanier wanted the Hermans case to go first, she said, was to put young Kyle Hermans on the stand and set "in the jury's mind an image that will never come out of their mind...of a 15-year-old boy climbing through a window to see his father dead on the living room floor." She said the Hermans case would have a "steamroller effect" on Merck's ability to defend itself against the other plaintiffs' claims.

Higbee said she didn't think it would have that effect but agreed to accommodate Merck's concerns. It was decided the court reporter would pull names out of a hat and the cases would be tried in the order drawn. The lawyers, except for one of Merck's, had joined the conference by phone. That lawyer and the judge would be witnesses to the ceremony.

"If this results in some plaintiff wanting to opt out of the case, I'll let them opt out of the case," Higbee said, before the court reporter drew names.

Lanier's case was drawn third.

"I can't do this," Lanier said. "I'm going to take advantage of the judge's affirmation that I can opt out, and I'm going to opt out." He hinted that forcing him out of the trial had been the "ulterior motive" for Merck's objections from the start.

The trial was set to start in a week, and it was hard to see how it could go forward if Lanier, who was to play the lead role in its first phase, was no longer participating.

"I think we're going to need a continuance to get somebody else ready for Phase I, in all candor," Lanier said.

"Mr. Lanier," the judge said.

"Yes, ma'am," Lanier replied.

"I'm not going to continue this case," Higbee said. "I'm going to let you talk amongst yourselves and then get back to me, but I intend to try something next week. We're bringing a lot of jurors in, and we're ready to go, and I'm just not going to give up their time and the staff's time... and not move another case."

"Mark [Lanier] is a big baby," Seeger said later. "I wanted Mark to pull out. I was, like, 'Let him go. I'll do general causation.'"

It had been over a year since Lanier had predicted (correctly) on national television that Seeger would lose Mike Humeston's case. The two men had patched things up, after a fashion, over dinner at Cipriani's in New York.

"He told me... what he did was wrong," Seeger said. "I told him, 'It was bullshit, and he shouldn't have done it.'" Lanier was new to dealing with the press, as they all were, Seeger said, and "I forgave him." Not entirely, it appeared.

When they returned from their break, the plaintiffs' lawyers were no closer to a solution. Lanier said again that he would pull out of the trial if he had to wait for two other plaintiffs' lawyers to present their cases in Phase II before presenting his. Seeger said he could step in for Lanier in Phase I, but he needed a month to prepare. Higbee suggested that Lanier try the Hermans case as a stand-alone, and that Seeger take the lead role in a bifurcated trial of the other three cases immediately afterwards. That would get around Lanier's objection to waiting in line to prove the specific link between Vioxx and his client's injury in a consolidated trial. It would also buy time for Seeger to prepare for the lead role in a bifurcated trial. Lanier balked at that proposal as well. He said he had put in more time and money on the Vioxx litigation than any other lawyer in the country—16 weeks in two trials and $4–5 million of his money. Both cases were on appeal, he said.

"I'll be quite candid with the Court," Lanier said, "I really don't think it is fair at this point for me to go try one single case and have a third one go up on appeal with Merck with another $2 million of my money and another six weeks of my time tied up in it."

The plaintiffs' lawyers would have divided costs four ways under the original plan.

In the end, Higbee made the call. She ordered Lanier to be ready to pick a jury the following week for a bifurcated trial of two cases—his and Seeger's. The other two cases would not be part of the trial.

"Come on, give us something," Higbee said.

"Your Honor, I can do that," Lanier said. "I can do that."

There were some very angry lawyers when the call ended.

"Lanier had the cards. He screwed us," said Ellen Relkin, whose firm, Weitz & Luxenberg, was one of the two forced out of the trial. But "it was a critical time in the litigation," she said. It had been months since the plaintiffs had won a case. "We needed a victory," Relkin said, and everyone knew Lanier was the man for the job. "He's a superb lawyer. He had the case down pat."

Lanier didn't think he'd screwed anyone. He said the other lawyers had begged him to take the lead in the trial.

"Everybody was asking me to," he said. "Otherwise, how could I? It wasn't our turn." Many other lawyers with trial-ready cases were waiting in the wings.

PLAINTIFFS' LAWYERS LIKE TO say that you need the holy trinity to beat the big guys: brains, guts, and money. There would be plenty of each in both camps when the trial got underway, and it would be a tense engagement.

Seeger was returning to Higbee's courtroom to try Mike Humeston's case for a second time. Shortly after the Humestons lost their case in 2005, the *New England Journal of Medicine* ran an extraordinary set of editorials questioning the integrity of a key Vioxx paper that had appeared in that journal five years earlier. The editors said the paper, which was written by Merck authors and consultants, had understated Vioxx's potential to cause heart attacks and other cardiovascular injuries. Higbee ruled that the editorials had undermined Merck's claim that it had warned of Vioxx's risks before Humeston's heart attack, and granted a retrial. She predicted there would be a different outcome this time. Merck's lead lawyer in the first Humeston trial, Diane Sullivan, would return for the rematch. Seeger despised her because he thought she had bullied and taunted him in the courtroom, often within earshot of the jury (and, no doubt, also because she'd won.) It seemed likely Sullivan returned the sentiment.

Lanier would represent young Kyle Hermans and the estate of Brian Hermans. Brian Hermans's parents had learned Vioxx could cause heart attacks only when Merck withdrew it and filed a case against the company. Over four years had passed since their son's death in September 2002, and the family hadn't recovered. Kyle Hermans, who had inherited his father's athletic gifts and been expected to go to college on a basketball scholarship, dropped out of sports after his father died. And his grades had slipped. Brian Hermans's death had left his son adrift.

Of course the early trials in a mass tort are always about more than just the individual plaintiffs. They're also about the thousands of others whose claims will never be heard by juries. That was doubly true of this trial, which the plaintiffs hoped would help Higbee fashion a powerful tool to try dozens of cases and bring Merck closer to the negotiating table.

"We research, we plan, we prepare, we leave no stone unturned."

CHAPTER 2

Preparing for Battle

Atlantic City, New Jersey, January 21, 2007

IT WAS 6 P.M. ON a wintry evening and Texas trial lawyer W. Mark Lanier was settling into Atlantic City's newest temple of marble and glass, a glitzy casino hotel called Borgata. The door to his airy 34th-floor suite was propped open and Lanier—clad in blue jeans, a cotton shirt, and loafers—was removing stacks of documents, legal pads, and office supplies from moving boxes and piling them on the floor. A steady stream of visitors trooped in to see "the boss." Lanier greeted each with a hug or a back-slapping handshake and a loud whoop of laughter. His trial team of lawyers and consultants was assembling for last-minute preparations, and the mood was giddy. The next day Lanier would face off against the drug maker, Merck, for a third time. He had won the last two times, and a third victory seemed within grasp.

I had stayed in touch with Mark Lanier after his victory in Angleton, calling every few months, often to ask why the plaintiffs weren't winning more cases against Merck. Lanier cultivates reporters assiduously and would respond within minutes from his BlackBerry or call on his cell phone, usually to say something like,

"Beating Merck is hard and the other plaintiffs' lawyers aren't as good as I am."

This could have come off as insufferably arrogant. But Lanier's pride in his skills was so unabashed it was disarming. I had learned some months earlier that he would likely return to New Jersey for another Vioxx trial, and I approached him about going backstage, as it were, to see for myself why he was beating Merck when others weren't. Lanier readily agreed. Over the weeks that followed, I tried to be the proverbial fly on the wall, as Lanier and his team plotted and prepped in his hotel suite, on the drive to and from court in his rental SUV, and in their cramped, overheated workroom a few doors down from the judge's chambers. Many in the group were uncomfortable with the presence of a reporter and her notebook. But Lanier had decided that I could be trusted to keep his secrets safe until the trial was over, and went out of his way to make good on his promise of access.

He had flown in that Sunday evening to a small airfield outside Atlantic City on his Learjet-60 with his jury consultant, Bob Leone; Dara Hegar, a young lawyer who functioned as his aide-de-camp; and his wife, Becky, and their two youngest children, Rebecca, 9, and Sarah, 7. The girls had been pulled from school to watch their father give his opening statement, and from time to time Lanier popped over to the rooms across the hall where his daughters lay sprawled across the enormous hotel beds.

Indeed, a domestic vibe pervaded the entire proceedings. Becky Lanier, a petite blonde woman in her 40s, was wrestling an overstuffed refrigerator into submission when I got there. (It was crammed with lettuce, tomatoes, and cold cuts for the bag lunches Lanier liked to take to court.) She had set out a bowl of fresh fruit and packets of pretzels and rice cakes. Someone had moved the hotel's coffeemaker and mugs to the floor, and in their place sat a wooden cutting board, a mean-looking bread knife, and boxes of cereal. A toaster would appear a few days later.

Other lawyers from Lanier's firm were ensconced down the hall from the pod of rooms that Lanier, Hegar, and Leone occupied. Lanier's long-time science consultant, David Egilman, had a large room one floor above, and had brought two research assistants with him. The two young ex-Marines who served as jacks-of-all-trades at Lanier's law firm, Juan Wilson and Jesse Alcorta, had driven a U-Haul truck filled with computers and supplies from the office in Houston the week before, stripped another 34th-floor suite of its sofas and plush chairs, and set up a "war room." Lanier's lawyers would work in it literally around the clock, and an assistant would be close by at all times to guard the documents and computers, even sleeping in a connecting room at night. Lanier's well-oiled trial machine was revved up and ready to go.

There had been more than a dozen Vioxx trials by this point. The evidence had been aired many times, the witnesses were grizzled courtroom veterans, and the strengths and weaknesses of each side's case were well-tested. Lanier himself had done a couple of those trials, as had the lawyers who would defend Merck the next day. Merck's lawyers had undoubtedly studied Lanier's previous trials for tips on his methods and style, just as he had studied theirs. Each side would set traps for the other while trying to avoid the ones meant for them. Practice makes perfect, the saying goes, and both sides hoped it would hold true for them in this trial. But, as Lanier well knew, it was a very complicated case.

"It's monstrously difficult to try," he said. Everything has "to go just right for it to work."

Victory was far from certain.

THE CASE TURNED ON what Merck scientists knew about Vioxx's risks and when. The plaintiffs contended that long before Mike

Humeston had his heart attack in 2001 and Brian Hermans his, in 2002, scientific studies of Vioxx had proven that the drug could trigger heart attacks, but Merck didn't tell doctors or patients. Merck's position was that it had seen no evidence of Vioxx's risks until the APPROVe study in 2004, in which Vioxx subjects developed cardiovascular problems at twice the rate of those on sugar pills. That's when Merck pulled Vioxx from the market.

It had taken experienced scientists years to sort through the company's spin. Juries had at most a month or six weeks for the job and were mostly made up of people who had ended their formal educations in high school. Merck's trial strategy capitalized on those facts, and on the inherent complexity of the science. To win, Lanier had to peel back the confusion and explain in simple terms the science underlying Vioxx, how its side effects had remained masked for years, and why Merck's government regulator had not exposed them. Lanier called these "education points," and he said there were 25 to 30 of them in the Vioxx case. They had to be explained in bite-sized pieces, repeatedly and thoroughly, he said, so the jury could understand them, and the process could not be rushed. A self-described "communication wonk," Lanier said research showed that you cannot teach someone more than three concepts in a day. (In federal court, where Judge Eldon Fallon allowed no more than two-and-a-half to three weeks for a Vioxx trial, Lanier believed, it was impossible to win trials because there wasn't enough time to educate the jury.) The explanations also had to be memorable—because, as he liked to say, "If they understand, but they can't remember it, it's not going to do me any good at all."

Lanier had pulled a lot of stunts over the years to make his points stick.

In the first Vioxx trial, after Merck's lawyers insisted for the umpteenth time that the company could not have done anything wrong because, after all, it had given the Food and Drug Administration every piece of information on Vioxx, Lanier mounted a dramatic spectacle to refute their argument. At an appropriate juncture in his cross examination of a Merck witness, Wilson and Alcorta, the ex-Marines who served as his trial assistants, had burst through the courtroom doors wheeling dollies piled high with bankers' boxes, and proceeded to pile them methodically in front of the jury box. The boxes contained some of the tens of thousands of pages that Merck had submitted to the FDA. It wasn't until the jury began to disappear from view behind the wall of boxes that Lanier called a halt to the demonstration. He had made his point: Merck could have given the FDA every piece of information it had about Vioxx (the plaintiffs maintained Merck hadn't), and *still* hidden Vioxx's safety problems from its regulator. He had shown the jury that "the best place to hide a leaf is in a forest," as Lanier's science consultant, David Egilman put it.

Lanier had also grafted the Vioxx story onto popular television dramas in his previous trials. In Angleton, he cast the jurors as investigators along the lines of the crime show "CSI," and charged them with finding the culprit responsible for the death of the plaintiff's husband.

"We know we got Republicans that are in favor of the death penalty, and we tailor the case so it sounds like a criminal death penalty case, because we know the jury will be good for that kind of case," Lanier's jury consultant, Bob Leone, explained.

Six months later, in New Jersey, in his second Vioxx trial, Lanier heaped ridicule on Merck's case and summed up his own with the help of the show "Desperate Housewives." Why "Desperate Housewives?" Leone's polling showed it was the second most-watched show in Atlantic County. Lanier plastered the faces of Merck's top executives onto the bodies of the show's stars and titled his show "Desperate Executives." Judging by the jury's verdict, it was a hit.

In the present trial, Lanier would use the metaphor of a cata-strophic traffic accident to explain the Vioxx debacle. Vioxx, he planned to tell the jury, was an 18-wheeler truck that Merck bar-reled past yellow and red traffic lights that had given ample warning of Vioxx's risks. Instead of obeying the traffic signals and slowing down or stopping to conduct more safety tests, Merck stepped on the gas and sold Vioxx even harder. It blanketed the country with TV commercials and celebrity endorsements, and the consequences were predictably deadly.

The story line was a tactical maneuver to sidestep Merck's "home court advantage." Merck was based just a hundred miles away in the small town of Whitehouse Station, NJ, and Merck's lead lawyer Diane Sullivan had made the most of Merck's New Jersey roots—and her own—in previous trials.

"She was so full of crap. She said she used to drive by Merck when she was a girl and hope that maybe some day she'd be a scientist," scoffed Leone, who was himself a New Jersey native.

Lanier needed a way to cast Merck's behavior in terms that could outrage even home-state loyalists.

"There are some things, I don't care where you are, that you would not tolerate, like speeding through a school zone. I don't care if you live in Mississippi or you live in Utah, if someone came in drunk, speeding through a school zone, you'd punish em," Leone reasoned.

Even a New Jersey jury would agree, he believed, that the driver of an 18-wheeler who ran red lights and collided with another vehicle deserved to be punished.

The one thing he and Lanier did not consider was trying the cases as straight product liability cases. They knew Americans hated personal injury lawsuits and lawyers.

"And you know why? Because corporate America is spending millions teaching them that," Leone said indignantly.

AT 54, LEONE'S CAREER as a lawyer was his third. (First-grade teacher and psychologist were numbers 1 and 2.) Though he was trained as a lawyer, Leone's role on the team was to *not* think like a lawyer, but to see the lawsuit and the trial as those on the outside might—to see them, in short, through the eyes of a juror. With a master's degree in experimental psychology and a PhD in clinical psychology, Leone approached the task of thinking like a juror as a cross between a scientific experiment and a military operation: "We research, we plan, we prepare, we leave no stone unturned," he said.

Leone guarded the details of his methods jealously. In general terms, here's how he did what was arguably the most important piece of his job—picking the jury.

Before a single juror was selected, Leone had made a thorough study of the residents of Atlantic City and neighboring towns, who constituted the jury pool, polling thousands on how they would vote to decide the case.

"You lay out different fact scenarios and figure out what they think," Leone said. "You say there's a pharmaceutical company named Merck and a person who had a heart attack on their drug. Who would you vote for? Suppose you knew that Merck knew about the heart attacks, who would you vote for?" and so on.

His pollsters asked the usual demographic questions about gender, age, race, religion, and occupation, as well as less conventional ones, such as "Do you exercise regularly?" or "Do you ride a motorcycle?" They were looking for associations between the poll subjects' views on the case and their other attributes, so that when it came time to pick a jury, Leone could tell from looking at those attributes which jurors would be good for the plaintiffs and which ones would be bad. The less logical the connection between the attribute and the opinion, the better it was, Leone said, because "the other side doesn't know what you're doing."

In many courts, jurors are selected after only a perfunctory oral examination, called "voir dire," by the lawyers or even just the judge. Judge Carol Higbee, before whom this case was to be tried, gave lawyers unusual latitude to gather information about potential jurors through a lengthy written questionnaire. This was Leone's opportunity to learn exactly what he needed to know to sort out plaintiffs' jurors from those likely to favor the defense. He used the information gathered from the polling and his training in the construction of psychological tests to devise his questions. The best questions were the ones that the other side considered "fluff," because "nobody but me knows that the question is differentiating between people," he said. The final questionnaire was the product of intense negotiations.

"I do a questionnaire. They [the defendants] do a questionnaire. The judge says, 'work it out,' and we send it back and forth. And we play games, 'I don't want this question, I want that question,' and we play games, we play games, we play games," he said, wearily. "It's a good fight. I usually win, but it's a good fight."

Some 300 Atlantic County residents had filled out the 26-page, 170-question jury questionnaire in Higbee's courtroom the week before. Both sides had a night to go through the answers before returning to pick the jury. Leone had hired 50 people to enter the data from the questionnaires, which was fed into his scoring model.

"Now I get a score for every juror—all 300 of them—on every area, 'How do they feel about pharmaceutical companies? How do they feel about lawsuits?' They get rated and they get ordered from 1 to 300, so it's not, 'is this person better than the other?' I got them in rank order. I can tell you who is the absolute best juror, and who is the absolute worst, and I can tell you who's number 144, and who's 145, at least according to me," Leone said.

He was pleased with the jury of 10 that was seated.

"If I was Merck, I would be seriously worried," he said.

"Here's their biggest problem," he continued. "They don't know what case we're going to try. They think they do. First of all, they've read our past transcripts, so they think Mark is going to do 'CSI' or 'Desperate Housewives.' [But] we never do the same thing twice.

"Even if they know we're not going to do it again, they don't know *what* we're gonna do. It makes a difference," Leone said. "We know what case we're going to do, and I know what kind of jurors I want for the case we're going to do."

IN HIGH-DOLLAR CIVIL CASES where expense is no object, opening statements are multimedia productions that weave illustrations, photographs, animations, graphics, and video clips into the lawyer's spoken statement. Lanier had collaborated on the visual presentations for the openings and closings in each of his Vioxx trials with Cliff Atkinson, author of a best-selling book on the creative use of PowerPoint software. They had begun brainstorming on ways to depict the traffic-accident theme a few months earlier, and Atkinson had come up with a series of animated slides. Lanier tweaked his opening until the very end, and Atkinson, a tall, slightly shy man with a big smile, was at the Borgata that evening to finish the job.

"Here's the agenda, guys," Lanier said, reading from a list he'd made on his computer. "I'd like to go through the opening itself, reread the juror profiles, I've got some notes I want to add to it, and get comments from the gallery while we're doing it."

The gallery at that moment consisted of Hegar, Leone, and Egilman, but would soon swell to include Seeger and his lawyers. Hegar dragged some chairs into a semicircle around the brightly lit round table on which Lanier had set up his computer, and Leone drifted over to Lanier's side. Atkinson was already at the table working on his own computer.

Because the trial was divided into two phases, and Vioxx's role in the Hermans and Humeston heart attacks wouldn't be considered until the second phase, the judge had ruled that the two sides could say little about the specifics of the plaintiffs' injuries in the first phase. But Lanier wanted to be sure the jury knew that a dead man figured in the trial.

"Well how are we goin' to do this?" Lanier asked Leone and Hegar, as they crowded around the computer to look at the opening slide.

It had the names of the plaintiffs' families—the Humestons and the Hermans.

"How about Keith and the estate of Brian Hermans?" Lanier said.

Hegar and Leone responded in unison, "Keith?!"

"Isn't that the boy's name?" Lanier said.

It was Kyle.

"I knew it had a K in it," Lanier muttered.

They settled on "Kyle and the Estate of Brian Hermans and Frederick and Mary Humeston v. Merck."

Atkinson's slides of a traffic wreck used a family minivan to represent the plaintiffs injured by Vioxx and culminated in the flattening of the minivan by the 18-wheeler Vioxx truck.

"You know you guys have to exchange slides in the morning? Diane will go nuts over the tractor-trailer ramming into the minivan," said Jeff Grand, one of Seeger's lawyers, who had joined the gallery. "I'm not saying she'll win, but she'll go nuts."

"Diane" was Merck's lead lawyer, Diane Sullivan. Judge Higbee required each side to share printouts of its slides with the other before showing them to the jury during opening statements.

"Let her go nuts," Leone said.

"Well, she won't see it ramming in," Lanier interjected, and without missing a beat, he suggested how they could sidestep Sullivan's potential objection that the slide was so graphic it was prejudicial.

"When we [print] these slides out, is there a way to [print] them out before impact?" he asked Atkinson.

"Not with the blood all over the ground," Leone added, helpfully, as the others chuckled.

If the collision wasn't visible in the printed slides, Sullivan wouldn't be able to object. Atkinson said he could print the slides out the way Lanier wanted, and he wrote himself a note to do that.

Lanier, who seemed to leave no detail to chance, asked Hegar, "Dara, are you making all of these notes?"

"Yes, I am," she said.

"I didn't see you write that down," Lanier retorted.

Hegar looked up, exasperated. "I just clicked my pen. Did you hear it?" she said. And when Lanier protested, she added, firmly, "Mark, we're good."

"Okay, hold on. I'm going to write it down too," Lanier said.

Hegar held her tongue, and they moved to the next slide.

A pert 32-year-old, Hegar was the only woman in Lanier's inner circle and adept at reading him. He joked that she was like Radar O'Reilly, the company clerk on "M*A*S*H," who frequently knew the commanding officer's next move even before he did. As Hegar told the story, she fell into the role early on. She was 25 years old, a year out of law school when she got a job at Lanier's firm, and it was her third week there. Lanier and Leone were heading out of the office to help with jury selection on another lawyer's case, and Lanier called out to Hegar, as they passed her in the firm's reception area, "Hey, you!" (It was before he knew her name, Hegar wryly observed.) "You ever been to a voir dire?" She hadn't. "Come with us!" he said, and she did.

She was with them in court when Lanier agreed later that day to try the case for ailing Houston trial lawyer John O'Quinn. The trial began on Monday morning, and it was a Friday afternoon, Hegar recalled. It was all hands on deck, she said. She served as Lanier's associate on the case, and had stayed in the role ever since.

"Mark, Bob, and I—it just clicked," Hegar said. "It's like a family. They're like my older brothers" she paused to laugh, "whom I have to take care of."

Indeed, Lanier relied on Hegar's obsessive attention to detail, her even temper, and her discretion to keep the waters around him smooth. During the trial, she was the first person he saw most mornings and the last at night. And while Lanier turned in at 9 or 10 most evenings, Hegar stayed up late into the night, making sure that the documents he asked for had been dug up, copied, and slipped under his door, ready for when he awoke to start work at 1 or 2 in the morning.

No matter how little sleep she'd had the night before, Hegar would be turned out every morning in an Ann Taylor black suit and white blouse—the uniform, as she called it—every hair combed, pearls in her ears, and mascara securely in place. Wearing sensible black heels, she would match Lanier's quick, long strides over the marble floors of the Borgata lobby, past the orange glass sculptures by Dale Chihuly and the serpentine lines of gamblers in sweatsuits and sneakers waiting to check in, down an escalator, and to their waiting rental car. As Lanier pulled out of the parking lot and dialed up his wife, Hegar whipped out her gloss and blush, and by the time he hung up she was almost done with her breakfast Power Bar. If Lanier made trying a case look easy in court, it was at least partly because he had Hegar backing him up.

MERCK'S STRONGEST ALIBI IN the Vioxx cases was the federal government. As the company's lawyers would tell the jury the next day, the experts at the Food and Drug Administration, which oversees drug companies, repeatedly confirmed the assessment of Merck's scientists that Vioxx was safe. Leone's jury questionnaire had revealed that seven of the ten jurors believed, falsely, that the FDA tested drugs. Lanier wanted to disabuse the jury of that notion as soon as the trial began. Leone had given Lanier notes on how to do that in his opening statement, and Lanier read them out loud for the group.

"FDA is a government agency responsible for everything from hairspray and toothpaste to prescription drugs and iron lungs," Leone had written. "They're understaffed and underpaid. They don't do their own testing. There's not enough money in their budget. They *have* to depend on the drug companies to supply the testing and the reports."

Lanier was incredulous. "Do they do hairspray and toothpaste? Really?" he asked.

"Suntan lotion!" Leone said. "Foot spray for athlete's foot!" He sounded like a carnival barker advertising the FDA's varied attractions.

"Okay, I want a new slide. Here's the slide I want to do," Lanier said, turning to Atkinson, "New slide. The FDA is over everything from hairspray and toothpaste to prescription drugs and iron lungs."

"Do me a hairspray picture," he told Atkinson. "We got older ladies on the jury. What's that old kind that old ladies use? Something 'net..."

"Aquanet!" Hegar and Lanier said simultaneously.

"Give me an Aquanet!" Lanier said.

"What kind of toothpaste are we going to plug," he asked the group. "What's a New Jersey toothpaste?"

"Colgate," said Leone, the group's New Jersey expert. "I grew up on it."

Atkinson added generic pictures of a bottle of prescription drugs, and an iron lung next. Lanier would summon the images the next day, one by one, as he rattled off the list of the FDA's responsibilities. By the time he was done, the images would cover every inch of the screen.

Egilman suddenly piped up from the back of the scrum, "Did you put food in there?" Getting no response, he said it louder, "Did you put *food* in there?"

"They're not the USDA," Lanier said, only half listening. He was still instructing Atkinson on where he wanted the iron lung.

"F-D-A, they're the *Food* and Drug Administration," Egilman shouted back. "F-D-A. They do food. It's the first word." Speaking slowly and enunciating every word, Egilman tried again, "You should do *spinach*. Do a picture of a California farm."

He had Lanier's attention now. A few months earlier, supermarkets around the country had pulled fresh spinach from their shelves, after an *E. coli* outbreak was traced to contaminated spinach grown in California. Five people had died and the FDA advised consumers everywhere to avoid the vegetable.

Lanier told Atkinson he wanted a picture of a bag of spinach to "explode" on the screen at the end.

"Because here's the way I'll say it," he said, putting on his courtroom voice—outraged, higher pitched, and deliberate, "Everything from hairspray to toothpaste, from prescription drugs to iron lungs. And heavens! F-D-A...F stands for *Food*! I'm not even going into all the *food* they're over."

"I like that," Leone said, quietly, and gave Lanier a final piece of direction that would hammer home the point that the overburdened FDA was no match for Merck. "You want to finish with 'They do the best they can.'"

YOU WOULDN'T HAVE KNOWN it from his demeanor, but David Egilman was embroiled in his own legal battle at the time, with another drug maker, Eli Lilly & Co. The dispute was about Egilman's role in the release of thousands of pages of Lilly emails, marketing studies, and scientific reports relating to Lilly's top-selling drug,

Zyprexa. The documents indicated that Lilly had known for many years that Zyprexa, an antipsychotic approved for the treatment of schizophrenia and bipolar disorder, was associated with obesity and high blood sugar, but had kept the information from doctors. (Lilly said there was no evidence Zyprexa caused diabetes, and that it had given doctors all relevant information.)

Lanier and other plaintiffs' lawyers were suing Lilly on behalf of clients who alleged they had developed diabetes after taking Zyprexa, and had been given the documents by Lilly on condition of confidentiality. Enter Egilman, who was asked to review the documents by one of Lanier's lawyers, and found them so disturbing that he arranged a roundabout way to release them to a few reporters. (I was among that group.) His role in the documents' release was revealed when *The New York Times* ran front-page stories on their contents in December 2006. The federal judge overseeing the Zyprexa lawsuits had denounced him as a "criminal" a few days earlier and Egilman was grappling that night with the prospect of going to jail if Lilly pursued charges.

It is customary for corporate defendants to get a court order protecting confidential trade secrets in the documents they turn over to plaintiffs in product liability lawsuits. Such orders are intended to apply only to documents containing true trade secrets, but almost universally companies designate almost all documents "confidential" in an effort to prevent the disclosure of embarrassing corporate conduct. Egilman refused, on principle, to sign consulting contracts containing a confidentiality clause, and maintained he had never agreed to keep Lilly's documents confidential. He derided the plaintiffs' lawyers for agreeing to do so.

"My father was in a concentration camp. I smell bodies burning. I cannot remain silent about it," he said.

("You'd be a little crusty too" if you grew up with that history, Lanier said the one time we discussed Egilman's family history.)

Egilman did not go to jail. Instead, later that year he paid Lilly $100,000 as compensation for the harm he had caused it by releasing the documents. The federal judge eventually unsealed the documents, ruling in September 2008 that "Lilly's legitimate interest in confidentiality does not outweigh the public interest in disclosure at this stage." And Lilly went on to pay a record fine of $1.4 billion to settle federal criminal and civil charges that it illegally marketed Zyprexa for use among elderly patients and children, who were particularly vulnerable to its side effects. The documents Egilman released had also described many of those marketing efforts by Lilly.

A driven, sometimes domineering, and impatient man, Egilman was often at odds with the plaintiffs' lawyers who sought his services. He considered them "lazy" and "incompetent." Lanier was the rare exception, he said. And he prided himself on cultivating an eccentric persona. One of the best David Egilman stories I'd heard came from Leone, who recalled his first encounter with Egilman years before, at a conference of asbestos plaintiffs' lawyers in Florida. Egilman had arrived at the conference in Tweety Bird slippers, a Hawaiian shirt, and tight biker shorts. He was to be deposed later that day and had dressed for the occasion, believing that his attire would lead the opposing lawyers to underestimate him. A rotund man—he referred to himself as "the fat man"—Egilman had cut quite a figure, according to Leone.

When he wasn't testifying in Tweety Bird slippers and biker shorts, Egilman favored black leather walking shoes with Velcro fasteners, khaki slacks, and t-shirts with political slogans. Rarely parted from his BlackBerry and headset, Egilman worked, and ate, constantly. He had been the first to break into the snacks when the group convened that evening.

LANIER'S GALLERY HAD GRADUALLY scattered. A few members lounged on the living room sofa, snacking on pretzels and nuts. Leone was pacing as he munched on an apple. Someone had turned on the big flat-screen TV in the next room for the Sunday night football game. And from time to time, everyone except Lanier, Atkinson, and Hegar disappeared to watch the game. At the end of the night, they gathered for a round of show-and-tell.

For weeks, Lanier had been busily buying trial "tools"—prosaic, everyday objects—that he would use the next day to explain unfamiliar concepts and dramatize how profits from Vioxx grew even as its dangers became clearer. "You want to teach someone something abstract that they don't know, you have to *show* it to them," he liked to say. By the time he got to Atlantic City, Lanier's stash included: an old-fashioned copper scale (purchased the week before on eBay); an assortment of small, brightly colored, plastic objects that looked like children's bath toys (they were party favors); a metal safe; Monopoly money; several sturdy mop buckets; and bags of drugstore remedies for conditions such as hemorrhoids, constipation, flatulence, bad breath, fingernail fungus, and insect bites. Lanier produced his tools, one by one, that evening for the group's inspection.

The question of where to position the tools in the courtroom the next day came up.

"We have to keep them hidden so Merck doesn't stand up and cry foul," Lanier told the others, "and I need to be able to pull 'em out in front of the jury."

Egilman let out a belly laugh. "Are they going to cry foul?" he asked.

"Yeah," Lanier said, and you could tell he was looking forward to the moment, "I'd like 'em to cry foul in front of the jury."

When Lanier fumbled as he tried to unlock the metal safe, Leone joked that if he couldn't unlock it in court the next day, Lanier should just tell the jury, "Only Merck knows the combination, and they won't tell us!"

Chris Seeger, Lanier's co-counsel in the case, had joined the group. He suggested Lanier go right up to Merck's lawyer, Diane Sullivan, and loudly ask, "Can I have the combination, please?"

"That's good. That's good!" Lanier said, and he mimicked himself asking Sullivan for the combination, to the group's guffaws, "'Just whisper it. It dun't matter,' and when she cusses me out, I'll say, 'Okay, thanks.'"

The goal of an opening statement, I was beginning to see, wasn't just to make your own side look good. It seemed you scored double points for making the other side look bad.

The group was gradually dispersing and by 9:30 everyone had left. Lanier wandered around in a daze. The monopoly money, the metal safe, the plastic buckets, and the remedies for bug bites and heartburn, Band Aids, and ankle braces were strewn about the room.

"Dara, will you help me?" he asked Hegar plaintively, as she walked back in the room.

"Of course I will, Mark," Hegar said, and they began pushing back chairs and putting away the tools.

"I have to have things really organized, or I go crazy," Lanier said.

(I came upon him many mornings during the trial tidying up his living room before he left for court—tossing out the empty Perrier bottles that dotted his coffee table, wiping down the bread crumbs on the counter, and grumbling a little petulantly, "why do people leave their trash for me to clean up?" He knew why. Except for the very early morning, when he worked in solitude, Lanier's door was open and everyone who stopped by to see him grabbed a fistful of nuts or a piece of fruit while they were there. By the end of the day, the living room looked like a college dorm room and Lanier was grumpy until he'd cleaned it up.)

For the first time that evening, Lanier's energy was flagging. He had slept only four hours the night before, and four the one before that. He was unshaven anf his voice was hoarse. He opened a bag of corn chips, inspecting its label as he ate, "Look at these chips: corn, canola oil. These are edible!" Lanier had had his own heart problems in 2001, soon after he won the first Vioxx case, and had gone from being a fast-food junkie to a fanatically picky eater. "I'm thinkin' a bowl of chili," he told Hegar, who was still putting things away, as he emptied a can of turkey chili into a bowl to warm in the microwave. A naturally hospitable man, Lanier insisted on making me a sandwich—ham, lettuce, and tomato on fat-free bread he'd baked the day before, with a pickle on the side.

We talked afterwards about how the evening had gone. Lanier said his primary goal had been to build camaraderie among the team and, particularly, to include Chris Seeger and his lawyers, who were representing the Humestons.

I did not know then all the details of the rift between the two men, or that Seeger had gone to see Lanier in Texas before this trial to reach an accommodation.

"I'm used to being the big dog, and you're used to being the big dog, how are we going to do this?" Seeger had told Lanier.

"You got to have one chief and one Indian," Lanier said, "and it's a great commendation to Chris that he was willing to be the Indian."

But Lanier had gone out of his way to treat Seeger as an equal that night. You would have thought they were the best of friends from the way they hugged, traded jokes, and finished each other's sentences.

"I like this. I like this a lot," Seeger had said when Lanier tried out his lines. "I don't care what anyone says. I like this part of you. It's very sincere."

"Give him a hug. Hug it out," Leone had shouted. Only later did I understand the layers of meaning contained within his joke.

Lanier and I also talked about Diane Sullivan, the lead lawyer on the other side. He had never tried a case against her before, but he already had a nickname for her, and it wasn't an affectionate one. He called her "Doofus." I asked him why he called her that, and like the skilled lawyer that he was, Lanier tried to back out of the question.

"Honestly, it's probably more that I'm a doofus. I'm really bad with names," he said.

I chuckled at this transparent attempt at spin.

"I can't remember if her name is Diane or Diana. But it starts with a D, okay?" Lanier said, chuckling himself. "This is like when my daughters' boyfriends come home, and I never can get their names right. I can get the first letter right."

Eventually he gave up, probably because he wanted to talk about why he found Sullivan distasteful. He said she had a tendency to stretch the truth, and that she was "abrasive to people." It seemed to annoy him particularly that juries didn't see those things about Sullivan. She was polite and friendly in front of them, he complained.

"You put all those factors together and mix em all up, for some reason when I call her name, I just think, 'doofus' and it comes out," he said.

Sullivan *had* successfully defended Merck twice in Vioxx trials, once against Mike Humeston, one of the two plaintiffs in this trial. It occurred to me that Sullivan's success may have contributed to Lanier's dislike of her, but I didn't think this was the moment to bring it up.

It was 10 P.M. when I left. Lanier would sleep for a few hours before wakening at 3 A.M. to put the final touches on his opening statement.

"You try to get into the heads of the people you are communicating with, figure out what they're thinking, and try to move them to where you want them to be."

CHAPTER 3

Opening Statements: The Plaintiffs

Atlantic City, New Jersey, January 22, 2007, A.M.

MY CELL PHONE RANG the next morning at 7:30.

"Yeah, I'm in the war room," a voice growled.

It was David Egilman, who never wasted time on greetings when he called.

"You can get a ride to the courthouse," he went on, "but you have to hurry."

Court wouldn't be in session until 9:30. I was still in my pajamas, and wearing them to court didn't seem like such a good idea. I thanked him for the offer and hung up. At 7:55, the phone rang again. It was Egilman, calling from the lobby.

"You ready yet?" he barked.

My ride options were dwindling, he told me. Everyone was leaving—*now*—for the courthouse. I took a cab to court that morning and learned an important lesson. Lanier's people worked late—and early—during the trial. And if I was going to keep up, I'd have to do that too.

The Atlantic County Civil Courthouse was a ten-minute drive from the Borgata, in a run-down part of the city. It was a squat building made of dun-colored bricks with a view of the city's neon landscape. Later that day I ventured out into the neighborhood, to what looked like the main drag, Atlantic Avenue, a short block from the courthouse. It was a cold and gray afternoon, and I was desperate for coffee that had a little more flavor and caffeine than the brew sold at the courthouse. I passed a Dollar Store and several small groceries. Their windows were covered with metal bars and the food on display looked forlorn. Finally I spotted a McDonald's across the street and stumbled into it. I didn't stay long. The customers all seemed to be high—on something other than caffeine—and one man and woman looked about ready to exchange blows. (McDonald's and the court-house coffee shop were neck and neck when it came to the coffee.) In the weeks to come, as the trial dragged on with no end in sight, the courthouse's blighted backdrop would reinforce my sense of living underwater, trapped in a bubble inside which only the trial was real and nothing else mattered or even existed.

That first morning, however, I walked into the courthouse with the greedy anticipation of an innocent, ready for the action to begin. The courthouse had two sets of heavy plate-glass doors. The first opened into a small foyer, and the second set onto a large atrium where two, sometimes three, burly, wise-cracking guards shepherded the waiting line of visitors through a metal detector. The building's two small elevators were a few steps away.

I found the third floor abuzz with lawyers. Plaintiffs' lawyers who had Vioxx cases of their own had come to size up Merck's defense. And like groupies flocking to a rock star, they came to see Lanier. Many months later, I asked one of them, Jerry Kristal, why Lanier had such appeal to other lawyers. Kristal was in his late 50s and himself a very successful trial lawyer. The year before, he'd tried (and won) a Vioxx case with Lanier in the same courtroom, and Kristal seemed surprised by my question.

"Any time you have a chance to see Mark, you go," he said. "It's like watching Michelangelo paint. At least for this generation of trial lawyers, he is, if not the best, at least one of two or three. You always learn something as a student of litigation."

Merck's lawyers were also present in full force. You could tell them apart from the plaintiffs' lawyers by their grim, unsmiling demeanor. The plaintiffs' lawyers were loud and boisterous, as if gathered to party. Merck's team looked as if it were attending a funeral and angry about it.

To accommodate the crowd, the trial was to be held in a courtroom usually reserved for small claims court. Courtroom 3A had high ceilings and the requisite portraits of judges on its walls, but it had none of the grandeur that I associated with courtrooms. Windowless and lit by panels of fluorescent lights, its floor was covered with a grungy blue carpet. Eight rows of folding seats, made of a lightly colored molded wood, were packed in tightly outside the courtroom well. Some of the chairs were broken. If not for the judge's bench and the jury box, it could have been a large classroom at a college with a depressingly small endowment.

But the courtroom's most notable feature wasn't something you saw. It was something you felt. It hit you the moment you walked in. The courtroom was frigid. The judge in the case was a large person, and though she blamed the temperature on an erratic heating system, both sides believed the courtroom was cold because that was how she liked it. It was so cold that the bailiff frequently wore a blanket around her shoulders. The court reporter had one on her lap. Spectators, even some of the lawyers, swathed themselves in heavy winter overcoats. Some people wore gloves. In her opening instructions, the judge advised the jury to "layer up" for the trial.

The judge's high wooden bench dominated the front of the courtroom. The jury box was to its right, and directly in front of the bench were two wooden rectangular tables. Those were for the lawyers. By custom, the table closer to the jury was given to the plaintiffs' lawyers—Mark Lanier and Chris Seeger would sit there. Just behind them, and still within the courtroom well, were chairs for Lanier's jury consultant, Bob Leone, and Seeger's partner, Dave Buchanan. Dara Hegar would sit in the first row of the gallery, directly behind Leone and close enough to whisper and pass notes to him. She had already claimed the adjoining seat for a cardboard box with documents. More boxes sat by her feet and under her chair, tucked behind her legs. Next to Hegar and her boxes, in clear view of the judge and jury, would be the plaintiffs—Mary and Mike Humeston, and the Hermans family.

Only a few feet separated the plaintiffs' counsel table from the defense table, where Merck's lead counsels, Diane Sullivan and Paul Strain, would sit. A phalanx of lawyers and paralegals from the four law firms defending Merck at this trial would fill the rows of seats behind them, surrounded by their own boxes of documents and with BlackBerries at the ready. As the trial wore on, an invisible line of demarcation would divide the supporters of the plaintiffs from Merck's supporters. Each camp kept to its own side of the line, and a demilitarized zone of vacant seats was studiously maintained in between.

But that first day every seat in the courtroom was taken, and it was each man (and woman) for himself. Those who couldn't find seats went next door to a smaller courtroom, which was being used as an overflow room. The trial would be shown live on Court TV's website, and the Court TV crew had hooked up a large TV monitor in that courtroom for the webcast. The number of reporters sent to cover the Vioxx trials had fallen considerably from the first trials, when every major news organization sent someone, but a Lanier trial still had news value and several newspapers and the national wire services were covering the opening. I snagged one of the seats set aside for members of the press in the last row of Courtroom 3A, draped my coat on the back of my chair, pulled out a yellow legal pad, and settled in.

THE PRESIDING JUDGE OF New Jersey's Superior Court (Atlantic County), the Honorable Carol E. Higbee was a placid woman with a plump, pink face. Higbee moved slowly when she walked into the courtroom, steadying herself against nearby objects and panting lightly to catch her breath. Her unassuming, down-to-earth manner made it easy to forget the power she wielded. Plaintiffs everywhere in the country could sue Merck in New Jersey, because the company was based there, and there were more Vioxx suits filed in New Jersey—roughly 17,000—than anywhere else. All of them fell under Higbee's purview.

Before the jury was brought in, the two sides wrangled for a while at the judge's bench over the slides that would accompany their opening statements. Lanier was forced to remove the picture of spinach from his slide about the FDA, for exactly the reason he had put it in: it evoked the FDA's nationwide recall of contaminated spinach. Toward the end, the two sides sparred over another of Lanier's slides. It was a priceless exchange and I laughed out loud as I read it later in the court transcript.

Hope Freiwald, a partner in the Philadelphia office of Dechert LLP and one of Merck's lead lawyers in the New Jersey cases, brought up the objection.

"Well, here's the big one," she told Judge Higbee. "It looks to me like they have Merck represented as the Iraqi army."

Freiwald was referring to a slide intended to represent the sales force of 3,000 that Merck deployed to promote Vioxx to doctors when it launched the drug in 1998. It was the largest sales force ever assembled by a drug company to promote a drug. Higbee's reaction, as recorded by the court reporter, was characteristically colloquial.

"Oh jeez!" she said.

In my mind's eye, I could almost see her rolling her eyes and hear the chuckle in her voice. She had been a plaintiff's lawyer before becoming a judge and gave lawyers on both sides plenty of latitude.

As Lanier had put it appreciatively the night before, "She lets lawyers be lawyers."

But this was her fourth Vioxx trial, and Higbee was nobody's fool.

When Lanier assured her he hadn't used a picture of the Iraqi army, she retorted dryly, "I hope it is not the Third Reich..." (Merck began as a German company.)

"It is the United States Marines or something," Lanier said.

"In berets," Freiwald said.

Lanier was cornered.

"They are the Green Berets," he said. "It is a picture of the army, U.S. Army. I promise you, it is the U.S. Army."

Diane Sullivan, Merck's lead lawyer, took over.

"It looks like the Iraqi army to me," Sullivan told Higbee.

And Freiwald tried a different tack, "It doesn't matter what army it is. It is a little more than over the top, Judge."

"No, it is not," Lanier countered.

Any moment, it seemed, the two sides would have to be separated and sent to their corners.

"I'm allowing it as long as it is not the Iraqis or the Nazis," Higbee said.

Lanier had won, but he couldn't resist tweaking the Merck attorneys.

"The Iraqis are on our side now," he told them (just in case they didn't know.)

THE MORNING WAS HALF over by the time the judge sent for the jury. While we waited for the jury, Lanier walked to the back of the courtroom, where Becky Lanier sat, flanked by her young daughters.

"Hey, Becky!" Lanier called out. "I need you. Bob [Leone] tells me my tie is not straight."

Lanier's wife stood up from her seat in the middle of the second-to-last row and Lanier squeezed his way past several pairs of knees to her. Almost a foot shorter than her husband, she reached up to loosen the tie knot and silently, she straightened it. Lanier's eyes were fastened to his wife's face. He was still looking at her when she finished her task and prepared to return to her seat.

"A kiss for luck," he said.

She met his gaze at last and responded with a chaste kiss on the lips. Smiling broadly, Lanier walked back to his chair in the well of the courtroom. It had been an oddly intimate exchange for such a public setting, and watching from my seat a foot away, I got the feeling that Lanier had been keenly aware of his captive, and curious, audience, and had been playing to it. His wife must have known it too. She was laughing as she settled back into her seat.

A couple of seats away, an old Houston friend scoffed playfully.

"My tie needs to be straightened! A kiss for luck!" she said, chuckling at the ploy Lanier had used to get a kiss from his circumspect wife. "He seems like such a smart boy, too."

Lanier was still adjusting his tie when the bailiff threw open a door in the rear of the courtroom, near the jury box.

"All rise!" she said, and led the jury in.

We rose, and stayed on our feet until all ten jurors had filed in and taken their seats. New Jersey law required a minimum of six jurors for civil trials. But the trial was expected to be long, and the judge had picked enough extras so she could be sure of having a jury if sickness or other events caused some jurors to drop out along the way.

They entered in reverse order, number 10 first. He climbed the steps inside the jury box to the upper tier of seats, walked to the far end of the box, and took his seat. Four jurors joined him on the upper tier, and they were followed by the five jurors who would sit in the lower tier. Juror number 1 was the last to settle into her seat.

By New Jersey custom, she would be the jury's foreperson. An older woman, perhaps in her seventies, she was Norwegian by birth. Her face was lined, and her hair was swept back in an old-fashioned bouffant. Behind her thick glasses, her eyes were alert. She sat with her hands folded in her lap and her back erect—the picture of rectitude.

Juror number 2 sat to her right, arms crossed across his chest, his face expressionless, almost stony. He was a policeman and one of two African Americans on the jury. To his right was juror number 3, white-haired and solidly built. He was a retired high-school teacher and still had the habit of authority about him. The other two jurors in the front row, numbers 4 and 5, had less forceful personalities. Juror number 4, a middle-aged woman who worked for the phone company, had large, dark eyes. She gave off a nervous energy as she crossed her legs and twisted her thin frame into the seat. She may just have been craving her cigarettes. Later in the trial, I sometimes spied her on the patio outside the courthouse, puffing on a cigarette in the cold before the trial began. Juror number 5 was a retired postal worker, an elderly, frail-looking, African American gentleman given to napping.

In the back row, directly behind juror number 1, was juror number 6. Balding and middle-aged, he worked in one of the local casinos, and as the weeks wore on, he receded more and more into the background. Maybe it was just the contrast with the man to his right, juror number 7, animated, brawny, and bearded, who identified himself as Egyptian and owned a diner in the area. At moments of high drama, he would lean his barrel-shaped body forward in the chair and smile widely. Next over was juror number 8, a woman with reddish hair and a pleasant face who had retired from the U.S. Mint in Philadelphia. To her right sat juror number 9, sweet-faced, dark-haired, and the jury's only twenty-something. He was a slot machine technician at the casinos and during jury selection, he had joked with the judge that jury duty would get him off the graveyard shift. He often looked entertained by the proceedings, and was a frank and unabashed admirer of Hegar's person. In the far corner of the back row, his body subtly angled away from the group, sat juror number 10. A compactly built man with graying hair and a dour face, he looked to be in his early 60s. One of his children worked as a salesperson for a drug company, which worried Leone.

HIGBEE GAVE THE JURY brief instructions and asked Lanier to begin.

Lanier stood up from his seat at the counsel table and nodded to the Merck lawyers a few feet away, before walking over to face the jury. He wore a dark blue suit, his short brown hair gleamed, and he radiated an earnest politeness.

"My name is Mark Lanier," he said, "and it is an honor to present this case before you." He glanced over his right shoulder to where Judge Higbee and her two law clerks sat and continued, "And before you, Judge Higbee, and your staff. And thank you all for your hospitality and thank you for letting us do this."

It's common for lawyers to begin by thanking juries for the service they are about to render. It's a way to show respect to the people who will render the final verdict. But by thanking the judge and jury for their hospitality, Lanier had also done something else. He had shrewdly stated the obvious—he was an outsider among them. It was impossible to hide. Lanier's speech was thick with the sounds of Texas.

He dropped his g's liberally, contracted his verbs, and peppered his speech with country colloquialisms. His manner belied his sophistication and often brought a smile to my face. I thought of it as his Texan charm offensive, and I thought he would probably need it before this New Jersey jury. New Jersey had been home to the pharmaceutical industry for more than a hundred years. At one time, three quarters of the world's drug companies were based there. The industry still generated more jobs and paid more taxes than any other in the state.

The jurors had met Lanier only once and briefly, during jury selection, when they had learned that the trial would be about heart attacks allegedly caused by Merck's painkiller Vioxx. That morning's opening statement would be their first extended encounter with him, and it marked the true beginning of Lanier's ardent courtship.

"I tried to think what I could do to try and make sense of this case to everybody in the way I understand it happened, so here's what I have done," Lanier began. "If we consider a car accident, that's something we're all familiar with. We have seen them. We have experienced them. I think in a sense that what we have here is a wreck."

A red 18-wheeler truck could be seen driving from left to right on the large screen behind Lanier, as he spoke. The side of the truck bore the orange and blue Vioxx logo, and in parentheses, the drug's generic name, rofecoxib. The truck was headed for an intersection, near which stood a building labeled "Merck." A second vehicle—a family minivan—was also making its way toward that intersection, moving up steadily from the bottom of the screen. As the truck and the minivan drew closer to the intersection and each other, the trucker's light turned from green to yellow. The light was red when the truck barreled through the intersection and the truck came to a stop only after it hit the minivan.

"We have a wreck here where someone has run a red light," Lanier said, "and we contend it's Vioxx."

Holding up a sample pack of Vioxx—the kind salesmen dropped off at doctors' offices to encourage doctors to prescribe Vioxx— Lanier continued, "And it is our contention that when Merck was selling this drug, for a substantial period of time, some of the people within Merck made decisions not to tell the whole truth about this drug. They kept studies secret, some studies. They kept some facts secret, they kept some worries and concerns secret." In an obvious nod to juror number 10, he continued, "They didn't tell all their salespeople. In fact, very few, if any, of their salespeople got the whole truth, and as a result, there was a lot of Vioxx usage that caused a lot of heartache."

A vehicle accident report floated into view over the collision scene at this point. It would be their job to decide if the light was red when Merck drove through and fill out the report, Lanier told the jurors.

"I'm going to contend to you that the evidence is going to show it was," he said.

In a few short minutes, Lanier had laid out in simple and graphic terms the nub of the plaintiffs' case: Merck had knowingly and recklessly put Vioxx patients in harm's way. It had known for years that Vioxx could be harmful, but it had withheld the information from patients and doctors. In the eyes of the law, corporations are considered people, and in Lanier's hands, Merck, the corporation, was acquiring character traits, like a person. It was wily and unscrupulous.

I HAD SEEN LANIER speak to juries twice before. But I watched this performance through new eyes. This time, I had been backstage and I knew something more about who he was away from the eyes of the jury. I had learned that no matter how casual Lanier seemed in court, his presentations were always meticulously planned. I'd also seen his visceral dislike of Merck's lawyers. But none of that was visible in the moment.

What struck me most was the intensity of his focus on the jury. It was as if, despite the crowd, for him, only the ten men and women of the jury were present in the courtroom. I thought it would be hard not to be flattered by such attention. When I shared my impressions with him later, I found that like so much else about how he tried cases, Lanier's behavior around the jury was both genuine and carefully calculated. Most public speakers, he said, avoided their listeners' eyes. He did the opposite.

"In my philosophy of communication, what you do is you try to get into the heads of the people you are communicating with, figure out what they're thinking, and try to move them to where you want them to be. You can look into their eyes and you can tell," he said.

Lanier's courtroom style drew heavily from another kind of public speaking—preaching.

"I'm a student of speech communication. I read the books, I read the studies, I attend lectures, and I can tell you that some of the best communicators are preachers," Lanier said. From preachers, he had learned that the most effective way to communicate orally was to tell a story, to use clichés, and to repeat his ideas frequently to help jurors remember them.

Lanier had trained as a minister in the "Churches of Christ," a nondenominational movement that traced its roots to the 19th century and in which he had been brought up. Though he forsook the ministry for law school, he still preached after a fashion. Every Sunday, for many years, he had taught a 45-minute Sunday school class at the Southern Baptist mega-church to which he belonged. Hundreds attended his class.

Like the opening statement, his Sunday school classes were built around a story that was amplified by catchy PowerPoint slides, and Lanier said teaching Sunday school was like being in court every week.

"Most lawyers try cases no more than once or twice a year, some once or twice every five years," Lanier said. "I speak 50 times a year for at least 45 minutes. That's 250 times over the last 5 years. I can do it in my sleep."

Lanier credited all that practice for the ease with which he meshed the spoken and visual elements of his opening statement. The feat appeared all the more remarkable because he spoke with his back to the screen on which the slides were projected. In fact, he could see the slides on his laptop, which sat out of the jury's sight, on the floor in front of the jury box. The laptop also displayed his notes and functioned as a teleprompter. Lanier controlled the slides with a remote control, tucked away in one hand.

Lanier's "philosophy of communication" extended to his attire. A self-described "clothes horse," he shopped widely for his clothing, in his hometown of Lubbock, Texas, at an upscale specialty store, called Malouf's; in New York, at Bergdorf Goodman; and many points in between. ("You should have seen the lavender striped shirt and lavender tie I wore this week," he told me once, "it just snapped you to attention.") He said he had so many clothes he could have gone through the seven-week trial without wearing a single suit twice. As a young lawyer, he had done just that before he learned that a large wardrobe was distracting to the jury. (In one trial, his suits and ties became a hot topic in the jury room.) Lanier's response was characteristically disciplined. He pared back his trial wardrobe to two suits and two ties that he alternated during the trial, no matter how long it lasted. To make the paltry clothing rations more palatable, Lanier treated himself to new suits every trial, and for this trial, he had bought two blue suits as well as six shirts, all of them white, a color he disliked and normally avoided. Jurors might still remark on his clothes, Lanier said. Perhaps they would wonder why he wore the same clothes almost every day. "Bless his heart. He's so in tune with the work, he's not even thinking about what he's wearing," jurors had said in past trials. Of course, they could not have been further from the truth. Lanier had chosen his clothes carefully to make sure they didn't steal the spotlight from the job at hand, which on that day was to give the jury an abbreviated history of Vioxx's rise and fall.

LANIER BEGAN WITH THE "green light" that launched Merck's development of Vioxx in the early 1990s.

The popular painkillers of the time—aspirin, Advil, and Aleve—worked well for most people, but in a small group of people they caused ulcers and stomach bleeding, Lanier told the jurors. That was because when these drugs blocked the enzyme that regulates inflammation and pain, called COX-2, they also blocked a related enzyme that maintains the stomach's mucous lining, COX-1. Scientists at Merck (and other companies) hypothesized that a painkiller that suppressed the pain-related COX-2 enzyme but left COX-1 alone, would cause less gastrointestinal bleeding and ulcers. That idea was the green light that initiated the development of Vioxx, Lanier said; that, and the promise of big profits. Some 66 million Americans were known to have arthritis, and Merck knew Vioxx would be a "high-dollar drug," he said.

Then in May 1998, a full year before Merck sold the first Vioxx pill, an external board of scientific advisors warned that new research suggested Vioxx may have a dangerous side effect: heart attacks. The light had turned yellow, Lanier said.

"Now, when the light turns yellow, we all know you gotta stop, or you at least need to be alert and try to figure out, should I be stopping, should be I be slowing, what do I need to do? Assess. Assess the danger. Assess where you are. Take time out and check," he said.

That didn't happen because "someone new started driving the company," Lanier said. For the first time in its history, the company's chief executive was not a scientist but a businessman, whose motto was "sales at all costs." He didn't want to slow down Vioxx's development with additional safety testing, Lanier said. Another drug company was also working on a stomach-sparing painkiller and Merck was racing to get Vioxx into patients' hands first.

"So what does Merck do? Light turns yellow, and they put pedal to the metal," Lanier said, and he nodded earnestly, as if to say he understood—and shared—the jurors' disbelief at Merck's behavior. Still nodding, he repeated, "They do," and hammered his point home with a new slide. It showed a speedometer with the needle fixed at its maximum speed, 160 miles/hour.

Lanier had brought the jury to a consequential moment in Vioxx's early history, where Merck's executives could have chosen to pursue the scientific questions raised by its advisors, or to look the other way and continue undeterred. They did the latter. Had they chosen differently, Lanier and the ten jurors might never have met.

Merck's external board of scientific advisers was worried about Vioxx because of research that suggested Vioxx suppressed one of the body's most potent defenses against heart attacks, a molecule called prostacyclin. The chain of events that leads to a typical heart attack begins with the cracking of the fibrous cap that covers the lumpy deposits of cholesterol and white blood cells, called plaque, inside coronary arteries. The cracking of the cap signals the body to patch up the tear with a clot, and the process of forming a blood clot gets underway. Disc-shaped cells called platelets rush to the site and produce a molecule called thromboxane, which recruits other platelets to the task. In healthy arteries, the layer of skin that lines the arteries produces prostacyclin to simultaneously "calm" the platelets and prevent them from forming a clot. If the body's clot-promoting and clot-busting systems are in balance, the clot is avoided. If they aren't, a clot can form; and if it grows large enough to block the artery, it leads to a heart attack.

Until Vioxx was developed, scientists believed that the production of both prostacyclin and the clot-promoting molecule thromboxane was regulated by the COX-1 enzyme. Research on Vioxx led them to suspect they were only half right: while the pro-clotting molecule thromboxane was regulated by the COX-1 enzyme, the anti-clotting prostacyclin was regulated by COX-2. Merck's scientific advisers inferred that Vioxx, which blocked the COX-2 enzyme but not the COX-1 enzyme, might throw off the balance of pro-clotting and anti-clotting molecules in the body. They hypothesized that a person taking Vioxx would be more likely to develop blood clots in the arteries, and to have heart attacks, than someone taking older painkillers, such as aspirin, which knock out both COX-1 and COX-2, and thus handicap, almost equally, the body's ability to make clots as well as to break them up.

Lanier had just described the leading theory of how Vioxx causes heart attacks, and it was a lot for the jury to take in, especially the first time around.

"Let me do it this way," he said, and reached under his table to retrieve the first of the "tools" he'd stashed out of sight of Merck's lawyers.

He emerged with the copper scales and two Ziploc sandwich bags filled with plastic party favors, and placed them on his table.

"You can tell I have kids," Lanier said, smiling, as he heaped the plastic party toys on the scales, diving after those that fell to the floor. The toys represented the chemicals he'd just described to the jury—prostacyclin and thromboxane.

"We're gonna put the prostacyclin. It thins the blood. We're gonna put those on this side," Lanier said, emptying the bag of green plastic toys into one pan on the scale.

"Now on this side, we're going to put the thromboxane that causes the clotting," he said, as he piled the orange toys on the other pan.

"Okay. Is that in balance, sort of? Give it a second to stop," he said to the jury, as the scales seesawed.

I craned my neck, feeling a bit like a child at a birthday party watching a magic act unfold.

When the two pans looked to be in balance, Lanier continued, "That's the way we are. We're in balance."

The older painkillers, such as Advil and Aleve, suppressed the production of both prostacyclin and thromboxane, Lanier reminded the jury.

"And so every time you took one out of one and one out of the other, things would stay in balance," he said, and demonstrated by removing a party favor from each of the copper pans.

Not so with Vioxx, which blocked the production of prostacyclin by as much as 80 percent, Lanier said.

"That would be two, four, six, eight," he said, counting out the green plastic toys that represented the prostacyclin molecules as he removed them from the scales, "for every two it takes out over here," and removed two of the red plastic thromboxane molecules.

The prostacyclin pan swung up as the thromboxane pan dropped. "The body is out of balance," Lanier said, holding up his palms, "Your body's got an ability to make the clots, but your body doesn't have the ability to thin the clots, and that's the problem."

"Without prostacyclin, you're a walking time bomb, and it's just a matter of time for a lot of people who have the risk factors before they have a heart attack," Lanier said. Merck knew this. "They understand this *before – they – start – selling – the drug*," Lanier said, matching each pause between words with a step toward the jury box. His voice was no longer conversational. It was loud and high-pitched.

The company's scientific advisors told Merck to do specific tests that would settle the question of whether Vioxx posed a risk to the heart, Lanier said.

"Merck says, 'No,'" and laughing softly, he continued, "In fact, Merck says 'We're not going to do those tests until we're selling the drugs, and then other people can do 'em, if they want 'em done.'"

The scales and the party toys would remain on, or just beneath, Lanier's table throughout the trial, a wordless reminder to the jury that Vioxx could disrupt the body's delicate balance with potentially lethal consequences.

EVEN IN THE EARLY studies, subjects who took Vioxx had more heart problems than subjects given older drugs or sugar pills. For the most part, the differences between the two groups did not pass tests for statistical significance, and in the absence of evidence to the contrary, it had to be assumed that there were more heart problems among Vioxx subjects because of chance. But by law, Merck still had to disclose the heart attacks to doctors and patients. Lanier said it did so as inconspicuously as possible, and put on his second show-and-tell of the morning to make that point.

From under his table he produced three large, brightly colored rectangular containers. The Food and Drug Administration requires drug companies to list all reactions that occur during clinical trials in one of three categories, and Lanier's containers corresponded to those categories. A large paper label that said "WARNING" was pasted to the red container. It was intended for the most serious side effects observed. The lime-green one was labeled "PRECAUTIONS" for slightly less serious side effects. Both of these containers were empty.

"And then there's one last bucket. It is kind of the catchall," Lanier said, placing a dark green container marked "ADVERSE REACTIONS" on his table, in clear view of the jury, and tossing a bottle of bug spray into the container.

"This is the bucket for Vioxx that's got stuff like insect bites," he said.

"Neosporin. Infected cuts," Lanier said, as he threw a tube of ointment into the bin.

"Some people were constipated. Some people were congested. Some people had gas," he said, tossing in a remedy for each malady as he ran through a litany of run-of the-mill conditions that were unlikely to have been caused by Vioxx and were therefore noted in the Adverse Reactions catchall. "Some people had a sore throat. Some people had hemorrhoids. Some people hurt their ankle. Some people got a toothache. Some people had stuffed-up noses. Some people had bad breath. Some people got scratches. Some people had toenail fungus." Lanier's pace quickened as the list lengthened. By the time he was done, there was an impressive pile of pills and potions in the container—from antihistamines to Preparation H.

"Now, Merck's got to report the heart attacks from these studies. Do you know which bucket they put it in?" Lanier said.

He picked up a plastic model of a heart that he'd used earlier to explain how heart attacks occur, and walked over to the red container that sat on the floor a few feet away.

"Warning: This pain pill can kill you," he said, holding the model heart over the Warning container, as if to drop it in. "It doesn't go in the Warning bucket," he said and took a couple of steps over to the next container and repeated the exercise. "Precaution: Yellow light, we're concerned, this pain pill might kill you. Noooo."

Lanier returned finally to the dark green Adverse Reactions container on his table.

"It goes over here with the bug bites and the broken ankles as just something that happened but doesn't seem to be related to the drug," Lanier said, and tossed the heart into the container, where it landed with a dull thud.

Looking over at Merck's lawyers, he continued, "They put it in the wrong bucket, and they start selling the drug."

In the back of the courtroom, Lanier's wife and one of his lawyers, Rick Meadow, exchanged a smile, as the plastic heart hit the bin. It had been a quintessential Lanier performance: funny, memorable, and brilliantly simple. I thought to myself it was no wonder the Merck lawyers despised him.

In the weeks leading up to the trial, Lanier had wracked his brain for a new way to explain the different sections of a drug label and why it mattered that Merck had put the Vioxx heart attacks in the Adverse Reactions section. He was out jogging one day when it hit him: "I could actually get buckets, put things in the bucket, [and] turn it almost into a joke."

Lanier was now about an hour into his opening, and half-way done. He had one last piece of show-and-tell for the jury before the lunch break—a Vioxx TV ad featuring a white-haired man in a plaid shirt and jacket taking his dog on an early morning walk.

"I don't want to play hockey, all I want are nights with less pain, mornings with less stiffness," the man said.

An announcer followed: "With one little pill a day, Vioxx can provide powerful 24-hour relief."

The commercial closed with man and dog arriving at their destination, a "dog park" where dogs ran off leash while their elderly owners sipped coffee and looked on. It was an idyllic scene. The announcer warned that people with asthma, kidney, or liver problems shouldn't use Vioxx, but made no mention of Vioxx's risks to the heart.

"You would think with all this hoopla about heart attacks, that [heart attacks] would be there in the warning," Leone said later. "And it's not in the warning in the first commercial, the last commercial, anywhere. We went through five years of their commercials, never ever do they put a warning," he said.

Lanier had wanted to underline that omission by telling the jury before he played the commercial to listen for the warning of heart problems, but the judge ruled he couldn't do that.

Lanier chose to emphasize instead how aggressively Merck had marketed Vioxx. In 2000, the first full year that Vioxx was on the market, Merck spent $160 million on advertising it to consumers, outspending PepsiCo's advertising budgets for cola and Budweiser's for beer. Vioxx was more heavily promoted to consumers that year than any other prescription drug in the country. The strategy paid off, as sales quadrupled from the year before to exceed $1 billion.

"It is an advertising blitz at a yellow-light time when the warnings are *there* for Merck," Lanier said, and he asked the court for a lunch break.

BOTH SIDES HAD LUNCH brought into their assigned conference rooms behind the courtroom. The plaintiffs' room was crammed with furniture—there was a large oval table, at least a dozen chairs, and metal file cabinets lining the walls. The floor was carpeted in rusty brown, the walls were painted blue, and it was blessedly overheated.

Lanier sat at the head of the outsized oval table that filled up most of the room, eating a homemade peanut butter and jelly sandwich and holding court on his obsession of the moment—Diane Sullivan's opening statement, why it would be "packed with lies," and how he planned to expose them.

"I want each one of these lies *immediately*," Lanier told his lawyers, between bites of his sandwich. "What I believe will happen is I will have 30 minutes, maybe 15 at the end of Diane's opening."

He would use that time to confront the top Merck executive who was his first witness with Sullivan's "lies." It was another illustration of how style was also substance for Lanier. Another lawyer might not have pushed to squeeze in fifteen minutes of cross-examination that afternoon. Lanier would, because he hoped the drama of even a brief cross-examination immediately after Sullivan's opening statement would send a loud message to the jury: Merck and Sullivan weren't to be trusted, but they couldn't fool Lanier—he was watching them like a hawk.

While Lanier talked, a minor rebellion was erupting around the table as his lawyers examined the lunch sandwiches—turkey, chicken, cheese, and roasted vegetables.

"You got any meatball subs?" Leone asked the young associate who was in charge of ordering trays of lunch from the Borgata.

"I don't want to lose my job," Meredith Gursky told Leone.

Gursky was under strict orders from Lanier to serve healthy lunches, and Leone's fondness for meatball subs was one reason why. Leone was diabetic, though you wouldn't know it from what he ate, particularly if Lanier, Hegar, or Leone's wife weren't looking. Chris Seeger was grumbling too.

"What's up with these non-transfat potato chips," he said, trying one.

Leone chimed in, "What's wrong with transfats?"

Rick Meadow, the rail-thin and exercise-obsessed lawyer who ran Lanier's New York office, held out hope to the group. "We're having pizza tonight," he said. (They grabbed dinner on their own, and thus were free to eat all the junk food they craved.) Lanier ignored them all and ate his sandwich.

As they prepared to return to the courtroom, Egilman, who stayed in the back room while court was in session, asked Leone about Lanier's performance thus far.

"How's he doing?" Egilman said.

"He's doing fine," Leone said.

It was Leone's job to know. From his seat, directly behind Lanier's in the courtroom well, Leone watched the jury, without seeming to, and passed frequent notes to Lanier. Lanier joked that Leone's copious notes were mostly "chaff."

"But you got to read 'em all, because you never know which one will have the nugget...that wins the case," he said.

THE TRAFFIC LIGHT HAD changed from yellow to red when Lanier resumed the tale of the Vioxx truck. He said the red light was from a study called VIGOR, whose results became known to Merck less than a year after it started selling Vioxx, in 2000.

VIGOR had 8,000 subjects—half on Vioxx and the other half on an older painkiller called naproxen. Merck did the study to show that Vioxx was, in fact, safer for the gastrointestinal system than older painkillers. That was Vioxx's primary claim to superiority over the older drugs, and VIGOR showed it to be true. Vioxx subjects had half as many gastrointestinal problems as those given naproxen.

But VIGOR also revealed that Vioxx had a serious downside. Vioxx subjects in the study had five times as many heart attacks as those on naproxen: there were four heart attacks among the study's naproxen subjects compared to 20 among those given Vioxx.

"Now, in the grand scheme of things, you might say, 'well, what do we have here?' It's not a huge incidence" of heart attacks on Vioxx, Lanier said. "But what you gotta think is that millions and millions and millions of people take the drug, and when you do the math, what you find out is just simply off the map."

Four and a half years before Merck took Vioxx off the market, the VIGOR study had predicted that Vioxx's toll on American hearts would run to the tens of thousands.

"That's what the VIGOR study shows. And Merck knows it," Lanier added.

Merck's lawyers interrupted Lanier's opening to argue heatedly that the results of the VIGOR study, which was conducted on subjects with rheumatoid arthritis, couldn't be extrapolated to the population at large. (People with rheumatoid arthritis are at slightly higher risk of heart problems.) Higbee overruled them. She said it was reasonable for Lanier to argue that the excess in heart attacks among Vioxx subjects in the VIGOR study, though numerically small, represented a much bigger number in the population at large.

Once the VIGOR study results were in, Lanier said, the light was as red as it could be.

"They should tell everybody, Time out, we've got a study that just came back, and this study shows five times as many heart attacks" on Vioxx as on the other drug, Lanier said. "We may not know why…but we know that it is there. So doctors, and people, be alert to that and make your own decision, 'do you want to take this drug?'"

He said Merck should have stopped sending out its Vioxx sales force, stopped the TV ads, and withdrawn the Vioxx label that lumped heart attacks with trivial side effects in what he called "the bug-bite bucket."

But Merck didn't do that, Lanier said. Vioxx was bringing billions of dollars into the company, he said. "And nothing was going to stop the Merck marketing machine," he thundered. "Nothing."

Merck "misreported" the results of the VIGOR study, Lanier said, and as he spoke, his eyes scanned his table, then the floor underneath it. Finally, he threw up his hands, as if in disgust.

"I don't have an illustration for this," he said, pacing the courtroom and staring at the objects on the court reporter's desk and the judge's bench until, apparently, he thought of something. He pointed to the screen on which the slides were being projected.

"I can't hide what's on that screen from you, but I'll tell you what I can do," he said, and walked around to the back of the projector, so its bulb shone on his suit jacket and his body obscured the slide from the jury's view. Shifting his weight from foot to foot, he continued, "I can stand here while I talk to you and you would get a glimpse, but you wouldn't get the whole screen. I can't stop you from seeing it, but I can certainly make it where it is hard for you to read what it is, especially if I'm standing here when I click to the new screen."

The mood in the room was shifting, as Lanier's outrage intensified into what looked like downright anger.

"The reason I use that as an illustration is because of this. Merck's got to report the VIGOR study. You can't keep that silent. So what they do is misreport," Lanier said. "They send it to the *New England Journal of Medicine,* and they leave out some important stuff."

Not all the heart attacks seen among Vioxx subjects in the VIGOR trial were disclosed in the *NEJM* paper, Lanier said. Many other heart problems were also omitted. In late 2005, the *NEJM's* editors had chastised the authors in print for the omissions.

"Don't play hide and seek with the data," Gregory Curfman, the *NEJM* executive editor, had said in deposition testimony denouncing the omissions. Lanier clicked on a new slide as he spoke. It showed a photograph of Curfman and a cartoon bubble containing those words issuing from his mouth.

Lanier said Merck blanketed the country with misleading letters to doctors.

"And Merck is going to want to tell you, Oh, ladies and gentlemen, use your common sense," Lanier said, throwing his head back and his arms up, and imitating the incredulous tones of a defense lawyer. "Would we send these letters out all over the country if we were trying to hide the results?" he said, and answered his question in a conversational tone, "Well, yes, you would, if the letters aren't true. And that's what I will show you."

Lanier looked over at where Merck's lawyers sat, and strode to the end of the jury box furthest from them.

"I'll be candid with 'em, and I'll be candid with you," he said. "Maybe, maybe your drug is fine. Certainly your people think it is fine, or a lot of your people do. But tell *me* the good, the bad, and the ugly. Tell all of us the good, the bad, and the ugly," Lanier said. His brow furrowed, lips tight, speaking at a higher pitch and faster, he went on, "Don't hide it from the doctors. Don't hide it from the public. Don't hide it from the FDA. Don't hide it from the scientists. Don't hide it from the magazine journals. Don't hide it from anybody."

With each sentence he had taken one short step, sliding along the length of the jury box, as if under the influence of a physical force that matched his rising emotion. He had covered half the length of the jury box, until finally he released his audience from the tension of the moment to finish off in an even tone, "Tell them the truth, so that people can make an intelligent decision."

The cadence of Lanier's speech and his moral outrage could hardly have been more like a preacher's.

Merck didn't tell people the good, the bad, and the ugly about Vioxx, he said, "and as a result, there are lots of people that had heart attacks in this country that shouldn't have."

"Don't get me wrong. Am I saying that when you take a Vioxx pill, it makes a clot in your body? Not directly," Lanier said.

But in people who were already at risk of heart attack, like the elderly, who were the natural market for Vioxx, it made blood clots and heart attacks *more likely* by blocking the body's own safeguards, he said.

Many studies after VIGOR also showed Vioxx had problems, but Merck didn't stop hiding the truth about Vioxx "until, finally, the wheels come off," Lanier said. It happened in September 2004 when Merck was testing Vioxx to see if it could prevent colon polyps in a study called APPROVe, he said. When the safety committee overseeing the APPROVe study determined that heart problems were occurring twice as often in the Vioxx group as in those given the placebo, it ordered Merck to halt the study. Merck did, and that's when it took Vioxx off the market.

Lanier said Merck blamed everyone for the problems Vioxx had caused, including Vioxx's victims themselves, and gave a mock preview of the argument that had helped Merck win most of the previous trials.

"They'll say, 'If people didn't have risk factors, if no one had this plaque in their arteries, then they wouldn't be having a heart attack to start with,'" Lanier said. He smiled and added, "Well, but this is America, everybody does, and Merck knows it. That's why they sell us drugs to lower our cholesterol."

Lanier shook his finger at the jury. "Don't let 'em talk their way out of the red light, because when all is said and done, they ran it," he said. "An accident report shows they ran it, and the accident report is drawn up right. And the eyewitnesses show that people driving for Merck had a red light and they kept going anyway. That's what I'm going to show you, ladies and gentlemen, in the first phase of this trial."

"What a disastrous business plan, to make a drug that you know hurts people and lie to doctors. You never would sell another medicine if you did that. It doesn't make common sense."

CHAPTER 4

Opening Statements: Merck

Atlantic City, New Jersey, January 22, 2007, P.M.

AS THE JURY WALKED out of the courtroom for a short break after Lanier's opening, a short, white-haired man approached the judge. Diane Sullivan's co-counsel, Paul Strain, looked to be in his early 60s.

"Can we get a moment of Your Honor's time," he asked.

The other lawyers clustered around Higbee's bench and leaned in to listen.

"Your Honor, during the opening argument, there were two extremely inflammatory things that I hope the Court caught," Strain said. "They warrant a mistrial."

Strain was referring to Lanier's remarks that tests of Vioxx among Alzheimer's patients showed Vioxx hastened the onset and progression of the disease.

"There's no evidence to suggest that, Your Honor. Even if there were evidence, that has nothing to do with this case," Strain said. "For anyone whose family may have been touched by Alzheimer's, there could be few things I can imagine more emotionally laden than that… That warrants a mistrial. We so move for mistrial on that basis alone, Your Honor."

Merck's studies *did* show that Vioxx hastened Alzheimer's, as one of the plaintiffs' lawyers pointed out and Higbee acknowledged. But Strain was right in saying that those results had nothing to do with the questions of Vioxx's alleged cardiovascular risks that were before the jury.

"Mr. Lanier, for the rest of the trial, it should not be referred to. I think it's not appropriate," Higbee said, and denied Merck's request for a mistrial. It was the first of dozens that Strain would make.

Just before the jury returned, Higbee summoned Strain and Sullivan for a second sidebar. Lanier's co-counsel Chris Seeger had complained that during Lanier's opening, Sullivan had derided Lanier's estimates of the number of heart attacks caused by Vioxx so loudly that the jury had overheard her. (The conversations between Judge Higbee and the lawyers at her bench, called sidebars, were supposed to be inaudible to the jury.)

"I want an end to that today. I don't want to go through another Humeston situation where I was called a name and it was, 'Oh, you're this kind of lawyer, you're that kind of lawyer,'" Seeger said, referring to the earlier trial of Mike Humeston's case.

Strain jumped to Sullivan's defense.

"I barely heard it," he said, of Sullivan's remark.

Higbee leaned forward in her chair and watched Seeger, the broad-shouldered former boxer, and the much smaller but still pugnacious Strain spar for a minute or two before intervening.

"All right, look, look. I'm not going to go into an issue of whether it was heard or not heard. I didn't actually hear it. So I'm not talking about anything done in the past," she said. "I'd ask in the future, all of you… Do not make disparaging remarks about each other. Do not make disparaging remarks about lawyers in general in the hearing of the jury. It is not necessary. Let's comment on the evidence. And that goes both ways for both sides."

His loss to Sullivan had rankled Seeger for a long time. When his fellow plaintiffs' lawyers came up to him at other Vioxx trials to ask how he was doing and to tell him he had deserved to win, he assured them that he had moved on. But that wasn't true.

"It's all I could think of for a year and a half. Literally to the point I couldn't sleep through the night. On the BlackBerry, I was keeping a list of every inappropriate thing she did," Seeger told me.

"I would cross her in the well of the courtroom, and she'd say, 'You're a [expletive] worm,' 'You're a [expletive] weasel,' 'Why don't you be a man?' 'Why don't you stop being a cry-baby?' 'You're a little girl.' She did that to me constantly," he said.

I found Seeger's account of Sullivan's schoolyard taunts incredible, and I asked him whether any one could corroborate his account. He said Sullivan had muttered the insults. When I went back to read transcripts of that trial, I found that Seeger had complained to Higbee several times about Sullivan's muttered remarks. In at least one instance, when Sullivan had allegedly muttered to Seeger, "Stop playing games," loudly enough to be overheard by the jury, Higbee had reprimanded Sullivan. She had summoned Sullivan to the bench, where Sullivan had protested her innocence. She said she had only used the phrase in a sidebar.

"I don't want the phrase used again in the courtroom at sidebar, or anywhere else," Higbee had said, adding "Miss Sullivan, you know, for some reason you let Mr. Seeger get under your skin. I don't know why."

To which Sullivan had responded, incorrigibly, *"Because he plays games, Your Honor."* (Italics added.) An apparently shocked colleague interrupted Sullivan before she could say more.

As he replayed such incidents during his sleepless nights, Seeger said he thought of all the things he should have said to the judge or the jury in response to Sullivan's tactics. This time around, he was determined not to let her get away with them.

He and Lanier had decided that when Sullivan broke the rules, Seeger would complain to Higbee immediately, "so she would be watching Diane as closely as we were."

I had seen Sullivan in the lobby of the Sheraton Hotel in Atlantic City on that November day in 2005 when she'd won the first Humeston trial. (The Merck defense team used the Sheraton as its base in Atlantic City, and I happened to be staying there as well.) Dressed in a track suit and sneakers, Sullivan was laughing as she walked with some of her colleagues through the lobby and out a revolving door, into the windy fall day. She had looked very happy, indeed.

At 46, Sullivan had the trim physique of someone seriously committed to exercise, and her pale skin was tanned to a bronze hue. She was dressed that afternoon in a navy blue suit, with a white shell underneath. It wasn't quite enough clothing for Judge Higbee's chilly courtroom, as Sullivan acknowledged right away.

"Good afternoon, folks," she said as she walked briskly to the jury box. "I'm Diane, Diane Sullivan, and I'm freezing." Her breezy smile revealed a crowd of slightly crooked upper teeth.

Lanier was a hard act to follow in court, but if Sullivan had any misgivings about being able to match him, they weren't visible to me. She had a winning track record of her own, including two Vioxx wins in that very courtroom. Gesturing toward Lanier, who sat just a few feet away, but without sparing a glance for him, Sullivan began with a jab.

"Now the plaintiffs' lawyer, he is a good storyteller, he had a lot of nice props and he was entertaining," Sullivan said, "and I think all of us folks who have kids, folks in their jobs, teachers, have heard some good stories from good storytellers, but when we get behind the facts and learn the facts, sometimes those stories don't stand up to the facts."

Lanier's story, Sullivan said, wouldn't be backed by the evidence in the case. Lanier leaned forward in his chair, put his elbows on the table and his chin on his fists. He was listening closely.

Every case has "one most important fact," Sullivan said, and Lanier had left that fact out of his opening statement.

"The plaintiffs have alleged that Merck failed to warn about a possible risk of heart attack," she said, "but [they] didn't show you Merck's warning labels that came with every Vioxx package and went to every doctor and went to patients, and I want to show you those now, if I can."

On the screen behind her, Sullivan projected a part of the 1999 Vioxx label that advised caution in using Vioxx among patients with past records of high blood pressure, fluid retention, and heart failure. A second slide showed the label's Adverse Reactions section—it listed heart attacks among the rare side effects seen in Vioxx studies. Lanier had ridiculed Merck for putting heart attacks in the label's "bug-bite bucket," alongside the insect bites, constipation, and toenail fungus also observed in the Vioxx studies. Sullivan retorted that Merck was just following the rules of the Food and Drug Administration.

"They are like the cops of the pharmaceutical companies. You can't do anything as a pharmaceutical company unless you follow FDA guidelines and regulations, and FDA has to approve ultimately anything you say in their label," she said.

And she suggested that Merck had actually done *more* than the FDA required.

"There was not a single study in 1999 that showed that there was an increased risk of heart attacks with Vioxx. But the folks at Merck, they gave doctors a heads-up anyway," she said.

Sullivan had started the game with her highest card: The United States government had known about and authorized everything Merck had done. Who were the plaintiffs to question Merck's judgment?

After the VIGOR study, Merck issued a second label in 2002, and Sullivan showed that next on the screen.

"What are the possible side effects of Vioxx?" Sullivan read from the label, and then, from among the list of side effects: "Heart attacks and similar serious events have been reported in patients taking Vioxx."

Sullivan told the jury Merck had mailed a copy of the revised label to every doctor in the country, with the changes highlighted in neon yellow. No pharmaceutical company had ever gone to such lengths to alert doctors to a revised label, she said.

In an apparent allusion to Lanier's allegations that the thrust of Merck's marketing efforts had been directed toward concealing Vioxx's risks, not illuminating them, and anticipating weeks of damaging testimony ahead, Sullivan told the jurors, "I think when all is said and done, I hope you shake your heads and you say, you know, maybe the folks at Merck didn't do everything absolutely perfectly, but they did warn and they did tell doctors in their labeling about...the possible risks of heart attacks."

In other words, no matter how badly it had behaved, Merck *had* done what the law and its federal regulator required by disclosing that people who took Vioxx had suffered heart attacks in clinical trials. It was up to doctors and patients to use that information as they saw fit. The company's hands were clean. That was Merck's bottom line.

A COURT IN NEW JERSEY was certainly the right place to make that kind of argument, and Sullivan took a few moments to milk the company's home-state connection to the jury. She had done that the last time the Humeston case was tried as well. The plaintiffs' lawyers had viewed her remarks about Merck's New Jersey roots as thinly veiled attempts to turn the jury against their out-of-state clients, and had complained to the judge. This time around, Higbee had ordered Sullivan to restrict herself to one mention of Merck's New Jersey connection in the opening. Sullivan ignored the restriction, and proceeded to fill the jury in on Merck's hundred-year history in the state, and high points of that history such as the manufacture of the nation's first vial of penicillin at a Merck plant in New Jersey 60 years earlier.

As she burnished Merck's reputation with the jury, Sullivan blithely violated another of Higbee's orders. In the previous Humeston trial, Sullivan had subtly suggested to jurors that a verdict against the company would threaten its effort to find a cure for cancer. This time Higbee had taken the precaution of ordering that, like New Jersey, the word "cancer" could be mentioned only once in Merck's opening statement. Sullivan mentioned it seven times in quick succession. Merck had just begun to market a vaccine against two strains of human papillomavirus that cause cervical cancer. Sullivan described it to the jury as "the *cancer* vaccine for cervical *cancer* that prevents *cancer.*" Just in case, the jury had missed the point, Sullivan brought it up again. She reminded jurors of Lanier's statement that Vioxx had been no cure for arthritis, just a palliative. Sullivan said Merck's scientists would have loved to cure arthritis. "They haven't figured that out yet, but they did, fortunately, as it related to cervical *cancer,* come up with a vaccine that prevents cervical *cancer.* The first time a company ever discovered a medicine to prevent *cancer,*" she said. Sullivan's message, though not explicitly stated, could hardly have been louder: we're Merck, and we cure cancer; can you really believe we'd knowingly sell a medicine that kills?

Not many lawyers would have chosen to violate a judge's orders so blatantly and repeatedly as Sullivan was doing, particularly not the orders of a mass tort judge, like Higbee. Merck had not one, but thousands of Vioxx cases before her. If Sullivan continued to represent Merck, she could expect to be in Higbee's courtroom many more times.

But Sullivan had a history of tangling with Higbee. During the first Humeston trial, she had reacted with angry outbursts when

Higbee made unfavorable rulings. On one occasion, she screamed at the judge, not stopping even when Higbee threatened to have her forcibly removed from the courtroom. (Higbee did not follow through.) There was a running debate among defense lawyers afterwards about whether Sullivan's outburst had been strategic, designed to bolster the chances of a mistrial at a time when the case was going badly for Merck. Sullivan went on to win the Humeston case, as well as a second Vioxx case in Higbee's courtroom, and had apparently concluded that she could break Higbee's orders with impunity. Court TV's camera captured Higbee pursing her lips ever so slightly at Sullivan's latest transgressions. She rebuked Sullivan mildly in a sidebar later.

"The word 'cancer' shouldn't be mentioned again during your opening," Higbee said. "You have already mentioned it probably ten times."

Sullivan had also mentioned New Jersey several times, Seeger interjected.

"He said he was from New Jersey," Sullivan protested.

Higbee smiled.

"All right, it is okay," she said.

Sullivan was smiling herself when she returned to her spot in front of the jury box.

AS MERCK'S LAWYERS HAD in every Vioxx trial before, Sullivan made the point that heart attacks were common, and plaintiffs could show no proof that their heart attacks happened because they took Vioxx.

"Over a million Americans have a heart attack every year. Almost 8 million Americans alive today have had heart attacks," Sullivan said.

"Cardiovascular Disease: Number One Health Problem in the US," her slide said succinctly.

"There is nothing different or unique or special or distinct about the heart attacks that the plaintiffs claim are caused by Vioxx, ...as compared with the heart attacks that happen to people all the time," Sullivan said, and ran through a list of conditions known to raise the risk of heart attack.

"Like being a man," she said. "Being overweight. High cholesterol. Stress. Family history. Physical inactivity. Diabetes. Elevated blood pressure. Smoking. And age."

As I listened to Sullivan, I was struck by the contrast between my response to Lanier's opening statement and to Sullivan's. Lanier's had kept me on the edge of my seat, listening and engaged. Sullivan's was deadening. It wasn't just that Sullivan didn't have Lanier's gift for telling a story, or his showmanship. Something else was also missing, and looking back, I think it was warmth. Perhaps it was her natural reserve, but Sullivan seemed cool, distant, a little superior. My wandering attention alighted on the back of Sullivan's head, where a section of her blonde hair had been sprayed stiff and sat motionless, stuck to her scalp. It was framed on either side by angel wings of fluffy, blow-dried hair. I watched the tableau with fascination for a while. Later I heard from others who had enjoyed an unobstructed view of the back of Sullivan's head on Court TV's webcast, that they, too, had been mesmerized by Sullivan's hairdo. The stiff and slightly ridiculous hair matched Sullivan's brittle courtroom persona.

To be fair to Sullivan's oratory, the deepening cold in the court room wasn't helping my concentration either. My woolen jacket and long winter coat were no match for Higbee's internal thermostat. I thought longingly of the coffee I'd bought at McDonald's over the lunch break. (It tasted like dishwater, but at least it had been hot.) I inventoried the clothes I'd brought with me to Atlantic City, and ruminated on how I might layer up for maximum warmth in court the next day. I must have nodded off for a few minutes, and woke up with a start. I looked around to see if anyone had noticed. It didn't seem anyone had, and I chalked up my nap to the courtroom's Arctic chill.

Months later, when the cold in the courtroom was just a memory, I went back to read and re-read the transcript of Sullivan's opening statement, and it hit me why I had had so much trouble following her in court: I had been looking for her arguments to make sense, to follow a decipherable internal logic. But Sullivan's style was to confuse and obscure more than to clarify, almost as if she believed that if she threw all of her arguments out there, some were bound to stick.

One of her main arguments was a standard legal defense in such cases, but as a layperson, I found it…fantastic.

When it withdrew Vioxx from the market in 2004, Merck said it was doing so because in a large, long-term, double-blinded clinical trial (the kind scientists consider most rigorous), the Vioxx group suffered twice as many cardiovascular problems as those on the dummy pill. In the language of medical research, the study, called APPROVe, had shown that the risk of developing cardiovascular problems was twice as high with Vioxx as without.

But in court, Merck maintained that Vioxx was a safe drug. Its lawyers said the company had always believed that, and still did. As for the study that led Merck to stop selling Vioxx, Sullivan suggested its results were barely consequential. It was only one study, she said.

"Sometimes a study is a fluke. Was it a chance? It could have been," she said.

Scientifically speaking, it was a farfetched assertion—tests showed the odds were minute that the safety problems seen in APPROVe were a "fluke." But there was a sound basis in legal strategy for Sullivan's claim.

"Once you start giving ground as a litigant, you're on a slippery slope," explained Jerry Kristal, the Weitz Luxenberg trial lawyer who had been Lanier's co-counsel during a previous Vioxx trial in New Jersey.

Under New Jersey law, Merck could be held liable for a plaintiff's heart attack even if Vioxx was only one of many factors that contributed to the heart attack. So admitting that Vioxx posed any risk, no matter how slight, would make it easier for plaintiffs to prove their cases in court, Kristal said.

In fact, Vioxx was remarkable in the annals of pharmaceutical history for the breadth and depth of damning evidence that accumulated against it over the years. Merck had had high hopes for expanding the uses of Vioxx beyond the profitable pain market to conditions such as Alzheimer's and cancer, and had tested Vioxx extensively. The evidence was so overwhelming, and Merck's position to the contrary so preposterous, that Judge Higbee invited the plaintiffs' lawyers some months after the trial ended to submit a motion to disqualify from testifying any expert who held that Vioxx was safe, on the grounds that the opinion had no scientific basis.

In her opening statement to the jury, Sullivan airily dismissed the significance of the VIGOR study's findings as well. (This was the study that found there had been five times as many heart attacks in the Vioxx group as in the group on an older painkiller, naproxen.) Lanier had told the jury those results should have brought Merck's aggressive Vioxx marketing to a halt until the drug's risks were better understood.

"The VIGOR study is, basically... one study out of over 120 studies that Merck did," Sullivan said, and the rest showed no statistically significant increase in heart problems on Vioxx.

And VIGOR had not shown Vioxx caused heart attacks, as Lanier alleged, Sullivan said. It had shown that naproxen, like aspirin, prevented heart attacks and Vioxx did not, Sullivan said. That explained why there were fewer heart attacks in the naproxen group than on Vioxx, she said. Naproxen would have had to be *twenty* times

more potent than aspirin, the gold standard in heart-attack prevention for Sullivan's explanation to hold. No previous study had shown
naproxen to have that property (though studies spurred by Merck's
claim later showed that naproxen did provide modest protection, but
far *less* than that provided by aspirin.)

"Merck did over 120 studies, some small, some big, some
medium... that didn't show any difference in people on Vioxx versus people on placebo or other medicines," Sullivan said. "And they
[the plaintiffs] want to talk about two, the VIGOR study that wasn't
against placebo and where there's still debate and discussion as to
whether naproxen reducing heart attacks is the explanation for that
study, and the APPROVe study that Merck didn't know about until
2004, which showed a very small increased risk and conflicts."

"You can't let people just cherry-pick out one study or two studies and draw conclusions based on it," she said, and returned to her
trump card. She said the FDA gave Vioxx its stamp of approval,
not once, not twice, but on four separate occasions. The last was in
August 2004, one month before Merck stopped selling Vioxx, when
the FDA approved Vioxx for use in children.

"You know, our system here is the best in the world," Sullivan
said. "Countries from all over the world try to emulate our FDA
regulatory standards, because we've got a pretty good system here for
testing and evaluating the safety of medicines, and they did a pretty
good job here, and you'll see it. And they...never concluded that
Vioxx caused heart attacks."

As her statement drew to a close, Sullivan violated several more of
Higbee's orders, in quick succession. One concerned a slide that Hig-
bee had not approved but Sullivan used anyway. It was a reproduction
of a *British Medical Journal* article by the Yale cardiologist Harlan
Krumholz, who had testified during Lanier's previous Vioxx trial in
Higbee's court. The article contained a photograph of Krumholz on

the witness stand. Sullivan questioned if Krumholz, who was slated to testify on behalf of the plaintiffs in this trial as well, was even qualified for the task—he had only published that one article about Vioxx, she said.

"And the article has nothing to do with science," Sullivan said, drawing the jury's attention to the accompanying photograph. "It relates to lawsuits, and it actually even has Mr. Lanier's picture in the article, and that should raise your eyebrows."

Lanier stood up. "Objection, Your Honor. It has your picture, too," he said.

"Not as clear," Sullivan said.

"They did fuzz you a little bit, Judge," Lanier conceded.

"You can ignore the issue of the pictures. I am sure they won't be of any interest to anyone," Higbee told the jurors, and Sullivan continued.

Lanier's casual comment obscured his real concern—that by juxtaposing the photograph and the article on her slide, Sullivan had successfully sowed doubt in jurors' minds about Krumholz's objectivity. Indeed, the plaintiffs' lawyers had objected strenuously to the photograph's inclusion on the slide during a morning conference with Higbee and Merck's lawyers. Higbee had not given Sullivan permission to show the photograph, and yet—there it was.

Seeger said that as soon as he spotted the photograph he had wanted to call Sullivan on her ploy.

"That's how it happens. She tells one lie, then two lies, and she's got the jury hating you," Seeger told Lanier.

But Lanier didn't believe in making a lot of objections. He believed they helped the other side more than his, because they called the jury's attention to things he'd rather they not remember.

"Let it go," he told Seeger, objecting to the photo only in passing, and then to make light of it.

A few minutes later, Lanier did object in earnest. Sullivan had returned to the findings of the APPROVe study and Merck's subsequent decision to withdraw Vioxx from the market.

"They pulled it from the market within days…they weren't going to put patients at risk," Sullivan said. "And some of their outside experts suggested, many of them, said, 'Well, you don't have to withdraw the drug from the market, just change your label and keep it on.'"

Lanier objected from his seat, so the jury could hear him, that there was no evidence that experts had advised Merck it didn't need to pull the drug.

"Counselor, let's not discuss withdrawal. Move on," Higbee told Sullivan.

She had ruled the issue off-limits to both sides.

But Sullivan wasn't done.

"Just to be clear, in case there was any misimpression, the FDA never asked Merck to take Vioxx off the market. It was a voluntary decision that Merck made, based on this very small increased risk the first time they learned about it, in 2004," Sullivan said.

Higbee cut her off.

"Counselor, did I just say not to talk about withdrawal?" she asked Sullivan

Sullivan would restate her point one more time for the jury, before finally moving on.

"Everybody knows you don't take a drug off the market unless you have to," a prominent defense lawyer remarked later. "It's a very bad fact when you're defending cases of this nature."

Sullivan butted heads with the judge again a few minutes later, this time over her roundabout reference to the fact that the plaintiffs were not from New Jersey. (The Humestons and the Hermans lived in Idaho and Wisconsin, respectively.)

Earlier, Lanier had told the jury that Merck's efforts to hide Vioxx's risks extended to intimidation of doctors who raised concerns about the risks. A well-respected professor at Stanford University, James Fries, had written to Merck's CEO complaining of such incidents and Lanier promised he would show the jury a videotape of Fries's testimony.

But Fries's testimony concerned one incident out in California, Sullivan said.

"Ask yourself," she told the jury, "What does this have to do with a doctor in Idaho and a doctor in Wisconsin [and the cases] that I have to decide?' "

Seeger objected immediately.

"Approach sidebar," Higbee ordered

"You have a ruling on this. We have an order signed," Seeger said.

Higbee concurred.

"Twice you said it," she told Sullivan.

Sullivan argued she was making a different legal point, one that Higbee had previously ruled out as well.

"You don't accept my rulings," she told Sullivan.

"Look, here is the thing, though... They're smart over here," Seeger said, referring to Merck. "They know what the rulings are. We have to live by them in this trial, and to sit and watch this already on day one... This is Humeston all over again."

Once again, Seeger's reference to the first Humeston trial had been strategic.

"I knew it would bring up the bad memories" of Sullivan's rule-breaking from the first Humeston trial, he said later. "The judge was agitated and I wanted to add to her agitation. The goal that early in the case was to remind the judge how bad she [Sullivan] was."

In a final violation of Higbee's orders, Sullivan closed with an appeal to the jury's New Jersey spirit.

"I grew up here in New Jersey in one of those New Jersey neighborhoods that the comedians make fun of, the New Jersey of landfills, factory smokes, and mosquito trucks, but there's a lot of good people that live in neighborhoods like that, just like there's a lot of good people who live in neighborhoods all over this state," Sullivan said.

"And in my neighborhood, maybe people didn't have a lot of money. People kind of looked out for each other. They kind of took care of each other's kids, they checked in on the old folks, and helped out if somebody was sick. And in my neighborhood, your good name was important to you. It was important what your neighbors…thought about you. Were you a good and decent person, could you be relied on, could you be trusted?" Sullivan said.

It was the same for Merck, Sullivan said, which relied on its reputation for its business.

"And that's why [the] plaintiffs' accusations don't make sense. What a disastrous business plan, to make a drug that you know hurts people and lie to doctors. You never would sell another medicine if you did that. It doesn't make common sense," she said.

The plaintiffs had made "a lot of accusations in the interests of winning a lawsuit for money," Sullivan said, and she promised the evidence wouldn't support them.

Higbee summoned Sullivan and Lanier to her chambers afterwards, and back at his suite in the Borgata, Lanier recounted to his crew what had followed.

He had changed out of his suit into a pair of jeans, and sat tipped back in a heavy upholstered side chair, legs swinging. The others lounged on the sofa or stood around, noshing.

According to Lanier, Higbee had chewed Sullivan out.

"The judge says, 'I'm not going to do this again with you. When I make rulings, I make rulings. You just violated them five ways,'" Lanier told the group. There were hoots and howls. The ghost of trials past had been in the courtroom, just as they had hoped. After the judge had spoken a bit, Lanier jumped in.

"Your Honor, if I might," he had said. "We're at the start of a long trial, and I don't like what I'm seeing. You set down rules for us. They're like shackles that we wear. Diane has thrown off her shackles but I am shackled to my chair. It's not fair to my client because we get beat up."

He'd even volunteered a solution.

"Where I come from, in Texas, we have what we call a twofer rule, and it's pretty effective" he had told Higbee.

The way it worked was that he would break two of Higbee's rules for every one that Sullivan broke, he explained, before reassuring the judge he wouldn't actually do what he was, in effect, threatening to do.

Lanier's account got better.

"Diane and I walk out and she says, 'You're a whiner. I thought you had balls. Looks like you don't after all,'" Lanier recounted.

"Sweetheart, I don't know where you got that from. I'm a eunuch," Lanier said he told Sullivan. "And I walked off." He was sure he had infuriated Sullivan by calling her, "sweetheart."

It was only the first day of the trial.

"Half the jury is thinking, 'am I all flash?'
Today we show 'em the beef..."

CHAPTER 5

"The Perfect Goober!"

Atlantic City, New Jersey, January 23, 2007

LANIER HAD SAID HE'D be awake and working with his door open early the next morning, but at 6:00 A.M. the door to his suite was still shut.

I had heard him planning his sleep schedule out loud the night before, "It's 9:09," he was saying to no one in particular. "If I go to sleep at 9:30, I can wake up at 1:30. Or I could sleep 'til 3:30 and get six hours of sleep."

Had he slept in, I wondered? If so, I didn't want to be the one to wake him up. Unsure of what to do next, I stood outside his suite. A moment later the door opened and Lanier poked his head out.

"Good morning, Snigdha. I thought I heard you," he said, and propped open the door to usher me in. "I don't have time to be hospitable. You'll have to be aggressive and get your own breakfast."

But I hadn't come for breakfast. Feeling something akin to the quiet thrill of a naturalist observing her subject in his natural habitat, I perched myself on an easy chair about ten feet from Lanier's desk, made myself very still, and watched him work.

Lanier sat in a pool of light at his desk, in sweats and a sleeveless undershirt, surrounded by stacks of slim manila folders. He was going through them, one by one, nodding to himself as he read, his mouth slightly open. It was still dark outside, and the room felt strangely calm.

From time to time, he looked up to talk, or at least to vocalize.

"Eewwweeeeeeeeee!" he said at one point. "Wish I had a few more hours."

"Have you ever been in a room when I've crossed?" he asked next. ("Crossed" was lawyer-speak for cross-examined.) I hadn't. Lanier intimated I was in for a good time, and we discussed which seat in the courtroom would provide the best view.

"You know we're right on this case," he said a few minutes later. "They really did do it. Maybe it's manslaughter but they really did do it." It seemed important to him that I be persuaded of the justice of his cause.

"Half the jury is thinking, 'am I all flash?' Today we show 'em the beef," he said.

The "beef" that day would take the form of an Australian named David Anstice, who had run Merck's U.S. drug business at the peak of Vioxx's sales. The folders Lanier was poring over contained the internal Merck emails and memos that he would use to show how Merck's marketing machine had made Vioxx into a best-seller. The emails and memos were among millions of pages of corporate documents relating to Vioxx that Merck had turned over to plaintiffs' lawyers in the legal discovery process.

I had watched the night before as Lanier's science consultant, David Egilman, Egilman's assistants, and a Philadelphia plaintiffs' lawyer who was particularly well-versed in the Merck documents worked on the folders in the war room down the hall from Lanier's suite. Dressed in a Humboldt University t-shirt ("It's where Einstein went to college," he explained), Egilman was in his element as he bossed the group.

"*Trust* me, in none of the cases do they have talent like this work-ing on them," he told me, grimly, a slice of pizza in one hand and a diet Coke at the ready.

They had made a list of Sullivan's "lies" and were pulling Merck documents to refute each one.

"Seeger was supposed to be doing this," Egilman said scorn-fully. (The night before in Lanier's suite, Seeger had offered to lead the effort.)

After so many trials, the plaintiffs' lawyers had a core set of documents they used in each trial to make their case. But lawyers from both firms, along with Egilman and his assistants, searched for fresh gems in the plaintiffs' database of Merck documents each night, as Lanier fine-tuned his case. Their finds were organized, copied, and indexed late into the night, and the folders were slipped under Lanier's door. He would sift through them when he awoke, picking out the "clean kills," which were unambiguously favorable for his case and easy for the jury to grasp, while discarding the rest. A final set of documents, annotated with his handwritten notes and highlighting, served as Lanier's road map to the day's cross-examination.

At 6:30 Lanier picked up the phone to call Dara Hegar. He could just as well have pounded on the wall that separated their rooms.

"Okay, I know I'm waking you up," I heard him say. "Egilman has a handwritten note from '98. Is it an exhibit or do we have to alert the 'bad guys'?"

Each side was required to inform the other about documents they might use with witnesses, and additions were often made until the wee hours of the morning. Merck—or the bad guys, as Lanier referred to them—had already been told about the note in question.

"This is powerful. Very powerful," Lanier said as he hung up. "Egilman has a great find."

Egilman showed up in person before long, dressed in a pre-court ensemble of shorts, t-shirt, and black socks that matched his black athletic shoes.

"You've got some gems I am using. Thank you, David," Lanier said.

Egilman tried to look modest as he walked over to where I sat.

"I was here before," he told me, smirking, as he clutched his Starbucks coffee cup in one hand and a scone in the other. "He sent me away."

I hadn't realized it before, but it appeared that in Egilman's mind we were competing for face time with Lanier and the ungodliness of the hours we spent around him. ("He has a boy-crush on Lanier," one of his assistants joked.)

Rick Meadow, who ran Lanier's New York office, wandered in next.

"The jury's not coming in till 9:30," he told Lanier.

"All night people have been getting me things," Lanier said. "You just got me the best thing—time!"

Meadow glowed. "That's what you need."

If Egilman had a crush on Lanier, he wasn't alone. Lanier was the star around whom the whole group orbited, and each member craved his attention.

"Grab you some breakfast, boy," Lanier said to Meadow. It was close to 7:30, and Lanier was fixing himself a bowl of cereal and milk with a banana. As he ate, he held court.

"Saturday, I'm at the container store, getting my buckets, my props, and tools. I email Dara, 'is there anything I need to get at the store for the trial?' She emails me back, 'yes, I desperately need more time.' I thought it was clever. I emailed her back, and said, 'I bought us some, but it's on back-order.'"

Lanier laughed expansively at the memory of how he'd topped Hegar's quip. I gathered he was done with his preparations and returned to my room to shower and dress. When I returned an hour later I found a small crowd gathered around the doorway to Lanier's bathroom. Lanier was entertaining his audience with a run-through of the Anstice cross-examination as he brushed his teeth.

In her opening statement the day before, Sullivan had suggested Lanier would unfairly grill Anstice, a marketing executive, on scientific issues outside his area of expertise. Lanier was worried Sullivan had set him up to look like a bully to the jury, and he had prepared a comeback.

"Here's the bottom line, sir. I didn't hire you, did I? I'm not the one who put you in charge of Human Health," Lanier rehearsed. [Human Health was the name of the Merck division that Anstice had run.] "Are we supposed to believe that Merck—one of the best pharmaceutical companies in the world—went to Australia to hire someone who doesn't know anything about human health?"

The lawyers laughed, as Lanier suggested an answer to the imaginary David Anstice.

"Just say, 'Mr. Lanier, I don't understand these things. I just run the company,'" Lanier said.

Bob Leone, his jury consultant, gave Lanier a thumbs-up.

"I'm liking it," he said.

Later I would ask Leone why Lanier had opened his case with a hostile defense witness instead of a pliant witness of his own.

"Mark's greatest gift is his cross-examination," Leone said. "So one of our techniques is we start out calling one of their witnesses. Put 'em on right away and destroy 'em, just destroy 'em. And Anstice is the perfect goober to do it to."

THE FIRST ORDER OF business in court that morning was from the day before. Each side put its objections to the other's opening statements on the record. The plaintiffs' lawyers had pored over the transcript of Diane Sullivan's opening statement and they complained that Sullivan had violated seven different court orders in her opening. Merck's lawyers retorted that Sullivan was only responding to Lanier's inflammatory opening. They said his references to Merck's Vioxx profits had been gratuitous. They had counted, and he had used the words "millions" or "billions" 48 times, they said. They complained his language contained religious allusions (it had), that he had brought up his children repeatedly (he had), and that he had compared Vioxx and Merck to cigarettes and tobacco companies, implying that like the tobacco companies, Merck could get a clean bill of health for its product by throwing money at experts to testify.

Higbee listened impassively. "The fact of the matter is that both counsel gave dramatic openings," she finally said. "It is hard to prevent it from happening." Both sides had referred to their families—Lanier to his kids, and Sullivan to her husband and football. "I don't have a problem with any of that," Higbee said. "What I have a problem with is someone deliberately violating my orders, acting in contempt of court, and acting unethically and unprofessionally by specifically violating what I ordered should not be done." Her eyes were fixed on Sullivan as she spoke.

"There were many things that the plaintiffs wanted to talk about that I didn't let them talk about... [and] I have blocked a lot of things that Merck wanted to do," Higbee said. "But Mr. Lanier followed my orders. Ms Sullivan did *not*."

Higbee reeled off the list of Sullivan's transgressions—the repeated mention of Merck's cancer research and its New Jersey roots, her sly reference to the plaintiffs being from out of state, and finally, Sullivan's decision to show the jury a controversial photograph without Higbee's permission. The photo had been taken in Higbee's courtroom, and showed Lanier questioning Yale cardiologist and plaintiffs' medical expert Harlan Krumholz during his previous Vioxx trial. Higbee was also in the picture. In a conference with the judge before opening statements, the plaintiffs' lawyers had objected to Sullivan's use of the photograph, believing, as she apparently did, that it would subtly taint the expert in the eyes of the jury. They thought they'd prevailed. Merck said they hadn't. Higbee wasn't sure. But the photo wasn't in the preview of slides the two sides exchanged. It turned out Sullivan had shown them a version of the slide *without* the photograph.

Higbee said she believed Sullivan had intentionally deceived her and the plaintiffs' lawyers. "There's no other explanation," she said.

This wasn't Sullivan's first run-in with Higbee. She had screamed at the judge on one occasion, when Higbee ruled against her in the previous Humeston trial.

"I attempted to set that aside. I accepted her apology. I tried to think it was just the pressure of that first trial," Higbee said. "Throughout that trial, Mr. Seeger suggested to me...that Miss Sullivan was making statements, looking at the jury and saying things about him, making disparaging remarks about him, and saying them loud enough and looking at the jury when she said them."

Higbee continued, "The fact of the matter is, I was concerned about Miss Sullivan and the fact that I felt she was overwrought, and I thought she was, in fact, a good lawyer, who was simply in— under a lot of pressure and—I gave her a pass, which I probably never should have done."

Sullivan stood at her table, looking down, avoiding Higbee's gaze. From time to time she shook her head.

"Miss Sullivan, you have acted in contempt of court previously and on this occasion," Higbee went on. "I can't deal with this for five weeks of the trial. I can't let this go unchecked...From now on, anything I say, I expect you to bend over backwards to make sure you don't violate an order...I am not going to deal with this kind of unprofessionalism. I am not going to let it taint this trial. It is a disservice...to the court. It is a disservice to the bar. It is a disservice to the client."

It had been a long and unexpectedly plain speech from a judge known more for her patience than her temper. (She has "the patience of a saint," Higbee's long-time bailiff, Mary Baskerville, would say later. "You really have to cross the line" to anger her.) Rule number 1 in her courtroom was "everybody be nice to each other." Where other judges might bully or shame recalcitrant lawyers into submission, Higbee listened quietly.

But Higbee silenced Sullivan when she tried to defend herself.

"You're not going to say anything. We're going to bring the jury in," she said.

"You won't permit me to make a record for myself on behalf of my client?" Sullivan said, incredulously.

"You can make the appropriate record at the appropriate hearing at the appropriate time." Higbee seemed to be threatening Sullivan with a contempt hearing, which could result in penalties ranging from a slap on the wrist, such as a reprimand, to a large fine, or in the worst case, a referral to the New Jersey bar.

Sullivan had likely believed she could get away with breaking the rules, but it seemed she had miscalculated. Still, she had succeeded in getting the jury to hear what she wanted, and Higbee's wrath may have been a small price to pay for that. Higbee did not follow through on her threat of a contempt charge in the end.

THE JURY HAD BEEN waiting in an anteroom for almost an hour by the time Higbee asked Lanier to begin.

"Your Honor, as our first witness we are going to call the Merck gentleman, Mr. David Anstice," Lanier said, pointing to where a tall, balding man with a long, angular face sat on the Merck side of the courtroom.

David Anstice walked briskly to the witness stand, raised his right hand somewhat theatrically, and took the oath.

"Good morning, Mr. Anstice," Lanier said, walking toward him, hand extended. "Mark Lanier."

"Good morning," Anstice replied, standing up from the seat he had just taken to shake Lanier's hand. He looked genuinely pleased at the gesture. Perhaps Lanier was glad to see him again?

"In fairness to the jury, this is not my first time to question you. I think this is my third. Is that about right?" Lanier continued.

"That's about right," Anstice said loudly, catching Lanier's drift.

The handshake hadn't been a social courtesy, but rather the opening shot in the day's battle. Already, I thought, Lanier had seized the high ground with his friendly greeting and its multiple messages to the jury: Merck has faced lots of Vioxx trials; I've tried many of those cases; and don't feel too sorry for Anstice—he's a pro at testifying; besides, look how nicely I treat the man. Anstice took a large sip of water from the tiny, clear, plastic Dixie cup provided by the state of New Jersey. The cup and the gesture looked wholly unequal to the job of steadying his nerves for what lay ahead.

I asked Lanier about that handshake as I was writing this account. A little over two years had passed but Lanier remembered the moment well, and a slow smile crossed his face, as he explained why he had offered his hand to Anstice that morning.

"First of all, I'm directing the action. I'm in charge," Lanier said. "He can't ignore me. He can't look at my hand and snub me." Also, Lanier knew it rattled Anstice's lawyers. "I have never seen another lawyer in sixty or seventy trials go up and shake their opponent's hand," he said. "And I knew everything in them is saying, 'Wait a minute, he can't do that! Objection, Your Honor, he's shaking his hand!' So they're set on their heels." And, Lanier said, it was a ritual salute to his opponent, "You know, before the sword fight, you bow before each other, then you turn around and take your paces back."

It was Lanier's way of declaring, "Let the games begin!"

The man whom Leone considered the "perfect goober" to launch the plaintiffs' case was dressed in full corporate regalia—a sharp blue suit, starched white shirt, and sober maroon tie. His hair was graying and cut short. He had a ruddy, pleasant face. It didn't advertise the drive and ambition its owner had doubtless needed to travel from the bottom of the globe to the very top ranks of a Fortune 500 company. But Anstice's origins were plain the moment he spoke. Despite years of living in the U.S., Anstice retained his distinctive Australian vowels.

As he questioned Anstice, Lanier wrote on the oversize tablet facing the jury, first in block letters, "DAVID ANSTICE," and then sprawling across the page, "President," "Human Health for the U.S." That was Anstice's title as Vioxx was under development and when it was first sold. It was the perfect setup for the routine Lanier had rehearsed in his suite that morning.

"I didn't hire you for that job, did I?" Lanier said with a smile.

"No, you did not," Anstice said, evenly.

"I'm not the one who went over your résumé and decided whether or not I was going to make you the president of Human Health of the United States of America, am I?" Lanier said, peering farsightedly at his hands in a parody of someone reading a résumé and grinning widely.

Anstice repeatedly patiently, no, Lanier had not hired him.

"You were hired by Merck?" Lanier said.

"Yes, that's correct," Anstice said.

The reason he was asking, Lanier said to Anstice, was that in her opening statement the day before, the Merck lawyer had suggested that he, Lanier, would question Anstice on matters related to science.

"Are you a science man?" Lanier asked Anstice.

"No, I am not a science person," Anstice replied.

"So as president of Human Health," Lanier said, pointing to his tablet, where Anstice's title was now circled in bright red Magic Marker, "You don't really know anything about Human Health, do you?" Lanier said.

"No, that's not correct," Anstice said.

"All right. Do you know some stuff about Human Health? Is it okay for me to ask you health questions?" Lanier sounded now like a parent humoring a difficult child.

"I am not a scientist, but I do have a general understanding," Anstice said.

"If at some point I ask you questions that are outside your area, you just gotta tell me, 'That's more science, I'm more a sales guy.' Fair?" Lanier said.

"Yes, I will tell you," Anstice said.

"Because, really, even though you were president of Human Health, you are a sales guy. That's what you are, isn't it?" Lanier was piling it on, but Anstice simply agreed.

If Lanier's strategy was to needle and provoke, Anstice's strategy was the reverse. He was trying to tamp down Lanier's high spirits with a kind of no-nonsense agreeableness that said, "Yes, yes, I know this is a show, now let's get on with it." Still, in just a few minutes, Lanier had managed to make Anstice look faintly ridiculous, and his touch had been as light as a feather. Anstice's lawyers sat quietly at their table, powerless to deflect Lanier's seemingly gentle barbs, at least for the moment.

LANIER LIKES TO TELL the story of the first time he deposed Anstice. It was March 2005. Merck had withdrawn Vioxx six months earlier and would soon face Lanier in the country's first Vioxx trial, in Texas. The deposition was going very badly for Anstice, according to Lanier, and Anstice's lawyer, Stephen Raber, a partner at the prestigious Washington firm of Williams & Connolly, was trying to push back. Raber accused Lanier at one point of standing over Anstice in an effort to intimidate him, and a few minutes later, he instructed Lanier to sit down. Lanier took exception to being ordered by Raber and refused. When Raber persisted, Lanier countered with a command of his own—he ordered Raber to stand up.

"Sit down," Raber repeated.

"Stand up!" Lanier retorted.

Back and forth, they went.

Thinking perhaps that a change of subject would strengthen his hand, Raber informed Lanier that his attire—jeans and tennis shoes—was "unprofessional."

"I represent a widow whose husband has been ripped from her life and her future because of what your company did with its drug, and she doesn't give a whit whether I'm wearing jeans or a tank top or *pajamas,* she just cares that justice be done," Lanier said he told Raber.

I suspect the tale gained some color in the telling, but both—the tale and the telling—were classic Lanier. Morally righteous yet slyly funny, our hero prevailed in the end. Lanier says Anstice took note.

"He realized his own lawyer was beat up. He realized I was the dominant bird in the room and on the pecking order and I wasn't going to back away," Lanier said, with satisfaction. Then he offered Anstice a compliment. "He doesn't get where he got in this world if he doesn't read people, and he doesn't read situations, and he doesn't see how things are going to play," Lanier said, "and so I think the big psychological underlay was laid in that first meeting, and from then on he's never really been one to challenge me."

ANSTICE WASN'T LANIER'S ONLY target in Higbee's courtroom that day. Lanier had Diane Sullivan in his sights as well. He had come up with an elegant device to do maximum damage to both, and he began right away.

"All right. Miss Sullivan made an opening statement to the jury. You understand that to be true, right?" Lanier asked Anstice, who said he did. "Okay, I found at least 47 different places, I believe, where Miss Sullivan..."

Paul Strain, dressed in banker's gray, was on his feet and objecting before Lanier could finish his thought. "We don't need lawyer speeches, just *plain* questions," Strain said.

"I'm framing the subject area," Lanier said.

"He is making a representation and that's improper," Strain said.

"I'm just framing the subject area," Lanier said, his jaw set and his back to Strain as he addressed the judge.

Neither looked ready to budge. Higbee finally intervened, "Let's hear the question."

"All right," Lanier said, turning to the jury, "I've got 47 different areas of representations that Miss Sullivan made to this jury that I want to write down and go over with you and see if you agree with *them* or if you agree with *me* that they're not true. Is that fair?"

Strain jumped up, "Objection, Your Honor," but it was too late. Twice in the space of less than a minute, Lanier had managed to tell the jury that Sullivan had lied in her opening statement—47 times! It was a devastatingly direct attack, and the cross-examination had barely begun.

Higbee summoned Strain and Lanier to the bench for a whispered sidebar, at which, predictably (and correctly), Strain argued that Lanier couldn't be allowed to claim that Sullivan had lied 47 times. In lawyer-speak Lanier was "testifying," or putting a fact into evidence, and only witnesses may do that. Higbee ordered Lanier to refrain from mentioning the opening statements, and Lanier returned to his position at the tablet. There, he proceeded to draw a vertical line down a fresh piece of paper, dividing it into two. He titled the column on the left "Merck Position," and the one on the right "Truth."

"All right," said Lanier, turning to face Anstice. "I'm going to ask you about 47 different positions that Merck has taken, and I'm going to have you compare them and see whether or not those are the truth," Lanier said to Anstice. He hadn't mentioned Sullivan or the opening statement this time, but Lanier had, for a third time, pounded home his message: "Sullivan lied 47 times yesterday."

"May I approach again, Your Honor?" Strain asked. "This is important to get this lawyer stuff straightened out."

This time Chris Seeger joined Lanier at Higbee's bench, his broad boxer's back partially obscuring my view of Lanier and Strain. Sullivan remained in her seat, reading and looking up from time to time, a tiny smile playing about her lips. Higbee rubbed her chin and looked off in the distance as the lawyers argued. The sidebar lasted four minutes—an eternity in courtroom time. When I went back to read the transcript, I saw that Strain had finally succeeded in getting a direct order from the judge that prohibited Lanier from bringing up "the 47 Merck lies" again.

"Start with number one, and if you get to 47, that's fine," Higbee instructed, with a smile.

Lanier returned to his tablet laughing, and began, "Number one. If Merck is taking the position in this case that Merck never misrepresented safety about Vioxx...that statement is *not* true, is it?"

"Yes, that statement is true," Anstice responded, calmly.

Anstice could hardly say otherwise, as Lanier well knew. That, after all, was the central dispute between the plaintiffs and Merck: had Merck given fair warning of Vioxx's risks, or had it not?

Lanier persisted. "Sir, the truth of the matter is that Merck *did* misrepresent safety, didn't they?"

"No, Merck did not," Anstice said, steadily.

Lanier had been writing on his tablet as he asked his questions. The column he had earlier titled "Merck's Position" now also contained this information: "1. MERCK DID NOT MISREPRESENT SAFETY." In the column labeled "Truth," Lanier had written, "MERCK DID MISREPRESENT SAFETY."

"FDA said you did, didn't they?" Lanier said.

"I don't believe so," Anstice replied.

Turning to Higbee, Lanier offered the plaintiffs' first exhibit into evidence. Anstice, who surely knew what lay ahead, removed his large, gold-rimmed glasses and from my second row seat in the courtroom gallery, I saw the bags under his eyes.

The exhibit was a "warning letter" from the FDA's Division of Drug Marketing, Advertising and Communications, to Raymond Gilmartin, then Merck's CEO and Anstice's boss. Lanier placed the letter on the overhead projector and grabbed his yellow highlighter. He would read it aloud, sentence by sentence, drawing and quartering Anstice with its contents as he went.

"All right. This is the warning letter, isn't it?" he asked Anstice. "Y'all are getting warned about something."

"That's correct," Anstice said.

"It says...the FDA has reviewed your promotional activities and your materials and concluded that they're *false*. Did I read that right?"

"Yes, you did," Anstice said.

The FDA sent the warning letter in September 2001, about a year and a half after Merck first received the results of the VIGOR study, in which the Vioxx group had five times as many heart attacks as those on naproxen. Merck had been telling doctors that this was because, like aspirin, naproxen prevented heart attacks.

"That is a possible explanation," the FDA's letter said, "but you fail to disclose that your explanation is hypothetical, has not been demonstrated by substantial evidence, and that there is another reasonable explanation, that Vioxx may have pro-thrombotic properties." In other words, there was no proof naproxen had prevented heart attacks in VIGOR, and it was quite possible Vioxx had caused them.

Merck's promotion campaign raised "significant public health and safety concerns," the letter continued, because it minimized and misrepresented Vioxx's potential risks.

"Now, by the way, I'm going to pause there. I know you're the number-two guy, but you're president of Human Health," Lanier said. "As president of Human Health, are you the man who is in charge of the promotional campaign for Vioxx?"

"Yes, I am," Anstice said, "and was at that time, at least."

By his own admission, the buck stopped with Anstice.

The jury was listening closely. I watched the heavy-set Egyptian-born deli owner—juror number 7—lean forward in his chair and scribble in a notebook.

"Now I asked you if the FDA accused Merck of misrepresenting safety, and we started with you saying no. Will you change your testimony now and agree with me the FDA did say that you misrepresented the safety profile for Vioxx?" Lanier continued.

Anstice said he would. It was the first of many occasions that day when Lanier would force Anstice to eat his words.

THE FDA HAD DETAILED three venues in which it had found Merck misrepresenting the safety of Vioxx—at two medical conferences where Merck salesmen had pitched drugs to pharmacists, in a corporate press release, and in "promotional audio conferences" where a Merck consultant spoke to fellow doctors about Vioxx.

Like other drug companies, Merck spent millions of dollars a year to cultivate influential doctors (so-called opinion leaders) as an extension of the company's sales force. The doctors were paid to talk about the company's drugs to their peers, and attendance at many of the talks counted toward the continuing education requirements that doctors must satisfy periodically. The talks took place in a variety of settings, ranging from the plush to the ordinary, including teleconferences that doctors could listen to from the comfort of their own offices. Those were the talks that the FDA had cited in its warning letter, and Lanier began by explaining what they were.

"Y'all would find doctors, you would educate those doctors," he said, his eyes fixed on the jury, and his voice dropping, "and you would *pay* those doctors to get on the telephone and have an audio conference where other doctors call in and listen to the Merck-paid doctor talk about, in this case, Vioxx, right?" he said.

"I would make the statement differently," Anstice said, blandly. "Merck had a practice across all of our products of asking senior doctors...to speak to other doctors because this was an important way for other doctors to get information."

"Well, Merck would *select* these doctors, you would *educate* these doctors, you'd *pay* these doctors. But there's one more thing you did with them, too, right?" Lanier continued, not bothering to acknowledge Anstice's answer.

Anstice looked at him, "What are you referring to?"

"Y'all would also *monitor* these doctors. They weren't free agents. You would have Merck people in there making sure they were toeing the company line, wouldn't you?" Lanier said.

Anstice acknowledged that Merck employees monitored the talks.

The FDA letter mentioned six audio conferences in which, it said, a Dr. Peter Holt, speaking on behalf of Merck, had minimized the risk of heart attack on Vioxx and broken the Federal Food and Drug Cosmetic act that governs how a company may promote its drugs. The audio conferences, each of which was moderated by a Merck employee, had taken place in June 2000, not long after Merck received the VIGOR results.

"Now, the June 8th audio conference by Peter Holt was in violation of the Act, wasn't it?" Lanier asked Anstice.

"That's what the FDA told us in this letter," Anstice said.

"And that's what you decided, too, isn't it?" Lanier asked.

"Yes," Anstice said.

"Because here's my question: after Peter Holt violated the FDA act and didn't tell the truth about this drug and its safety profile on June the 8th, and you monitored it, your employees were there, y'all didn't fire him after that, did you?" Lanier asked.

"Correct," Anstice said.

"A man you have selected, educated, paid, and monitored, you monitor him, you hear him violate the message, what you do is you pay him to do it again a week later, don't you?" Lanier said

"That's right," Anstice said. He hadn't spotted the trap in Lanier's question.

"June 8th, he violates it," Lanier said. "Y'all pay him to do it again less than a week later, and then after that, you pay him to violate it again three days after that, don't you?"

Anstice had finally caught on "We were not paying him to *violate*," he said. "We were paying him to speak at conferences."

"Knowing that he is violating, because you've got a monitor there, and you're the people who have educated him and told him what to say, didn't you?" Lanier pressed. "And then you paid him to give three more of these on June 21st of 2000, didn't you?" Lanier said.

"Yes," Anstice said. He had stopped fighting Lanier for the moment, and Lanier had made his point. Peter Holt's Merck minders knew full well that Holt downplayed Vioxx's risks in his educational talks—and they didn't punish him for doing that, they rewarded him with repeat engagements.

According to the FDA warning letter, undercover FDA inspectors at two medical meetings had also caught Merck's salesmen offering the misleading naproxen explanation for the heart attacks in the VIGOR study.

"You shouldn't be training your salespeople to...tell people that naproxen is the reason there are extra heart attacks on the Vioxx end, should you?" Lanier said to Anstice.

"And we were not training our people," Anstice said. "Our representatives were not meant to be discussing the VIGOR study in this way at all."

"You're saying these were just the cream-of-the-crop, the specially selected people that are talking to hundreds of doctors and professionals at these three- and four-day seminars were, were just freelancin'?" Lanier said.

"I don't know what they were doing," Anstice responded.

"Did you ever chase down who those sales reps were?" Lanier asked Anstice.

Anstice said he hadn't.

"These people weren't out there freelancing. This is what you trained them to do," Lanier insisted.

Anstice said again that wasn't so, and left the witness stand unsmiling for a morning recess. I imagined him recovering in Merck's back room. Were his lawyers fanning him? Pressing cold compresses on his forehead? Giving him a stiff drink? Or telling him to buck up, because the torture wouldn't last forever? When Anstice returned to the witness stand, he looked even grimmer than when he'd left it. Lanier had spent the break refueling with a PB&J sandwich and basking in the congratulations of his team.

"SIR, YOU KNOW WHAT an MVX is?" Lanier said to Anstice.

"Yes I do," Anstice replied. It was Merck's internal voice-mail system, and it could be used to send a message to thousands of employees at the same time.

Lanier held a typewritten script for a voice-mail message from Anstice to the Vioxx sales force concerning Vioxx and the VIGOR heart attacks. Though it had been shown to juries in many previous Vioxx trials, Merck had tried to keep it out of this trial, arguing that there was no evidence Anstice had recorded and sent the message. But Higbee had overruled the objection, and Lanier placed the script on the overhead projector for the jury to follow along as he read aloud. It was dated September 13, 2001, four days before Merck received the FDA's warning letter.

"I can understand why some people are confused about the results of VIGOR...if they don't understand the data," Anstice's voice mail script went. "I can even understand why physicians, Wall Street, and even lawyers might be confused. To understand VIGOR, you must understand that naproxen is cardio-protective, like aspirin. In VIGOR, Vioxx did not increase the number of [heart attacks], naproxen decreased the number of [heart attacks,] because it has cardio-protective properties."

"Did I *read* that correctly?" Lanier said, his voice laced with sarcasm.

"You read that correctly," Anstice said.

"That's the very same thing that your sales reps were sayin' that they got written up over. You told them...in VIGOR Vioxx did not increase the number of MIs [myocardial infarctions, or heart attacks], naproxen decreased because it has cardio-protective properties," Lanier said. "You were tellin' em what they were sayin'..."

Anstice glowered at Lanier. "This is *not* an instruction to the sales representatives to discuss the data with doctors," he said, "and this is *not* how our representatives received their instructions to do their work."

Lanier pushed some more, "Sir, you *trained* your sales force to say that Vioxx didn't cause MIs."

"No, we did not," Anstice insisted.

It was the closest Lanier had come to tying Anstice directly to Merck's misrepresentation of Vioxx's risks, and Anstice was angrier than I had seen him all morning.

WHEN IT STARTED SELLING Vioxx, in mid-1999, Merck assembled a sales force of 3,800 representatives, the largest in the industry's history, and gave them given extensive training on how to persuade doctors to write more Vioxx prescriptions. Anything that got in the way of closing the deal was dubbed, logically enough, an "obstacle." Thus doctors' concerns about Vioxx's side effects, its $3/day price tag (compared to pennies a day for some of the older painkillers), its effectiveness, were all "obstacles," and over Vioxx's five-and-a-half year history, Merck developed many tools to train sales reps in overcoming those obstacles. There were role-playing exercises, games, and regular instructional bulletins. There was also a video called "Be the Power," which drew heavily from the movie *Star Wars*. Lanier and Leone loved to show it to juries.

Triumphal trumpets resounded through the courtroom as the lights were dimmed and the jury sat back to watch the video. They saw a galaxy of stars stretching as far as the eye could see, and these words scrolling down the screen, "Not long ago, in a universe not too far away, an elite group of pharmaceutical representatives faced a situation not unlike our own. This is their story..." The protagonists of the story, Vicky and Vince, (aka the "V-Squad") were sales representatives who sold Vioxx. Their heroic mission—to persuade doctors to prescribe more Vioxx—required them to overcome a series of obstacles, including one called "Safety Concerns." A nervous-looking actress played the part and confessed she was worried that Vioxx caused heart attacks. It took many encounters and the V-Squad's strenuous assurances that Vioxx was safe before "Safety Concerns" was vanquished and she melted away.

With the lights back on, Lanier turned to Anstice. "Sir, before we watched the training video, I asked you this question, word-for-word: 'You trained your sales representatives to say that Vioxx doesn't cause MIs.' Your answer was, 'No, we did not.' You're wrong. You did train them to say it doesn't cause MIs, didn't you?"

"No," Anstice said, turning to the jury. "I don't know that this is a training tape which is instructing people how to answer questions in the field." His color was rising.

"Let's be clear. This is a Merck video," Lanier said.

"Yes, this is a Merck video," Anstice agreed.

"These don't come cheap and easy. This was written. This was produced. This is put onto film, and I won't say it is high quality, but, you know, it's not like cinema, but it is a good job, isn't it?" Lanier said.

"Yes," Anstice said, "and it appears to be a filler in training." The real instruction on what salesmen could or couldn't say to doctors would have been contained in the printed brochures they used with doctors, he said, not in a filler video. That was his story, and he was sticking to it.

David Anstice had started the morning looking collected. His face had been impassive, his tone even. But under the hypnotic drumbeat of Lanier's pointed questions, Anstice's composure was cracking. You could see it in the twitching of his nose, the wariness of his gaze, and the frequent pursing of his lips. His sips of water had become more like gulps, the better, perhaps, to contain his anger and humiliation. Senior corporate executives are used to being treated with deference. Lanier was treating him like a liar and a fool.

Leone liked to say that it didn't take many lies—two, three, maybe four—for jurors to decide that the witness was a liar, reasoning that "if people lie about one thing, they lie about others." It looked as if Lanier had caught Anstice (and Sullivan) in several lies by the time the judge called a lunch break.

I HEADED TO THE PLAINTIFFS' overheated back room to thaw out. The plaintiffs' lawyers could take the direct route there—through the courtroom well and out the back door that the jurors used to enter and leave the courtroom. Not wanting to offend Judge Higbee or anyone else with any power over the proceedings, I took a more circuitous route. Threading my way up the courtroom aisle, I walked out into the dimly lit corridor and ducked into the smaller courtroom next door to gain access to the back corridors. I hurried past the tightly shut door of Merck's prep room and after a couple of quick lefts, arrived at the door, also always shut, of the plaintiffs' room.

A jubilant Chris Seeger showed up a few minutes later. His nemesis, Diane Sullivan, had finally received her just deserts. "That was fun!" he gloated, "Diane is so discredited right now."

Lanier walked in next and sat down at the head of the table, talking to himself. "Is that all I want?" he said. He had bought two small boxes of Cheerios and a pint of fat-free milk at the courthouse's tiny second-floor coffee shop. "Dara, what are you seeing in the jury?" he asked Hegar, who was sitting, as usual, in the chair closest to him.

"Number 3 worries me," she said. Number 3 was the retired schoolteacher.

"He was so friendly to me in line," Lanier mused. They had run into each other at the coffee shop.

"Here's the strategy that we're pursuing," Lanier explained to Egilman's young assistant, who was headed to law school in the fall. "You start with the strongest witness first. Marketing is the strongest part. The jury decides they are lying, cheating scumbags. When you get to science, they don't believe a thing Merck says. As you watch this, ask yourself, 'are we being successful in showing you really can't trust them, and you got to watch your back.'"

I noticed that as in Lanier's suite that morning, the mood over lunch, though animated, was also strangely relaxed. Given the high emotion in the courtroom, I'd expected a little more tension. Lanier appeared to enter a protective bubble at will, sometimes participating fully in the conversation, and at other times sitting quietly, immersed in his BlackBerry, or talking to Hegar, who was just as engrossed in hers. Leone, meanwhile, looked like he hadn't a care in the world as he laughed and traded quips with anyone who'd respond. They had all prepped and prepped and prepped for this competition. It was here now, and like professional athletes, they were in the zone.

As the lunch break drew to a close, Leone joked with Egilman. "He's not finished yet," Leone said of Anstice, "There's still some blood left in him."

"There's still blood, not much truth," Egilman retorted.

"He's been practicing. He's getting better," Leone said, offering what sounded like a dispassionate, professional opinion of Anstice's performance, before reverting to form, "I hope he didn't fill up. I hope he left some room. He's going to be eating documents."

WITHIN WEEKS OF RECEIVING the VIGOR results, Merck's marketing division produced a large, glossy brochure called the "Cardiovascular Card" (or CV card) and distributed it to every Vioxx sales representative in the country. Sales representatives were told to use it with high prescribers (crucial to expanding Vioxx's market share) who expressed concern about VIGOR's cardiovascular findings. "The Cardiovascular Card will allow you to set the record straight," read the April 28, 2000, bulletin introducing the card, with unintended irony.

According to the CV card, Vioxx was at least as safe, if not safer, than older painkillers like ibuprofen. Patients on the older nonsteroidal anti-inflammatory painkillers were eight times as likely to die from cardiovascular problems as those on Vioxx, the CV card said. These were remarkable assertions in light of the newly completed

VIGOR study, in which Vioxx subjects had five times as many heart attacks as those on the older painkiller, naproxen. The VIGOR results did not merit a single mention in the CV card.

An incredulous Lanier stood with CV card in hand and asked Anstice, "Doesn't that seem kind of unfair that you don't tell [doctors] about the biggest study you have ever done that shows five times as many heart attacks, you totally leave that out?"

"I don't think it is unfair," Anstice said. The studies shown in the CV card were clearly labeled as osteoarthritis studies, he said, whereas VIGOR was conducted on subjects with rheumatoid arthritis. (Osteoarthritis is the less serious, and more common, kind of arthritis.)

Did doctors who were shown the CV card even know about the VIGOR study, Lanier asked Anstice. They did, Anstice assured the jury. Merck had put out press releases on the study. Couldn't the sales reps have at least toted along Merck's press releases on the study, Lanier asked. They couldn't, Anstice said, and he offered a seemingly bulletproof reason. Merck believed federal law prohibited sales representatives from discussing the VIGOR study until its findings were reflected in the FDA-approved drug label.

Anstice was half-right about what his sales representatives could and couldn't say about VIGOR at the time. They *were* forbidden to promote additional benefits of Vioxx until the FDA vetted the evidence and approved changes to the drug label. Thus they could not have touted the stomach-sparing benefits of Vioxx seen in VIGOR without the FDA's formal approval. But as Higbee would later instruct the jury, Merck did *not* need the FDA's permission to spread the word among doctors that Vioxx had been associated with sharply higher risk of heart attack than an older painkiller in the VIGOR study.

The CV card remained in use until the Vioxx label was amended two years later. Sales representatives were reminded to use the cards whenever debate about Vioxx's potential risks bubbled up in the news. "<u>Do not proactively discuss any of the recent press stories,</u>" warned one such bulletin to sales representatives. It counseled sales reps to move quickly from dealing with doctors' safety concerns to more favorable ground: "Remain focused on your efficacy messages for Vioxx." Merck's market research had shown repeatedly that patients in pain cared most about getting rid of the pain, and far less about the painkiller's safety, and that doctors would prescribe the biggest, baddest painkiller they could find.

After the drug was pulled, an FDA medical reviewer told Congressional investigators that the data in the CV card was "ridiculous," "scientifically inappropriate," and irrelevant to an analysis of Vioxx's cardiovascular safety.

THE THANKLESS JOB OF defending Anstice from Lanier had fallen to Sullivan's number-two, the pugnacious and persistent Paul Strain. Strain was short for a man, and early on, Bob Leone remarked that Strain reminded him of the Lucky Charms cereal leprechaun. Leone liked the image so much that for the rest of the trial he referred to Strain almost exclusively as Lucky Charms or the leprechaun.

By the time the proceedings broke for lunch, Strain had brought them to a halt 25 times to lodge objections, often interrupting Lanier midsentence, with cries of "Lawyer argument!" or "This is just improper!" or once, "There's been another violation!" Anstice may have been going up in flames, but he wasn't going to go easy, if Strain could help it. As the day wore on, Strain's tone grew more querulous and petulant. I half expected him to reach over the few feet that separated their tables and shake Lanier hard. (Alas, that never happened.) Higbee was bending over backward to accommodate Strain, but she sent small signals of her displeasure, such as the occasional public reprimand when Strain interrupted Lanier, or, increasingly, a tinge of reluctance in granting Strain's frequent requests for a sidebar. But grant them she did, and I watched them unfold with avid interest.

First came Strain's angry objection, then Lanier's impatient rejoinder, followed by Higbee's uninflected instruction, "Counsel, approach the bench," or if the two were still sniping, "Counsel, stop! Stop, both of you," and finally came the scrum, as Chris Seeger joined Lanier and Diane Sullivan joined Strain to listen and argue, shake their heads, and pat their man on the back while scowling at their opponents. The arguments were conducted in whispers, but it was apparent the disputes were fierce. Sometimes order broke down completely. The court reporter, Regina Tell, whose job it was to record every word of the proceedings, would wave her hands frantically and shout, "One at a time! One at a time," and when that didn't work: "Judge, I can't hear anything!" If the lawyers still didn't respond, Higbee would cast a glance at the jury and say, "Guys, stop! The jury can hear you both." Then she might rule which side could continue and which had to wait its turn.

As I watched, I wondered who was winning these battles. Strain was thanking Higbee so loudly after each sidebar that I thought he had to be scoring big. But Higbee, whose face betrayed no emotion that I could see, not even exasperation, was letting Strain argue his point *ad nauseum,* and then, almost without exception, she was overruling him. Strain was doing what every trial lawyer is taught to do after a conference at the judge's bench: he was flashing a smile at the jury and thanking the judge profusely, even when she had chewed his argument to shreds.

Lanier was just as mindful of how the sidebars were playing with the jury. In one of the day's most entertaining whispered exchanges, Lanier complained to Higbee about Strain's displays of gratitude. "I have a frustration," he told her. "Whenever we turn away from the bench, he gets far enough away to say thank you, like you ruled for him…He has been doing it all day."

"The king of the gamesmanship, the king of the thank you, Your Honor, is Mr. Lanier," Strain responded, sarcastically. He had a point, of course.

"Don't raise your voice when you say that. You whisper on the things that you don't want the jury to hear," Lanier countered.

"We'll enter into a contract—neither one of us is going to say thank you after Your Honor's ruling. I'm fine with that, Your Honor," Strain suggested finally.

Ever the Boy Scout, Lanier proposed a different resolution. "We can say it now in unison, thank you," he said as the sidebar ended. "Out of politeness, thank you."

"Thanks very much," Strain said, and they all walked back to their seats.

Though Lanier's team joked that Strain suffered from "legal Tourette's," they were rankled by his manner.

"It wasn't just that he was objecting," said Seeger's law partner, David Buchanan, who knew the history and reasoning of Higbee's Vioxx rulings backward and forward, and frequently made the trip to her bench to fight off Strain's attacks. "He was objecting with a tone that showed disdain for the question. He was trying to suggest that the plaintiffs weren't playing by the rules, and to highlight that he was angry."

Even Anstice betrayed glimmers of irritation at Strain's belligerent manner, with a slight rolling of the eyes, or an impatient laugh when he asked that a question be repeated after yet another eruption from Strain's corner of the courtroom. Lanier sensed Anstice's discomfort. As a salesman, Anstice was sensitive to the importance of appearances, Lanier would say later, and Strain's objections, "made it look like David couldn't handle himself and things were out of control."

If, as the plaintiffs' lawyers believed, Strain's objections were intended to throw Lanier off his game, they were backfiring. Lanier's concentration was almost unshakeable. And Strain's angry agitation only highlighted Lanier's affable, cool control of the courtroom.

Moshe Horn, a veteran former prosecutor at the Manhattan District Attorney's Office who now worked for Seeger Weiss, summed up what Strain was up against like this: "Mark owns Anstice, Anstice knows that and Merck knows that."

LANIER SQUEEZED ONE LAST drop of advantage from the day, with a little help from Bloomberg News. The wire service had sent a veteran reporter to cover the trial, and his story on the day's events included a complete account of Higbee's wrath at Sullivan. It closed with reaction from Seeger and Lanier.

"There are rules. This isn't a brawl," Seeger complained.

Lanier said he was "appalled" by Sullivan's conduct and extolled Higbee's virtues. "The judge showed remarkable patience," he said.

The next morning Lanier crowed to Leone, "Did you see my quote in Bloomberg?" Leone hadn't, but it didn't matter. "The judge will see it!" Lanier continued, and misquoting slightly, he gleefully told Leone that he'd told Bloomberg: "I think the judge has shown remarkable restraint."

"And *I* am Mark Lanier and *I* follow the rules," Leone said, not missing a beat as he spelled out the not-so-hidden meaning of Lanier's quote.

"Yeah!" said Rick Meadow.

"That's the new Lanier," Leone said, and he chuckled some more.

"They have dropped enormously,
and it's very sad to watch from the outside."

CHAPTER 6

A Company Gone Bad?

Atlantic City, New Jersey, January 24, 2007

I HEARD IT SAID OFTEN, by Merck supporters and critics alike, that with its reputation for impeccable science, Merck was the last place they would have expected a debacle like Vioxx to occur. Merck's scientists were the best in the business, they said, and its safety record (until Vioxx) had been impeccable.

It was a view Lanier implicitly endorsed. In his opening statement, he had told the jury Merck went bad after Roy Vagelos, the longtime chairman and CEO of Merck, was replaced by Raymond Gilmartin. Vagelos was a physician and research scientist and had run Merck's research labs before becoming CEO. Gilmartin was an engineer and business school graduate. Lanier said Gilmartin had brought a new corporate culture to Merck, which empowered Merck's marketers at the expense of its scientists. At key moments in Vioxx's history when scientific prudence might have dictated further research and fuller disclosure of Vioxx's potential risks, Lanier said, Merck forged ahead with its aggressive marketing. Gilmartin's team was determined to protect the Vioxx brand from the taint of safety problems and to safeguard Vioxx sales.

The pharmaceutical industry was among the most profitable in the U.S., and Merck its largest and most profitable company when Gilmartin arrived in 1995. During Vagelos's two-decade tenure at Merck, (as president of Merck Research Labs from 1976 to 1985 and then as chairman and CEO from 1985 to 1994) the company's research labs had churned out a steady stream of new drugs, including two "blockbusters," industry parlance for drugs whose annual sales exceeded $1 billion. One of them, Mevacor, had revolutionized how doctors treated high cholesterol. It was the world's first statin. *Fortune* magazine named Merck the country's most admired company seven years in a row. It was a golden era for Merck and the drug industry, as an unprecedented convergence of new technology and new buyers fueled the growth of profits.

The post-World War II investment in fundamental biological research had created a substantial base of new knowledge on the molecular workings of the body, and in the 1980s it yielded a stream of new drugs that took precise aim at specific molecules to interrupt the disease process. Many of these drugs had milder side effects than their predecessors, making them palatable for broad use. Most treated chronic conditions from heartburn to high cholesterol and were meant to be taken for months, years, even a lifetime.

At the same time, newly generous insurance benefits in the 1980s created a pool of patients willing and able to pay top dollar for the new drugs, as insurance plans excluded prescription drugs from the deductible and required only a small, flat co-payment (usually $5) for each prescription. Insulated from the cost of the drugs, insured patients were indifferent to the high price of their drugs and to the industry's recurring price hikes, which far exceeded the rate of inflation. Drug company profits soared.

But by the early 1990s the party had ended, as insurers and hospitals reined in their drug spending (by setting up drug "formularies" that steered patients away from the most expensive drugs), and the government demanded discounts on drugs purchased by the federal-state Medicaid program. Drug makers grudgingly negotiated lower prices with both private and public institutional buyers. In 1993, when President Bill Clinton threatened price controls under his health-care overhaul, drug makers pledged drug prices would not go up any faster than inflation. The Clinton health-care overhaul never materialized, but the industry's untrammeled freedom to raise prices had been dealt another punishing blow.

Competition from cheaper generic drugs also hurt the drug industry's profits in the 1990s. For most of the post-war era, law and regulation had protected those profits by guaranteeing drug makers exclusive market rights on their new drugs. Here's how the system worked: When a company found or invented a chemical with promising potential, it applied for a patent and obtained a monopoly on the fruits of its invention until the patent expired, up to 17 years later. In practice, the drug maker's monopoly could last indefinitely. A separate set of government regulations made it prohibitively expensive to develop copies of the drugs even after the patent expired. Then in 1984, Congress passed a law that eased those regulations and made it easier for generic drug makers to market copies of drugs once their patents had expired. The law's impact was dramatic. Before its passage, only a third of drugs faced generic competition, and it usually took years for the generics to materialize. After the law, generic competition became the norm. It came swiftly after the patent term ended, and within the year (and later, months) generic substitutes would take over the market and wipe out profits from the brand-name version of the drug.

Merck's blockbusters would not face generic competition until the late 1990s and its profits were still growing. But the push-back on prices from institutional buyers, such as hospitals and managed care organizations, meant they were growing only half as fast as they had in the late 1980s. The company began to miss earnings targets and was forced to cut jobs.

"Everyone must understand that we are in a war, a war with the external environment affecting our business and with the competition, which is trying to surpass us," Vagelos told his senior executives that spring. The profits of the future would depend on developing drugs more quickly and making up declining profit margins with "dramatically" larger sales volumes, he said.

Vagelos would not stay to lead his troops through the war. Merck had a mandatory retirement policy and Vagelos left when he turned 65 in 1994. After Vagelos's hand-picked successor resigned abruptly, the board of directors took over the hunt for his successor. It chose the 53-year-old CEO of Becton, Dickinson & Company, a medium-sized manufacturer of syringes, gloves, and diagnostic equipment. Raymond Gilmartin received a mixed reception from investors and analysts. Some said they were "bewildered" and found it "unbelievable" that the world's largest drug maker would now be run by a man with no experience in the drug industry. Others said Gilmartin would bring a "fresh perspective" to Merck's problems. Vagelos seemed to bless the choice when he told the *New York Times* Gilmartin was "clearly the best person for the job." Hospital suppliers, such as Becton, Dickinson, had seen their pricing power erode under pressure from big buyers in the 1980s, and Gilmartin had proven adept at cutting costs and management layers. Vagelos suggested the experience would serve Gilmartin well at Merck, which, like every other pharmaceutical company, was trying to become more efficient.

But cost-cutting alone couldn't secure Merck's future. The company needed new "hit" drugs, and it needed to get much better at selling them *hard*.

With the changes in patent law and cost-cutting by managed care eroded pricing power, marketing had become the new lynchpin of profitability in the drug industry. Drug makers had to make the most of their monopolies before their brand-name drugs were sidelined by inexpensive generic competitors. In a marketplace crowded with virtually indistinguishable competitors, there were two ways to do that—aggressive marketing and aggressive discounts. Not surprisingly, drug companies preferred the first. The new focus on "lifestyle" drugs for baby boomers (think drugs to treat baldness and erectile dysfunction, to name just two), and the new freedom to market directly to patients as a result of changes to the FDA's rules, gave the industry's marketers products and tools (such as television ads) peculiarly well-suited to promotion.

Under Vagelos and his predecessors, the research labs had been the seat of power at Merck. But as research prowess alone could no longer guarantee market share or profits, Gilmartin set about the task of redistributing power at Merck and giving marketers a bigger share. He boosted the marketing division's budgets and professional skills, training Merck's marketers in data-driven methodologies that had been perfected already to sell consumer goods from Coke to cars. In the new Merck, marketers would no longer be bystanders but powerful players in charting the company's strategic course and making sure the company followed it. As part of that effort, marketers would work closely with scientists during the drug development process and after the drug was on the market.

Gilmartin's belief that better coordination between scientists and marketers would translate into bigger profits was widely shared in the drug industry. In his book *Generation Rx*, Greg Critser recounts a 1991 conversation between the newly installed CEO of Pfizer, William C. Steere, and a top company lobbyist, Steve Conafay. "[The CEO] told me he had three priorities," Conafay told Critser. "The first one was get marketing and research closer together. The second one was get marketing and research closer together. And then he said the third one was get marketing and research closer together." Steere had integrated marketers into Pfizer's drug development teams in the 1980s, well before Merck.

Marketing's new clout was cemented by changes in the top ranks, where three marketing executives (an increase over the one under Vagelos) sat on the 11-member Management Committee and helped Gilmartin run the company. David Anstice was among the three. Reassigning him from Europe, Gilmartin promoted him to lead Merck's marketing operations in its largest and most important market, the United States. In that position, Anstice was a key participant in the shift of power from science to marketing at Merck.

MERCK HAD HIGH HOPES for Vioxx when it began developing it in the early 1990s. An estimated 100,000 persons were hospitalized in the United States each year due to gastric bleeding brought on by nonsteroidal anti-inflammatory drugs such as ibuprofen and naproxen. More than 16,000 of them died. The market potential for a safer alternative to the NSAIDs, which are among the most commonly used medicines in the world, appeared huge. Moreover, Merck's scientists believed Vioxx would be the first of the new breed of safer painkillers to hit the market. Being first counts for a lot in the drug business. The first entrant of a new class of drugs commands a higher price than later entrants and it gets a leg up in the all-important contest for doctors' attention and prescriptions. But the honor of being first went to a close chemical cousin, Celebrex, which came on the market in January 1999. Celebrex was developed by drug maker Searle (later Pharmacia) and promoted jointly by Searle and Pfizer.

Vioxx was launched six months later, and in style. Merck rented an island under the Bay Bridge in San Francisco, hired a 20-piece swing band and spent $1 million to fete its sales representatives and motivate them to sell the new product. David Anstice himself flew out to speak to the sales representatives, and he promised them that despite its slow start, Vioxx would pull ahead of Celebrex, and Merck would soon own the painkiller market. A videotape of the speech shows a younger, heavier, slightly awkward Anstice beaming as he delivered his lines.

"I *am* in it to win it," he declared. *"You can bank on that!"*

Borrowing from David Letterman, Anstice rolled out a top ten list of reasons why Vioxx would pull ahead. Among the items on his list were the following: Merck had enlisted hundreds of practicing physicians and academic opinion leaders as consultants, advocates, and speakers; it had assembled the industry's largest sales force ever to sell a single product—3,800 people, 25 percent larger than the Celebrex sales force; the sales representatives were getting what Anstice described as "an absolute corker" of a compensation package; Merck had conducted a "clinical trial" to put Vioxx in the hands of 800 primary care physicians and familiarize them with it even before it was available on the market; and sales representatives would be provided 17 million units of Vioxx samples to distribute to 25,000 physicians over the following seven months. A great deal was riding on Vioxx's success—patents on many of Merck's older drugs would soon run out—and Anstice and his marketers were not leaving any aspect of Vioxx's future to chance.

A YEAR LATER, CELEBREX was still ahead of Vioxx, and had even beaten out the older painkiller ibuprofen to become the top-selling painkiller on the market. But Vioxx was not far behind. And Merck forecasts showed Vioxx poised to overtake Celebrex in 2001, as long as Merck was able to "neutralize" concerns about Vioxx's safety.

Celebrex had its own problems. Unlike Vioxx, it had not delivered on the COX-2 promise of being gentler on the gut. But, also unlike Vioxx, Celebrex was not associated with a higher risk of cardiovascular problems than older painkillers, until much later. In December 2004, two and a half months after Merck pulled Vioxx from the market, a large study by the National Institutes of Health found that Celebrex was two to three times more likely to cause heart problems than sugar pills. (There was talk at the FDA of requiring Pfizer to withdraw Celebrex, but on the advice of a panel of outside scientists, the FDA did not take that step, instead asking Pfizer for a strong warning on the Celebrex label.) But in 2001, Pfizer's sales force had a devastatingly simple message: Celebrex was the safe COX-2 and Vioxx the unsafe one.

Merck's best hope of neutralizing Pfizer's tactics was the Food and Drug Administration. If, after dissecting the results of VIGOR and other Vioxx studies, the FDA agreed with Merck that the VIGOR results were proof not of Vioxx's problems but of naproxen's powers, Vioxx might yet beat out Celebrex to become the top painkiller in America.

In 2000 and 2001, while the FDA was conducting its review, the official Vioxx label continued to characterize the risk of suffering a heart attack as remote. Heart attacks appeared only in what Lanier called the label's "bug-bite bucket," alongside insect bites, hemorrhoids, and other conditions that had been observed in clinical studies but were unlikely to have been caused by Vioxx. But as the FDA's review progressed, it became apparent that FDA scientists believed Vioxx's safety problems were real and serious.

Anticipating that the FDA would call for tougher labeling, Merck executives prepared a five-year operating plan for the Vioxx franchise in July 2001, in which they mapped out how sales would be affected if the FDA asked Merck to move the heart attacks from the "bug-bite bucket" to the label's Precautions or Warnings sections. The plan included a graph depicting estimated annual sales under each of the three disclosure scenarios. The graph had become a staple at the

Vioxx trials, and Lanier quizzed Anstice about it that day, placing it with practiced ceremony on the overhead projector, and shielding its curves, at first, from the jury's eyes with a blank sheet of paper. The graph was blandly titled, "Upside/Downside Sales Forecast."

"So, financially, your people made a calculation on the difference it made to your company in sales if you got to keep the heart where it is, in Adverse Reactions, right?" Lanier said to Anstice.

"Yes, they were making such a forecast," Anstice replied.

Something about Anstice's tone appeared to irk Lanier, and he turned from the projector to face Anstice, "Not 'they.' This is y'all. This is your department, isn't it?"

"Yes. Not the scientists at Merck. The marketing and financial people," Anstice said, facing the jury, his tone still level.

Lanier took a few steps toward Anstice and pointing with both his arms, for emphasis, at Anstice, he said, "David Anstice's people."

"Yes," Anstice said.

"When you say 'they,' it sound like it is someone else. The buck stops with you, doesn't it?" Lanier said.

"Absolutely," Anstice said

It had been a humiliating exchange, and Anstice looked pale as Lanier returned to the graph on the overhead projector and proceeded to unveil it.

Three curved lines snaked across the courtroom screen, going up for the first two years, before gradually descending in roughly parallel fashion. The line closest to the bottom of the graph represented projected sales if the potential for heart attacks on Vioxx was moved to the Warnings section of the label. The line in the middle represented sales if the heart attacks were described in the Precautions section of the label (for less serious side effects), and the line at the top represented sales under the best scenario for Merck, in which forecasters would remain in the least serious, Adverse Reactions, label category.

The graph showed that by 2006, annual Vioxx sales were projected to range from just under $1.5 billion if the FDA required Merck to disclose the risk of heart attack in the label's Warnings section, to just over $2.5 billion if the disclosures remained in the least serious label category, according to the graph.

"Isn't it safe for us to assume that the difference in moving the heart issues from the Adverse Reactions bucket to the Warnings bucket is projected to cost your company a billion dollars a year in sales?" Lanier said, dropping his voice an octave as he neared the magic 'billion.'

"Yes," Anstice said, then addressed the jury, "but that is not what was driving our behavior."

"In other words, this is just something y'all did," Lanier drawled, "but you didn't—this wasn't because it was going to affect how you acted at all, you just wanted to *know*."

"Yes. You have to know what the different scenarios are," countered Anstice stoutly. "Our scientists make conclusions about the label based on the science."

The sales forecast affirmed the plaintiffs' own position that had Merck fully disclosed Vioxx's risks, it would have sold a lot less of the drug. The graph showed that Merck had motive to hide Vioxx's risks, said the veteran plaintiffs' lawyer Jerry Kristal.

"That's a killer for them," Kristal said gleefully afterwards. "It's hard to recover."

The jury in the first Vioxx trial had based its $229 million award of punitive damages on another projection found in the same long-term business plan. That was the amount Merck believed it would lose in sales if the label change were to occur four months sooner than it had previously anticipated.

Three months after Merck's marketing and sales teams prepared the long-term sales forecast, Merck's worst fears came to pass. The FDA informed the company that FDA scientists believed Vioxx's heart effects, as seen in VIGOR, warranted prominent disclosure in the label's Warnings section. A furious exchange of emails ensued at the top levels of Merck, and Lanier wrapped up this section of his cross-examination with them.

"It begins with an email from Ed Scolnick, who is over the science end, right?" Lanier said.

"Yes, that's correct," Anstice replied.

"And it is sent on Monday, October 15th, 2001, right?" Lanier said.

"Yes." Anstice said.

"And it is sent to you, David Anstice, right?" Lanier said.

"Yes," Anstice replied.

"The subject is the Vioxx label, true?" Lanier said.

"Yes," Anstice said.

Lanier had placed the email chain on his overhead projector and was highlighting it line by line. Before long, the emails were glowing neon yellow from his attentions.

"And what Edward Scolnick tells you is, 'Be assured, we will *not* accept this label,' right?" Lanier said, reading Scolnick's words, with feeling.

"Yes, right," said Anstice, his manner becoming more muted as Lanier's became more dramatic.

"So, the FDA sent y'all a label, and he wanted you, evidently, to be assured that y'all would not accept it," Lanier said, again.

"Yes," Anstice said, with a tiny shrug of his shoulders. "It is his decision what to do with labels, but he was telling me that he would not accept it."

"Because the FDA sent you a label saying that the heart attack information ought to go in the Warnings bucket that would cost you a billion dollars a year, right?" Lanier said.

"They had sent us that," Anstice said. "But that was not the reason he was objecting, I believe."

The company's top scientist railed against giving a strong warning that Vioxx could cause heart attacks, but, according to Anstice, Scolnick's opposition was based on scientific principle, not on the knowledge that Merck would lose $1 billion in sales as a result. It was pure chance that Scolnick's opinion was aligned with the company's financial interests.

Anstice had emailed Scolnick back, and the jury could now see that response on the screen.

"E-mail from you to Ed Scolnick. I guess it was, what, 30 minutes later?" Lanier said.

"Yes, it was," Anstice replied.

"You said, 'Ed, thanks.'" Lanier said, adding parenthetically, "Is that what you called him, Ed?"

Hardly surprising, given that Ed was Scolnick's given name, but Lanier had Anstice on such a short leash now, that he could say just about anything and get away with it.

"Yes, that's what I called him," Anstice said, with a glance toward the jury.

"I just received a copy five minutes ago and will digest it tonight. We knew it would be ugly, and it is," Anstice had written back.

Lanier showed the jury Scolnick's reply, "It is ugly cubed. thye are bastards" *(sic)*

Merck fought the label, as Scolnick promised, and in 2002 the company succeeded beyond its wildest hopes. The revised label didn't just soft-pedal Vioxx's risks—it thoroughly confounded them. On the one hand, it suggested the need for caution by citing the VIGOR results. On the other, the label provided results of two placebo studies in which, it asserted, there were fewer serious cardiovascular events on Vioxx than on the sugar pills. (Researchers later showed the claim was misleading.) The label advised doctors to take these results into consideration when prescribing Vioxx, then added that the significance of their contradictory findings was "unknown."

For a doctor, that's as good as the FDA saying "forget about the cardiovascular risk," said Lanier's science consultant, David Egilman, who had practiced as a general physician himself for many years. "Physicians do not have the time or the training," he said, to interpret the underlying data, and if the FDA couldn't say what it meant, they had to assume it was "meaningless."

The amended label was a far cry from the "ugly label," which had declared unequivocally that in VIGOR, the risk of developing a heart attack had been five times higher on Vioxx than naproxen, and had cited a second, smaller study whose findings were consistent with VIGOR as additional support for its grim view of Vioxx's risks. There was no mention of that study in the final label. And the FDA moved the disclosures from the Warnings section in the "ugly label" to the less prominent Precautions section in the final label, a change that added hundreds of millions of dollars to Merck's bottom line. No wonder, then, that Scolnick pronounced the new label a "miracle" label.

It had taken close to two years to bring the "miracle" label to fruition, during which time neither the official label nor Merck salesmen told doctors that the largest study of their drug had shown Vioxx subjects to be more prone to heart attacks than those given an older painkiller. And millions more patients were put on the drug without knowing it could harm them.

I'D HEARD THAT ROY VAGELOS still held strong opinions on the affairs of the company he once ran. In July 2009, I flew to meet him on Martha's Vineyard, where he summers. It was a stormy day and my flight was very late. I found Vagelos waiting on a bench outside the chain-link fence at the edge of the airfield, a rolled-up copy of the New York Times in hand. He was dressed in shorts and a short-sleeved pink shirt—a slight, spry figure a few months shy of his 80th birthday. As we walked to the airport restaurant, we chatted about the bouillabaisse he was making that evening and his newborn grandson.

I had hoped Vagelos would be willing to share his opinions about Merck, and Vagelos did not disappoint. We talked for an hour and a half over hamburgers and coffee, amid the din of waitresses shouting out lunch orders, dishes clattering, and a noisy blender at the bar.

"Stepping down from Merck was like dying for me," Vagelos began, as soon as we had ordered lunch. "It was a calamity for Merck."

How so? I asked.

"Anybody can make an error in the selection of a leader, but living with it for a decade is a disaster," Vagelos said. "They have dropped enormously, and it's very sad to watch from the outside. "You wonder how these companies survive when they don't know what to do."

In a few short minutes, Vagelos had thoroughly disavowed Gilmartin and the "new" Merck.

The conversation turned inevitably to Vioxx. I told Vagelos that credible research had indicated potential safety problems even before Vioxx was put on the market, and that internal emails documented Merck's deliberate decision to *not* do follow-up studies. Vagelos listened without comment, and sounded agitated when he broke his silence. "You have to understand and believe me when I tell you that I don't know any of this," he said. Gilmartin and the head of research, Edward Scolnick (whom Vagelos had hired) made it clear when he left that they weren't interested in his opinions or advice. "Let me tell you how bad it was," he said. "I was invited back to Merck to give a lecture early this year. That was the first time I have been invited to Merck in 15 years." (Scolnick and Gilmartin had both retired.) A few weeks before we met, Vagelos had gone back to Merck again, after a Merck scientist asked if Vagelos would be willing to review some of the company's research projects. "And I said, 'if you'd like, *of course* I would be willing.' So I returned about six weeks ago and spent most of the day with the research group," and Vagelos repeated, "First time in 15 years." The architect of Merck's scientific (and financial) renaissance was, at once, angry, sad, and disbelieving that his successors had, as he put it, "blotted out the past."

Vagelos's ties to Merck went back to his teenage years, when he worked after school in his parents' luncheonette in Rahway, New Jersey. It was a few blocks from Merck's headquarters and a popular lunch spot for the company's scientists, who made a big impression on the teenager. "For the first time I saw people truly excited about the intellectual aspects of their work," Vagelos wrote in his book *The Moral Corporation*. After graduating from the University of Pennsylvania, Vagelos trained as a physician at Columbia University's College of Physicians & Surgeons. He got his start in research at the National Institutes of Health and went on to chair the department of biological chemistry at Washington University's School of Medicine in St. Louis. In 1975, Merck hired Vagelos to reinvent its research labs, which were in the midst of a protracted dry spell.

A colleague at the university warned Vagelos he would be selling toothpaste and hairbrushes when he got to Merck.

"Really?" Vagelos said he responded.

He couldn't be sure it wasn't true. And he had his own misgivings about leaving the pursuit of "pure knowledge" in the university world. He was worried about how deep Merck's commitment to research really ran.

Vagelos said he asked Henry Gadsden, then Merck's CEO, "What would happen if things went sour in the business?"

"Roy, we would cut back in marketing and sales and all the staff groups," Vagelos said Gadsden told him. "But I would do everything in my power not to cut back on research, because research is our future." Vagelos took the job.

In *The Moral Corporation*, Vagelos wrote that when he got to Merck he spent much of his time talking with individual scientists. He was looking to get a clear picture of "what was or wasn't working at the bench level of research," he wrote, and to help researchers negotiate roadblocks. Vagelos said he talked to scientists everyplace he could. "I would talk to them in lunch lines, and they would tell me things that I would *never* hear in a formal meeting," he told me. "And I'd call them at night and tell them my reaction, because I could think about it, you know."

Like others in the drug industry, Merck scientists were still using traditional chemistry-based research to identify and develop drugs when he arrived. Vagelos dragged them into the modern age—coaxing, cajoling, and persuading his new colleagues to give the tools of molecular biology a chance. He hired hundreds of new scientists, recruiting from the best universities, and year after year, obtained bigger budgets for the research labs. Both of the new blockbusters, Mevacor and Vasotec (which lowered cholesterol and blood pressure, respectively), were developed using the new methods Vagelos championed—object lessons for the old guard on the power of the new.

"The heart and soul of the biotech-pharmaceutical industry is drug discovery. That's what it's all about," Vagelos said. "You have to allow scientists to move in the direction of science, and then you have to help them...aim [the science] in the direction of disease. Some places can do it. Most places cannot....I loved to do that. That's what I loved to do."

Yet Vagelos, too, had recognized in the early 1990s that Merck could not rely on research alone to prosper. Toward the end of his tenure, Vagelos spent $6 billion to acquire the nation's largest mail-order drug company, Medco Containment Services. He was hoping to turn employers' cost-containment efforts, which had devastated margins in Merck's core business of selling drugs, to Merck's advantage. Like Gilmartin, Vagelos had also envisioned a bigger role for marketing at Merck. He had chosen a marketer, Richard Markham, to succeed him. He even floated the idea of merging Merck with the industry's most aggressive marketer, Pfizer, on the theory that the combination of Merck's science and Pfizer's marketing muscle would create an unbeatable powerhouse. (The idea was stillborn—neither Pfizer nor Vagelos's senior team at Merck were interested.) Still, Vagelos's embrace of marketing was always uneasy. A case in point: Vagelos advocated cuts in the size and role of the Merck sales force, even as he considered merging with Pfizer.

When I asked Vagelos what he thought of Gilmartin's efforts to bring Merck's marketers closer to the scientists, Vagelos responded that *he* had banished marketers from involvement at the early stages of drug discovery. The marketers were squelching ideas because they didn't understand the potential of the underlying science, he said.

"We don't need your information, because it's not valuable," he told them.

In the years since he left Merck, Vagelos has burnished his anti-marketing credentials. In 2008, he chaired a task force of the Association of American Medical Colleges, which called on medical schools to ban or limit such inducements as meals, gifts, and drug samples that drug companies use to ingratiate themselves with young doctors and, in Vagelos's words, to "buy prescriptions."

These are standard practices in the drug industry. Hadn't Merck used them when he had been CEO, I asked Vagelos.

"It couldn't have happened when I was there," Vagelos said, looking horrified. His voice climbed an octave, "Are you kidding?"

Of course those marketing practices, writ large, had been the key to making Vioxx a blockbuster drug.

THE VIGOR STUDY'S CARDIOVASCULAR findings were not a complete surprise when Merck received them in early 2000. Before the first Vioxx pill was sold, prominent outside scientists had warned Merck that Vioxx may be harmful for the heart and suggested Merck quickly undertake studies to answer the question. As Lanier had already told the jury in his opening statement, the response of the scientist in charge of the Vioxx project was unequivocal—Merck would not be doing such studies. In an apparent allusion to those early concerns, Scolnick wrote his colleagues shortly after he received the VIGOR results, "The CV [cardiovascular] events are clearly there…It is a shame, but it is a low incidence. It is mechanism-based, as we worried it was."

"Had you been one of those *worried* about the idea that Vioxx might cause heart problems?" Lanier asked Anstice, after he read the email for the jury.

Anstice said he had not been among those worried.

"Okay," Lanier said, and paused to face Anstice, his back slightly swayed, apparently weighing his next words. "Once these results came in, Merck did not, you did not, or anybody at Merck, make a decision to *stop* running your advertisements, did you?"

"No," Anstice said emphatically. "We did not stop our advertising."

"In fact we have an exhibit," Lanier said, and reached over to his table to retrieve a black binder several inches thick. "Your Honor, it is Plaintiffs' Exhibit 270, which we move into evidence." It was a detailed record of each and every Vioxx ad in print or on radio or television, over the drug's five and a half years on the market.

Lanier examined the binder for a minute before walking to Hegar's seat in the front of the courtroom gallery and heaving a copy up to carry to Strain. Hegar walked to the witness stand and delivered a second binder to Anstice herself. It was quite a production, as indeed, it was intended to be. Lanier and Bob Leone had joked about just this moment in Lanier's suite that morning.

"I'm going to need the Vioxx advertisement notebook. Bob, will you carry that for me?" Lanier had said as he prepared to leave the suite.

"You bet. I'll hand it to you personally," Leone had said.

And Lanier had responded with a smile, "That's what I was thinking."

Lanier hauled the binder close to the jury box, held it up, and paged through some of its thousand pages.

"Sir, what we've got here is print advertisements for '99, print advertisements for 2000, 2001, for 2002," Lanier said.

"Yes, I see it," Anstice said. He had made the mistake a minute earlier of not immediately taking Lanier's word for the binder's contents.

"For 2003, for 2004, all the way until we get to page 300, right?" Lanier continued. He was unstoppable now, "And then starting on page 300, we've got the television advertisements."

Strain stood up to see what he could do. "Your Honor, I'll be happy to—whatever counsel proposes what it is, just represent what it is, and I'll stipulate to that," Strain said, cooperatively.

"Great," said Lanier, and proceeded to describe the binder's contents again.

"And I certainly agree that's what it looks like, Your Honor," Strain said.

Lanier wasn't quite done. "And then the only other thing I would add is, for example, you can look at the TV ads and print ads and see that y'all were running advertisements every single day for the entire duration of the product, right?" he said to Anstice, who wisely accepted Lanier's assertion.

It looked like the torture-by-advertising-binder portion of the show was over. Lanier had walked back to his table and set the binder down, when he said, slowly, and with just a hint of puzzlement, as if he wasn't quite sure he had his facts right.

"Those ads that you were running, you never pulled those ads for any day," Lanier said, "not even the day that we have here, when Ed Scolnick says..." He had whisked the email sent by Merck's top scientist about the heart attacks in the VIGOR study back on the projector and was reading its choicest bits again: "The CV events are clearly there. It is real. It is a shame but it is a low incidence."

"You never pulled the ads one day, did you?" Lanier said.

"I don't recall advertising being stopped," Anstice said. "Correct."

LANIER'S PERFORMANCE THAT DAY was, by turns, low-key, almost casual, and melodramatically angry, even grave. He was a little less cordial than he had been the day before. It turned out he was taking his cues from the jury.

"One of the things I have to really guard against when I try a case is that I get so involved...that I can walk in already righteously indignant," Lanier explained. "And yet a jury would not understand if I were righteously indignant at the start of a trial. Now once you start counting the jurors that cross their arms like this," he said, and crossed his arms across his chest to demonstrate, "you can count on them getting indignant, and fed up, and as that starts happening, and witnesses start crumbling, then I can show a little more indignation as well." By day 3 of the trial, several jurors could be seen laughing or shaking their heads at Anstice's answers, and Lanier deemed the jury ready for that display.

David Anstice, for his part, had grown both cooler and angrier. As I listened to them spar, I reflected that Lanier and Anstice were playing entirely different games. Lanier was playing to the American taste for plain speech with his blunt sentences. His one- and two-syllable words packed an emotional punch. Anstice's style was rational and slightly formal. It had likely served him well in his climb up the corporate ladder, but it sounded shifty in the courtroom.

"I think [Anstice's] attitude was 'I just need to get my story out there, and try not to take on too many hits. If I get my story out there, surely they'll understand I did nothing wrong,'" Lanier mused later. "That would be my strategy if I were him. It just doesn't work, though."

The contemporaneous record preserved in Merck's memos and emails contradicted Anstice's testimony, Lanier said. When confronted with those documents, "Anstice either had to admit to the truth or *obviously* lie to the jury," Lanier said, "and either one was fine for me."

I told Lanier I found myself feeling a little sorry for Anstice when I watched his testimony for a second time on videotape.

"Well, that's because the facts kill him. The *facts* kill him," Lanier chortled. "I mean he ought to be taking on shots. I mean they screwed up. They major screwed up and hurt a lot of people. I just use him to show it."

"How many more of these do you want to do?
I bet the answer is zero."

CHAPTER 7

Digging the Hole Deeper

Atlantic City, New Jersey, January 26–30, 2007

IT WAS FRIDAY, THE end of a long first week, when Anstice took the stand again. The rhythms of the trial had become my own by then. Each morning, around 8:30, I caught a ride from the Borgata to the courthouse with Lanier and his crew. Fifteen minutes later, Lanier's rented SUV was pulling into the parking lot across from the courthouse. I slid out of the back seat, where I had been sandwiched between Bob Leone and Rick Meadow, and jaywalked to the courthouse—tagging several feet behind Lanier and Dara Hegar and trying to keep up with Leone and Meadow. My physical position perfectly mirrored my position in the group. I was *in* the group, but not *of* it, an outsider with temporary privileges. At a few minutes before 9 A.M., we passed through the metal detector and entered the cold, dimly lit recesses of the Atlantic City courthouse.

We waited in the lobby for one of the two small, slow elevators to take us to Judge Higbee's courtroom on the third floor. Leone entered the elevator, looked around and said loudly, "Four, please."

The joke was that there were only three floors. "Ha, ha, Bob," Hegar or Lanier might say. But Leone was happiest when some unwitting stranger looked for the number 4 on the elevator panel and politely informed him, "There is no fourth floor." Leone would respond with disbelief, until one of the others set the stranger straight. His enthusiasm for the joke was so unflagging that I found myself laughing every time.

The courtroom was quiet at that early hour. But you could feel the hostile chill that permeated the trial as soon as you walked in. The two sides were setting up shop for the day's work, and avoiding each other assiduously as they did so. They used doors separated by the width of the courtroom to come and go from their workrooms in the back, and avoided eye contact when their paths crossed. Paul Strain, alone, could be counted on to breach protocol with some regularity and use the aisle on the plaintiffs' side of the courtroom to enter the courtroom well. Sometimes he brushed by Hegar or Lanier on his way. They pretended he didn't exist, but you could tell from their stiffening backs and from Strain's own tense demeanor, that each was intensely aware of the other's proximity. I sometimes wondered how they could bear it. Afterwards the plaintiffs' lawyers would complain, "That Paul Strain..." It was quite something to watch.

I was not exempt from the partisan distrust, as I had learned on David Anstice's first day in court. Seeing Anstice in the flesh, I did what any self-respecting reporter would. I introduced myself. Anstice responded pleasantly, and we chatted until an officious man in a suit materialized at Anstice's elbow. Anstice was urgently needed in the back, the man said. Anstice looked puzzled, but with the air of a man used to minding his handlers, he left the courtroom. His escort shot me a glance as he shepherded Anstice to safety.

"Back off," the look said.

You were either friend or foe in that courtroom, and apparently, if I wasn't one, I had to be the other.

By the end of the week I had taken to sitting next to Rick Meadow, the head of Lanier's New York office, in the gallery's second row. It meant I had someone with whom to exchange glances or notes when tempers flared and I found my stomach twisting itself into knots.

If the courtroom had a neutral zone, it was the small rectangle between the witness box and the judge's bench, home to Regina Tell, the ace court reporter and a vivacious, funny presence in her own right. Tell would be at her post testing her equipment to be sure each side was receiving her transcription in real time, and the lawyers took turns chatting her up. That Friday morning, I watched as Leone sauntered over to Tell for a long, involved conversation about her transcription machine. He had wandered away when David Anstice hurried across the courtroom to take his seat in the witness box. As Anstice exchanged pleasantries with Tell, Leone coolly sauntered back to resumed his conversation with Tell, without so much as a nod to Anstice.

Leone's cold shoulder was calculated.

"I always tell our guys, 'don't be friendly with the other side,' 'cause if the jury sees that, they think it's all one big game, we're all friends here, nobody is really against anybody," he explained once. "If the jury is in the room, let's be clear. We're not there to joke around and play with 'em. It's a serious case. It's a serious wrong. We're talking about a hundred thousand heart attacks, and we're talking about dead people."

LEONE MADE A POINT of ignoring one other group of people in the courtroom—his shadow jury. They sat in the back of the courtroom, their jeans, sweatshirts, and inexpensive winter jackets conspicuous in the sea of lawyerly blue suits around them. They had been chosen to match the demographics of the actual jury, and help Leone keep a running score on how each side was faring with the actual jury. Trained interviewers questioned them after court on what they thought of each day's witnesses and testimony. The shadow jurors (or gallery jurors, as Leone preferred to call them) also rated the lawyers and witnesses on a scale of 0 to 10 daily. The jurors weren't told they were working for the plaintiffs, so they wouldn't be tempted to tailor their opinions. To guard against subtle bias in their questioning, the interviewers also weren't told who their client was. True to his background as an experimental psychologist, Leone was running the shadow jury like a double-blind experiment.

Bob Leone's wife, Kelly, who described herself as a "housewife," served as an undercover go-between, and sat in the courtroom's last row with an employee of the consulting firm that had hired the shadow jurors. To all appearances, she was unconnected to the plaintiffs, and the Leones went to some lengths to preserve that illusion. They drove separately from the hotel to the courthouse. In court, husband and wife avoided eye contact, and never once did I see either acknowledge the other's presence.

Not knowing of her role, I greeted Leone's wife warmly when I saw her in court on the first day of the trial. I was thoroughly snubbed in response. A few days later Leone chided me for talking to his wife, and gave me stern instructions to stay away from her and his shadow jury. I did as he asked. But I found myself smiling whenever I caught sight of Kelly sitting in the back of the courtroom, posing as an uninterested observer of the proceedings her husband was helping to orchestrate.

THE MAIN ITEM ON the agenda that Friday was Strain's direct examination of Anstice. But before he passed Anstice to Strain, Lanier intended to inflict a little more damage.

Among the exhibits Lanier pulled from his folders that morning was a 2001 email that reflected Merck's worry that publicity about Vioxx's cardiovascular problems was making its TV commercials less effective in recruiting new patients. The unfavorable publicity reached new heights when two prominent cardiologists joined the debate over Vioxx's safety problems in August 2001. Writing in the pages of the *Journal of the American Medical Association (JAMA)*, Eric Topol and Steven Nissen, chairman and vice chairman of cardiovascular medicine at the Cleveland Clinic, argued that the real-world hazard from Vioxx may be even more grave than studies suggested. That was because patients who took Vioxx in the real world were more likely to have heart disease than subjects in the Vioxx studies (which were conducted largely in people without heart disease). Topol and Nissen urged doctors to use caution in prescribing Vioxx *and* Celebrex to patients with heart disease, and called on Merck and Pfizer, the drugs' makers, to perform well-designed clinical trials to settle the matter. (Clinical trials had not shown Celebrex to be risky thus far, but Topol and Nissen argued that may have had more to do with trial design than with Celebrex's innate safety.)

The *JAMA* paper was big news in the general media. Vioxx and Celebrex were used by tens of millions, and Topol and Nissen were noted cardiologists. Moreover, their analysis bore the imprimatur of *JAMA* and its editors.

"We're staring at a major public health issue," Topol warned on the front page of the *Wall Street Journal*.

Company scientists had tried to dissuade Topol and Nissen from publishing their paper. Now, Merck's marketers did their best to blunt its impact. They prepared talking points for use with the media, and dispatched an overnight letter to the entire membership of the American Medical Association, challenging the article's conclusions. And they distributed a video news release of sound bites to television stations around the country for use in local television news broadcasts. Its message: Merck had data that Nissen and Topol did not, and that data showed Vioxx was safe.

Three weeks after the paper's publication, on the afternoon of September 11, 2001, Anstice informed CEO Ray Gilmartin that weekly sales reports showed the "coxib class [to which Vioxx belonged] is really suffering…clearly as a result of cardiovascular issues."

The article ultimately proved less damaging than Merck had feared, as shown by another email sent two months later, which Lanier pulled out. It concerned Vioxx TV commercials featuring the popular Olympic ice-skater Dorothy Hamill.

"After the *JAMA* article, a lot of us questioned whether DTC would still have the same ROI [return on investment] for Vioxx," the email read. DTC was short for direct-to-consumer advertising.

"As you can see in the attached, our Dorothy Hamill campaign (assessed post-*JAMA*) might be the highest impact ad we've had for Vioxx. We estimate that our campaign is generating at least the 4:1 confirmed this summer (measured based on the number of new patient starts driven by DTC.)"

In other words, every dollar spent on the campaign was generating $4 in new Vioxx prescriptions.

Lanier put the email on the projector and read it out for the jury, line by line.

"Did the thought ever occur to you during this period of time on any of these TV ads to go ahead and put in at least a mention about the heart problems that might be associated with [Vioxx]?" Lanier asked Anstice, returning to a theme he had struck earlier in the cross-examination.

"No," Anstice said. "That would not have been appropriate, because the information was not in our label at that time."

(Merck held that neither its salesmen nor its advertising could have warned about the cardiovascular risks of Vioxx until the amended label was approved by the FDA in 2002. In fact the FDA's rules required a drug manufacturer to change its label immediately if it had evidence that its drug was associated with a dangerous side effect.)

Lanier pointed out that Merck hadn't put a warning in the TV ads even *after* it amended the Vioxx label.

"*Honestly,* you never put it in there, did you?" he said.

Anstice hedged, "We did not put it in some of the ads. However, patients had access to the information."

"Not 'some of the ads,'" Lanier said. "You ran over *23,000* TV ads around this country...and not one time did *any* ad for the lifetime of that drug on TV ever say *anything* about heart troubles. That's the truth, isn't it?"

"The ads themselves did not," Anstice said.

I could see Leone shaking his head and laughing. Lanier was building up to the moment both men looked forward to in every trial: playing a Vioxx commercial for the jury. It would be the second one of the trial.

"A commercial is only a minute, they listen to every word, [the jurors hear] no warning. That gets them a little mad," Leone said. And, each time Lanier played another commercial, the jury got madder still.

The commercial du jour, naturally enough, featured Dorothy Hamill, and as the lights dimmed, Lanier instructed Anstice to "listen for the warning." It opened with pictures of Hamill on the ice at age 8, followed by pictures of her as a very young woman at the Olympics. And Hamill confided in a voice-over that she hadn't expected to win at the Olympics. Or to suffer from arthritis, she continued. As an older Hamill lithely glided across the screen, a soothing voice closed the sale, "Vioxx is here. With one little pill a day, Vioxx can provide 24-hour relief. Ask your doctor if Vioxx is right for you."

Even before the lights were turned back on, Lanier turned to Anstice, "Okay. Nothing about heart attacks," he said.

"No, not in that clip," Anstice said.

"Not in that ad," Lanier retorted. "That's the whole ad. I didn't take out part of it."

"That happened to be a whole ad," Anstice agreed.

"Nothing about, 'Go see our website to learn about heart attacks,' was there?" Lanier said.

"It didn't state it in that way…but there is a reference to our website and an 800 telephone number in that ad," Anstice said.

Lanier had the email about the Hamill ad back on the screen.

"When you sit here and you compare and you do this mathematical calculation, we're going to make $4 for every dollar we spend for running the Dorothy Hamill ad," he said, "do you take into account that if you put in that Dorothy Hamill ad 'Some studies have indicated that you've got a five times greater chance of having a heart attack on our drug than if you take a different drug for your arthritis?' Don't you think that might affect your four-to-one ratio a little bit?"

"Well, in that hypothetical situation, it might," Anstice said.

"The reason you didn't put it in there is because you would lose the benefit, the money benefit, isn't that true?" Lanier said, mildly.

"No, that is absolutely not true," Anstice said emphatically.

Lanier had once again made tangible the price for Merck of telling patients the truth about Vioxx—it was lost sales and profits. Anstice might argue that those financial calculations didn't affect Merck's decisions. But the longer he stayed on the stand, the less credible that position seemed.

Lanier returned to the ads as he closed his cross-examination an hour later. He stood several feet away from Anstice, rubbed his hands together thoughtfully, and spoke in a soft tone.

"Your company ought to tell us the truth about the drugs, shouldn't they?" Lanier said.

"Yes, and we do," Anstice said, firmly.

"Sir, your Dorothy Hamill ad did not have anything about heart attacks, did it?" Lanier said, pointing to the screen where the commercial had played.

The company website gave that information, Anstice said.

"But your company ought to tell us the good, the bad, and the ugly about your drugs," Lanier continued. "You would agree with that, wouldn't you?"

"Yes, and we do," Anstice said.

Lanier nodded and gazed at Anstice for a moment. His stance and silence exuded righteous disgust. He turned to Higbee.

"I'll pass the witness, your Honor," he said quietly.

The good news for Anstice was that he had earned a temporary reprieve from Lanier. The bad news, it soon become clear, was that he was now in Paul Strain's hands.

There was a sense of celebration on the plaintiffs' side of the courtroom, as the jury filed out and Strain began to rearrange the furniture in the courtroom well for his examination of Anstice. One by one, Lanier's team came up to pat Lanier on the back or exchange a laugh. He was talking to Jerry Kristal, with whom he had tried his last Vioxx case in that courtroom, when I approached him.

"I have a great wife," he was telling Kristal. He had been exchanging emails with her on his BlackBerry.

"I just passed the witness. I want to come home. I want you," Lanier had written. Becky Lanier had written back instantly, "I want you more," to which Lanier countered, "I want you most."

"Let's see how she can beat that," he said to Kristal.

Becky Lanier's answer shot back through the ether. Lanier grinned widely as he read it to himself, and held up his BlackBerry for Kristal to read. It was apparently too risqué to be read out loud.

STRAIN BEGAN HIS EXAMINATION after the brief break.

"I'm as you know the one who keeps interrupting," Strain said to the jury. "So..." His voice trailed off.

It hardly seemed like the best way to introduce himself, but it had the advantage of being truthful. For four days, Strain had been like an angry junkyard dog, baring his teeth at the plaintiffs every chance he got. He'd even snarled at the judge when she tried to call him off. Now he had to show a more likeable face and forge a connection with the jury as he set about the task of patching up Merck's image.

In her opening statement, Sullivan had portrayed Merck as a company dedicated to such high-minded goals as curing cancer and AIDS. She had dismissed as ludicrous plaintiffs' allegations that Merck had known of Vioxx's risks and hidden them from the outside world.

"What a disastrous business plan, to make a drug that you know hurts people and lie to doctors," Sullivan had said. "It doesn't make common sense."

But as Lanier had shown, hiding Vioxx's risks proved to be a fine business plan for Merck. And Strain began his rehabilitation of Merck's image by attacking the overarching theme of Lanier's narrative—that Merck was a good company gone bad, in which money, rather than science, drove important decisions.

"Mr. Anstice, how long have you been at Merck?" Strain asked.

"I have been at Merck for 33 years next month," Anstice said.

"Okay. So, you had a lot of experience under Dr. Vagelos and a lot of experience under Mr. Gilmartin?" Strain said. (Roy Vagelos was CEO of Merck from 1985 to 1994, and Ray Gilmartin succeeded him.)

"Yes, I was at Merck throughout their entire leadership period." Anstice said.

"I would like you to just tell our jurors...whether there was any change in culture at Merck when Dr. Vagelos retired and Mr. Gilmartin took over. Was there any less focus on safety, any less focus on patient safety?" Strain said.

"No, I do not believe that there was any less focus on patient safety," Anstice said and proceeded to extol the integrity of Merck's scientists, and their concern for patients.

In case that testimonial weren't enough for the jury, Strain plodded on:

"On the issue of whether...Merck moved away from a focus on safety, did or did not Mr. Gilmartin continue the same doctor responsible for all that progress and science and medicine under Dr. Vagelos...as head of Merck Research Laboratories?" Strain asked. (He was referring to Merck's top scientist, Edward Scolnick, known to the jury at this point chiefly for his intemperate emails to Anstice.)

Anstice dutifully responded that Gilmartin had retained Ed Scolnick as head of Merck's research labs.

By eliciting testimony that Merck was as focused on patient safety under Gilmartin, the CEO with an MBA, as it had been under the physician-CEO Vagelos, Strain had blundered. Three years before it got the Vioxx warning letter, Merck had been cited by the FDA for repeatedly minimizing the risks of several of its other drugs. Higbee had kept that reprimand letter out of the trial thus far, because it did not concern Vioxx. Now, Strain had opened the door to its use. Both FDA warnings had come on Gilmartin's watch. Merck had not received one under any previous chief executive.

"I have argued to this jury that there was a very clear change in the safety protocol within Merck, that marketing started driving the truck, that marketing was driving and eventually responsible for this wreck," Lanier would argue to Higbee Monday. "This jury truly thinks now that for 35 years Merck has consistently, throughout all of these years, been clean, been pristine, been great. The only problem was these three areas in that one FDA letter. That's just not the truth."

Higbee would rule that Lanier deserved the chance to set the record straight by showing the additional FDA reprimands to the jury.

But on this Friday afternoon, apparently oblivious to the implications of his line of questioning, Strain turned next to the one warning letter the jury did know about. The FDA had cited three instances in which Merck had misrepresented Vioxx's risks, and Strain tried to show they were isolated infractions which Merck had remedied promptly.

With Anstice on the stand, Strain read from the FDA's response to Merck's efforts, "This matter has been satisfactorily resolved and is considered closed."

"Did I read that correctly?" Strain asked.

"Yes, you did," Anstice replied.

"In other words, just what you were saying or trying to say during cross-examination, correct?"

"Yes," Anstice replied.

This was Merck as model corporate citizen—law-abiding, conscientious, and eager to please.

AT THE VERY BEGINNING of his examination, I had found Strain's slow, methodical manner a welcome, almost soothing, change of pace from Lanier's kinetic style. But it wasn't long before his heavy step and his plodding circuit, between the lectern on which he kept his notes, to the overhead projector, back to the lectern, up to the witness box to hand Anstice exhibits, and back again to the lectern, made Strain seem too old for his job. He was distracted, frequently referring to his witness as "*Dr.* Anstice," or just "Doctor," prompting Lanier to stand up at one point.

"Just for the record," Lanier said, "This is *Mr.* Anstice, not a doctor."

Even the mechanics of producing his exhibits seemed to challenge Strain almost beyond his capacities. He had trouble finding the correct documents. Then he fumbled for the sections he wanted to put on the projector for the jury. ("They're spending millions of dollars in attorney's fees and they can't find their freaking documents!" Lanier joked later.) Indeed, it was a far cry from Lanier's hyper-organized system, each exhibit in a folder of its own, set out in the order he expected to use them, with the relevant parts of the exhibits marked in a rainbow of neon stickers. On one hunt for a missing exhibit, after rooting around his lectern, Strain turned to Lanier to ask if perhaps Lanier had the missing exhibit.

Lanier replied mildly, "You have a set and we have a set."

"I'm all thumbs," Strain said to Higbee after another such incident. His comment was a little too close to the mark.

Moreover, Strain was dull. His questions were long, winding, and oblique. By the time he got to the end of one, you might not remember how it had started. Even Anstice looked confused.

Lanier said Strain was suffering from a problem common to big-firm defense lawyers: he hadn't made the transition from arguing his case in *writing* to arguing it orally.

"I'm at a point in my career now where I try cases against lawyers who are with the big firms that have the best brains that are really worth all the money, because those are the ones the defendants go to. They went to the best schools. They got the best grades," he said. "Now, I've taught at law schools, as a visiting guy, I'll show up, I taught a torts class at Harvard three weeks ago. Now here's what happens. In law school, the best grades go to the best writers, because you write your exams. Now Paul Strain, he's probably a wonderful writer. That's the way his brain works, and so he prepares his trial thinking, 'Okay, what are the questions? What are the answers I need so that

I have this clear logical progression of evidence?' But you use different communication techniques if you want to communicate orally as opposed to in writing."

For example, you use slogans and rhymes, Lanier said.

"If Johnny Cochran had written an appellate brief, and told the judges on appeal who are reading it in their dark, cave rooms, 'if the glove don't fit you must acquit,' you know the judges would have read that brief and thought, 'give me a break.' But when he says it in front of a jury, he's brilliant."

Strain wasn't an "oralist," as Lanier put it, but that wasn't his only handicap. He seemed ill at ease with the jury, and with his witness. Where Lanier addressed the jurors as, "y'all," Strain referred to them in the third person, as "the ladies and gentlemen of the jury" or "our jurors." Occasionally he used humor to court the jury, but his attempts felt painfully stilted, as when he tried to kid Anstice, first about his Australian accent, and then this:

"And the other thing, very important, I want you to tell our ladies and gentlemen of the jury, I know and none of them know, what is the name of town where you were born in Australia?" Strain said.

"The name of the town I was born in was Waga Waga," Anstice said.

"Would you say that one more time, because we must have misheard?" Strain said.

"Waga Waga," repeated Anstice, dutifully. "It means place of many crows."

"Crows?" Strain said.

"Crows," Anstice replied.

When testimony resumed on Monday, after a break for the weekend, Strain returned to the subject, as he greeted Anstice, "We know you didn't have time to slip down to Waga Waga over the weekend."

"No, I did not," Anstice replied, a bit awkwardly.

Lanier had taken every opportunity to underscore Anstice's foreign origins for the jury. He had done it with an air of innocence, and under the guise of making sure that Anstice understood the cultural references in his questions. (Do you have Saturday morning cartoons in Australia, he asked Anstice at one point; and another time, do you drive and understand how the traffic lights work here: you drive through a green light and stop at a red light. "Like he's never been in the States," Leone would chortle later. "He's probably been here for 30 years.") Strain, I think, was trying to take the sting out of Lanier's ridicule, but he was so clumsy it was embarrassing.

For all that, I thought Strain scored a big hit when court resumed Monday, as he walked Anstice through Merck's rollout of the amended Vioxx label in 2002. According to Anstice, Merck mailed a label and patient instructions to 300,000 doctors within two days. The company also distributed millions of informational "tear sheets" for doctors to give patients, and it sent its sales reps pounding the pavement with instructions to visit every last doctor in their territory within 14 days (a task that would normally take six weeks) and "proactively" tell them about the changes in the label. The Merck machine at full throttle was an impressive sight.

The plaintiffs said the real reason Merck disseminated the new label so aggressively was that the new label also contained VIGOR's gastrointestinal findings, and enabled Merck to promote Vioxx as a safer alternative to the older painkillers and to the other COX-2 painkiller, Celebrex, which had failed to show similar superiority. No matter, Strain had still helped his case.

LANIER WASTED LITTLE TIME in getting to the previous warnings Merck had received from the FDA when he got his turn with Anstice Monday afternoon.

"You were asked questions about Merck and its safety program, and whether safety has changed over the three decades or so you've been there," Lanier said. "Do you remember that?"

"I remember discussing that topic generally, yes," Anstice responded.

"And you made a statement to the jury toward the end of that examination where you told this jury that... over your 35 years at this company, this company's perspectives on safety had never changed," Lanier said. "Do you remember that?"

"Yes, and I believe that," Anstice said.

"Sir, you know that's not true based on your correspondence with the FDA, don't you?" Lanier demanded.

Anstice disagreed.

"That warning letter we were looking at earlier was not the first warning letter you had ever gotten from the FDA, was it?" Lanier said

"No, it was not," Anstice acknowledged. "I had received a previous one prior to the introduction of Vioxx."

Roughly three years before it warned Merck against misrepresenting Vioxx's risks, the FDA had raised similar concerns about Merck's marketing of *five* other drugs. The earlier warning letter, which was sent in June 1998, accused Merck of minimizing the risks of those drugs in brochures and other promotional materials. The letter noted that the FDA had raised similar concerns previously about the marketing of other Merck drugs (the letter mentioned top sellers such as Zocor, Pepcid, and Fosamax), and that Merck had promised to discontinue those practices. But Merck had not, the FDA said.

"The truth of the matter is, sir, that after Mr. Gilmartin took over...the FDA repeatedly wrote you and finally warned you that they were concerned about a 'continuing pattern and practice of widespread corporate behavior to avoid complying with the regulations concerning disclosing risk information.' That's what happened, isn't it?" Lanier said.

Anstice hemmed and hawed, but the letter was plain for the jury to see, and its implications were unsavory.

As plaintiffs' lawyer Jerry Kristal explained, though the *Vioxx* warning letter (which Lanier had shown to the jury at the start of Anstice's cross-examination), described only a few instances in which the FDA caught Merck misrepresenting Vioxx's risks, that letter got the jury wondering, "Are they [Merck] doing it more often? Are they good at getting away with it?" The warning letter presently before the jury suggested the answer to those questions was "yes."

In one form or another, Lanier had been trying to answer those questions for the jury throughout his cross-examination, and he returned to them with a vengeance in his final hours with Anstice, showing repeatedly even after it received the FDA's warning letter, Merck presented only the favorable explanation for the VIGOR heart attacks—that naproxen prevented heart attacks—and said nothing about the possibility that Vioxx may cause them. This was the very "lack of fair balance" that the FDA had called "false" and "misleading" in its warning letter. As he showed Anstice example after example of press releases, advertisements, letters to physicians, and bulletins to the sales force, Lanier asked Anstice the same question each time: where does it say that Vioxx may cause heart attacks? And each time, Anstice had to concede that explanation was missing.

On his oversized tablet, Lanier summed up Anstice's testimony for the jury:

"Ads—don't give both

Bulletins—don't give both

Press Releases—don't give both

Sales Reps—don't give both"

Anstice glowered, Strain objected, but Lanier was merciless. Leone egged him on. From his chair a few feet away, he peppered Lanier with one- and two-line notes.

"So you think when the FDA said it's not right to not give both sides, you think it means only in the 3 places you got caught, but it was okay everywhere else?!!?" said one note.

"Okay so just ask Anstice: Was there a change in the Marketing Culture Philosophy once Gilmartin got there?" said another.

Lanier worked Leone's comments into his questions.

Merck's omissions mattered because its voice was the loudest in the marketplace and drowned out every other, even those of prominent experts such as Topol and Nissen, and medical journals, such as *JAMA*.

"It's like dropping a penny down the well, and if the well is really deep, you may not hear the splash," said David Graham, a senior FDA scientist who, like Topol and Nissen, had sounded the alarm about Vioxx's risks early on. "Most [doctors] don't have time to read [research] papers. What they know about the safety of a drug comes from sales reps, who leave samples and lunch for the office."

IN ADDITION TO THE sales reps and the aggressive consumer advertising, Merck, like other drug companies, made its voice heard through the hundreds of physicians it paid to act as Vioxx advocates. These were physicians whose ties to universities or high-profile practices made them "opinion leaders" in their communities (or nationally), and whose "educational talks" were proven to influence physicians to prescribe Vioxx more often. Merck paid them in many ways, such as with speaking fees, consulting contracts, and research grants.

When opinion leaders dissented, Merck's marketers worked aggressively to "neutralize" them. In a 2005 report on National Public Radio, I described the case of one such critic, a physician affiliated with Stanford University named Gurkirpal Singh. Singh had been a senior researcher on a seminal study of the gastrointestinal effects of nonsteroidal anti-inflammatory painkillers and spoke extensively on behalf of Merck when Vioxx was launched. But the cardiovascular results of VIGOR left him uneasy about Vioxx's safety, and he pressed Merck for detailed results.

"I was worried, because obviously this was something new. This was something we had never seen before," Singh told me. "I wanted to know how many heart attacks, how many strokes, how many deaths were occurring in each of the groups, and what were the actual number of patients at risk."

Merck did not release the details of the VIGOR results for more than eight months in 2000, and frustrated, Singh started talking about Vioxx's potential risks in talks to doctors, paid for by Merck and later by Celebrex's manufacturer, Searle. Inside Merck, marketing officials gathered detailed intelligence on Singh's talks and held vigorous email discussions of how to contain the fallout. It was decided that Louis Sherwood, a marketing executive, would call Singh's boss at Stanford and ask him to rein in Singh. Sherwood, formerly a professor at the Harvard Medical School and dean of a medical school in New York, was now a senior vice president at Merck and reported directly to Anstice. Sherwood made his move in a phone call to Stanford professor James Fries in October 2000.

"I don't usually receive phone calls at home on a Saturday from representatives of drug companies," Fries told me in 2005. "So it was definitely unusual."

He said Sherwood accused Singh of making "wild and irresponsible" statements about the cardiovascular side effects of Vioxx, and hinted there would be repercussions for Fries and Stanford if Singh's statements didn't stop. He said he was left with the sense that Merck's financial support to Stanford might be at risk.

In an email to his colleagues at Merck, Sherwood reported he had spoken to Fries, and added, "I will keep the pressure on and get others at Stanford to help." He also advised one of the marketing executives on how to pressure Singh himself, "Tell Singh that we've told his boss about his Merck-bashing. And tell him 'should it continue, further actions will be necessary' (don't define it.)"

Back at Stanford, Fries examined Singh's lecture slides and talked to others who had heard Singh's presentations and he found no basis for Sherwood's complaints. Fries also learned that Sherwood had made threatening phone calls to researchers at seven other institutions after they raised doubts about Vioxx's safety, as well as to their department chairs or medical school deans.

Incensed, Fries wrote a three-and-a-half page, single-spaced, letter to Merck chairman Raymond Gilmartin describing a "consistent pattern of intimidation of investigators by Merck staff," and urging Gilmartin to address the issues he'd raised. Anstice was copied on the letter, as was Ed Scolnick, who headed Merck's research division. Sherwood explained his actions in a memo to Anstice.

He said there was "certainly no orchestrated campaign or specific program" to deal with what he called "problem individuals," then implicitly confirmed the existence of one by listing groups of Merck executives who managed Vioxx critics.

"I will only get involved when our representatives...regional medical directors, Merck research lab physicians...or key individuals in the therapeutic business group have felt frustrated by their inability to reach out or to 'balance' selected individuals," he wrote.

Sherwood suggested his interventions were often successful.

"Without trying to appear immodest, I believe I am the most respected physician in the pharmaceutical industry among academic chairs and deans...Therefore, when I call them on a matter of urgent concern, they generally take it seriously...This has been a source of strength...as I have been able to exert balanced leverage in some difficult situations."

When I spoke to Sherwood in 2005, he said he had "never threatened to withdraw funding or hamper anyone's faculty appointment." He said Fries may have mistaken his criticism for a threat.

"I thought y'all were open with all your information and data?" Lanier said to Anstice, as he reconstructed the Singh affair for the jury with the help of Sherwood's emails.

"Yes, and we are," Anstice said.

"He was out there telling Vioxx might cause heart attacks, wasn't he?" Lanier said of Singh.

"I don't believe he was necessarily saying that. I think he was raising issues around edema and hypertension, and asking if they, perhaps, were connected to the VIGOR results," Anstice said.

"To the VIGOR results of heart attacks?" Lanier inquired.

"Of heart attacks, right," Anstice said.

"Okay. So he is saying that maybe your drug is causing heart attacks and he wanted to get more of the data to try to look at it, didn't he?" Lanier said.

"He was looking at it, and I believe he did get the data he needed," Anstice said.

James Fries had sent a copy of his letter to Merck's top scientist, and Edward Scolnick reacted to it in an impassioned email to a subordinate, which Lanier read out loud for the jury.

"This Fries incident is a disaster for Merck. Worse than the VIGOR results themselves," Scolnick had written.

"The VIGOR results were a disaster for Merck, too?" Lanier asked.

"I don't believe they were," Anstice said.

"I hope and pray it does not change forever the image of the company. But it may," Lanier said, reading from Scolnick's email. "Once the hounds smell blood, I am afraid the scent will attract other hounds and sharks. If it were me, I would fire relevant parties summarily."

"But you didn't fire him, did you?" Lanier said.

"I did not fire who?" Anstice asked.

"Anybody over this," Lanier said.

"No, I did not fire anybody over this," Anstice said. "I concluded it was not necessary."

WHEN IT WAS OVER, the other lawyers said it was Lanier's best cross-examination ever of Anstice.

"How many more of these do you want to do? I bet the answer is zero," Lanier said to Anstice, who reddened and laughed uncomfortably before stepping down from the witness stand.

CHAPTER 8

Defender of the Franchise

Atlantic City, January 31–February 5, 2007

IT WAS ONE WEEK into the trial, and Lanier was feeling good about the jury.

"They question the credibility of Merck's lawyers and Merck. They think marketing was out of hand," Lanier said. "Now we need to bring them home."

He was hoping his next witness—the polished and highly presentable Alise Reicin—would help him do just that. A Merck scientist, Reicin was a regular on the Vioxx trial circuit, and her testimony went to the critical question that confronted every Vioxx jury: was Merck's science worthy of the jury's trust? The company said its scientists had not found any evidence of safety problems until the one study in 2004 that led to Vioxx's withdrawal. Lanier would use Reicin's testimony to argue that Merck's science had been corrupted by the same profit pressures as its marketers, while the company's lawyers would argue Reicin exemplified the rigor and purity of Merck's science.

The Reicin jokes were flying in the plaintiffs' back room days before she arrived in court. Lanier's crew called her the "witch from Columbia," in a nod to her teaching stint at Columbia University, and to her personality, which they found strident. (The plaintiffs' bar, a predominantly male club, was not known for its sensitivity to sexist stereotypes.) Leone said she rode a broom, while Lanier announced Reicin was at vampire school to freshen up on her courtroom skills.

The night before Reicin was to testify, the plaintiffs' lawyers gathered in Lanier's suite to talk strategy.

"The goal for you is to dirty her up," Lanier told Seeger, zestfully.

"I'll try to do it as nicely as I can," Seeger said.

"Absolutely, you'll be a gentleman," Lanier said.

I thought privately that if anyone was going to get roughed up the next day, it would be Seeger. I had seen Reicin make quick work of cross-examining lawyers before.

Lanier would take over after Seeger and do the bulk of Reicin's cross-examination, in the fifth round of what plaintiffs' lawyer Jerry Kristal called their "death embrace." Neither had prevailed thus far, but it wasn't for lack of trying. Reicin was the rare witness who was as deft at evading questions as Lanier was at lobbing them. And she did it without breaking a sweat, smiling all the while.

VIOXX HAD MADE MANY of Merck's senior executives very rich, as the value of their stock options soared in tandem with its sales. Reicin was only a few years out of medical school when she joined Merck in 1996, and too low in the company pecking order to receive a big options package. But Vioxx had smiled on Reicin too. She was smart, ambitious, and hard-working, and Vioxx's safety problems had created many opportunities for a smart, ambitious, and hard-working scientist to distinguish herself. When VIGOR's cardiovascular results threatened to derail Vioxx sales, it was Reicin who rushed to find the slim underpinnings of Merck's "naproxen theory." She went on to serve as the savvy advocate of the theory and the drug to the scientific community and stock analysts, and climbed the corporate ladder as she did so.

The night before Lanier cross-examined Reicin in the Texas trial a year-and-a-half earlier, he was reading her personnel file and came across her performance evaluation from 2001, the year after Merck learned the VIGOR results. It began with this memorable sentence: "Dr. Reicin's major efforts this past year were focused on defending the Vioxx franchise…" Lanier recognized the sentence immediately for the gift it was.

"That's what she was doing—defending the franchise, in science, at the FDA, that's what got her all the big promotions," he would say later. "And bless her heart, like Pavlov's dog, now she was doing it in court."

The next day, Lanier asked Reicin if her job at Merck had included being a "defender of Vioxx." When Reicin demurred, Lanier produced the evaluation, and ever since then Reicin had been introduced to juries as "the defender of the franchise." ("We like to give labels to people, because it's hard for the jury to remember names," he explained helpfully.)

It was a particularly useful label for Lanier's purposes because it went right to the heart of Reicin's credibility as a witness. It was as if Lanier were saying to the jury: Yes, Reicin has all the fine degrees that the Merck lawyers say she does—an honors degree from Barnard, an MD from Harvard, another degree from MIT—however she stands here before you not as a purveyor of objective scientific truth, but as a spinner of facts. She is a marketer posing as a scientist.

Reicin arrived in court the next morning dressed demurely in a brown suit and a white turtleneck, wearing pearls in her ears and at her neck and a frosted orange-brown hue on her lips. Her pleated skirt grazed her knees and her jacket was secured with a belt. Why were all the women associated with Merck so painfully thin, I wondered? Reicin was even thinner than Diane Sullivan and Hope Freiwald, two of Merck's lead lawyers in the trial.

Egilman had wandered out of the plaintiffs' back room to get a glimpse of Reicin, and offered his sartorial analysis. She was dressed to look like a wealthy Jersey suburbanite, he said. What's more, she wore that very suit and those metallic green shoes every time she testified, Egilman said. Such vital details demanded a second source, and I turned to Hegar, who immediately confirmed them and provided an additional nugget. She promised that Reicin would wear a black suit the next day. It was her *other* trial outfit, Hegar said. Reicin, it appeared, appreciated as keenly as Lanier that the courtroom was a stage and that the right wardrobe was critical to getting into character.

I asked Lanier and Leone later what they thought of Reicin's clothes.

"She wears what she's told to," Lanier said dismissively. Reicin's attire did nothing for him.

"The pearls add credibility," Leone mused, "They're retro, like Audrey Hepburn." Not bad, I thought, being mentioned in the same breath as Audrey Hepburn. I'd take that, if I were Reicin. Any outfit that evoked the whispery innocence of Hepburn, even fleetingly, in so cynical an observer as Bob Leone had to be rated a smashing success.

THE PLAINTIFFS' LAWYERS HAD agreed that before Reicin took the stand Seeger would prime Higbee to rein in Reicin by refreshing the judge's memory about Reicin's three previous appearances in her courtroom, and in others around the country. They called the maneuver "poisoning the well," and Seeger did it artfully, beginning with a recent, and ingenious, refinement in Reicin's testimony.

In the early trials, many Merck executives, including Reicin, made a point of telling juries that they had used Vioxx themselves, the implication being that surely they wouldn't have used it if they had believed it was unsafe. If judges did not allow such testimony,

Reicin found other ways to communicate her personal comfort with Vioxx.

"Here is the problem," Seeger told Higbee, "She told the jury in the last case that her style for designing a clinical trial is determining whether she would put her own father in it. That's a new tactic."

"It's a back door to [saying] 'I believe in this drug enough to take it myself. I believe in it enough to give it to my dad,'" Seeger's partner David Buchanan added.

"That never existed the first seven times she testified," Lanier chimed in.

"Cross-examine her on it," challenged Diane Sullivan.

"What can they cross-examine on it?" Higbee said. "The last time you testified you didn't say it?"

Strain tried a more conciliatory approach. "It's not a back door to anything, Your Honor..." he said.

But Higbee wasn't buying it. "No reference to a relative," she ruled, and Seeger moved on to the next item on his agenda.

"Judge, I think you have ruled on this, no talking to the jury on sidebars," Seeger said. "You may remember she used to say to them, 'Oh, I'm cold. How are you? Are you cold?'"

"She did that in Cona-McDarby," Lanier said immediately, referring to the cases brought by Thomas Cona and John McDarby, which he had tried previously before Higbee.

(Jerry Kristal, who had tried Cona-McDarby with Lanier, would corroborate Lanier's account later. "Most witnesses, if there is a bench conference, they look away [from the jury] or look down, or pretend to read," Kristal told me. "*She* would nod and smile at the jury. She clearly was trained to do that. It was so phony.")

"Make sure she doesn't face [the jurors]," Higbee told Strain. "When the sidebars are on, she should turn and face the lawyers, not be making any kind of communications with the jury."

Strain could hardly reject the judge's ruling, but neither could he accept even the whiff of a suggestion that Reicin's past behavior warranted such an instruction.

"I'm not for a moment saying she did, Your Honor," Strain said.

"I'm not saying she did either. I'm just saying she shouldn't," Higbee said.

Ah, that wily Higbee. She knew Reicin deserved to be admonished, and she knew that Strain knew it as well, but she played along with his face-saving protest.

Reicin had one other defining trait as a witness: she rarely answered questions with the "Yes" or "No" that cross-examining lawyers were entitled to demand from witnesses. Instead she treated each question as an opportunity to advance Merck's view of the case. When the questions were inconvenient, as they frequently were, Reicin did what a good politician (or lawyer) might do in that situation: she simply answered the question she wanted to be asked.

"The judge knows she's the queen of the non-answer, the queen of the dodge," Lanier had said the night before, as the plaintiffs' lawyers plotted how to keep Reicin on a short leash. The sidebar ended with a final ruling by Higbee: Reicin was to answer the plaintiffs' questions with a simple yes or no. No speeches, Higbee ordered. The plaintiffs had gotten much of what they wanted from Higbee. How her rulings would stand up to the reality of Merck's star witness on the stand remained to be seen.

SEEGER BEGAN HIS CROSS-EXAMINATION by establishing Reicin's identity as "the defender of the franchise."

"Now, this is your personnel file, correct?" Seeger said to Reicin, preparing to read from a performance evaluation.

"Um, I don't know. I have never actually seen my personnel file," Reicin chirruped.

Since she had been questioned about its contents in courtrooms across the country, Reicin's claim was hardly credible, and Higbee made note of that a few minutes later when Strain stood up to ask that Reicin be allowed more time to read the file before responding to Seeger's questions.

"Dr. Reicin has seen the document before," Higbee said dryly.

Seeger's tour of Reicin's personnel file included a description of her job in 2001. It was the year after Merck got the VIGOR results and Reicin's job included: working with marketing on strategy and promotional materials, working with public affairs, joining the company's elite Worldwide Business Strategy Team as a formal member, and supporting global marketing efforts through participation in symposia and meetings with "key thought leaders." Reicin insisted that her contributions to these business and marketing efforts were strictly scientific.

Seeger moved next to a table in Reicin's 2003 evaluation, which showed the relative importance of her various duties that year, assigning each a percentage weight. Most of Reicin's Vioxx work that year involved government regulation and crafting business strategies to boost Vioxx sales.

"You see the point, it kind of focuses on how much of your time is spent doing these things," Seeger said, as he showed the table to the jury.

"Correct, so there's obviously a few things missing, because they don't equal 100," Reicin replied.

Merck had deleted sections of the evaluation that weren't related to Vioxx, and a portion of the table was blank, except for the words "Redacted—other product." Vioxx accounted for 60% of Reicin's job, and it was the only part that the jurors could see.

"That's right, they don't equal 100, but I can't get into the redacted things," Seeger said.

"They would have been other scientific things I did," she said.

"Dr. Reicin, do you want to fill in the points that are redacted for us, because I'm not allowed to ask you questions, so I appreciate it if you don't testify about…" he said.

The statements were redacted under the Court's order, Strain objected.

"Yes, but at your request, and now she is trying to tell the jury what they say," Higbee said, before turning to address Reicin directly. "That's inappropriate, Miss Reicin. Answer the question as asked."

Reicin looked puzzled and a little hurt, but she smiled brightly.

As the morning wore on, Higbee stepped up her efforts to rein in Reicin.

"Miss Reicin, you know, we want yes-or-no answers," Higbee said, after Seeger had made several unsuccessful attempts to get an answer to a straightforward question.

"I'm doing the best that I can," Reicin said.

"You're not doing very well," Higbee said. Though she said it without heat, coming from the mild-mannered Higbee it was a withering response.

More than any witness I had seen before, or since, Reicin vied with the cross-examining lawyer, and the judge, for control of the courtroom. She refused to concede the simplest facts. She tarried over documents. Best of all, she looked as if she were trying to cooperate, cocking her head to listen to each question and nodding attentively at appropriate junctures. Before answering questions, she half-turned her body to look at the jury, and wet her lips or smiled from behind the curtain of hair that fell coquettishly across her face. When she finally spoke, her voice was low. There was no hint of Reicin the seasoned corporate infighter. She may have been "as tough as nails," as Leone liked to say, but she looked like a damsel under duress.

Reicin's performance won rave reviews in the plaintiffs' back room at lunch. Despite themselves, the plaintiffs' team had a grudging respect for Reicin. Egilman reeled off a list of Reicin's attributes as a witness, barely pausing for a breath.

"She knows her stuff well, she's a good communicator, she smiles even when she's getting chewed out, she stays on message and speaks in sound bites, she knows the pitfalls and avoids them, and she points out every mistake Chris [Seeger] is making," he said.

The review was so glowing I wondered for a moment if I had walked into the Merck lunchroom by accident.

At least Leone was still in character. "Fasten your seat belts, she's lyin' through her teeth," he said. "She's an evil woman."

Reicin, Leone believed, had known from the start that Vioxx was to blame for the heart attacks in the VIGOR study, and naproxen had little or nothing to do with them.

THAT EVENING, LANIER RATTLED off, from memory, the long list of Merck documents he wanted delivered to his desk—pronto. He had spent the day on the sidelines in court, listening as Seeger and then Paul Strain examined Reicin, and he had been plotting his attack.

"I *personally* want to read each of those," he said. "I'm going to make some reaches. I want to make sure my butt is protected."

Lanier had read the documents many times before, but was hoping to find ammunition he had overlooked.

"I'm going to pound her into the dirt," he declared. "We're going to kill her, guys. We're going to *annihilate* her."

When I walked into his suite at 7:30 the next morning, Lanier was on the phone. He seemed to have a steady stream of friends whom he entertained with stories from the trial, usually in morning and evening calls. I heard him say that he had been up since 1:44 in the morning, and that he expected to get Reicin after lunch that day. He said he thought his cross-examination would run through the following day, but that Reicin, an observant Orthodox Jew, had to be off the stand in time to get home before sunset, for the Sabbath.

"I'm not allowed to say she's a practicing Jew," Lanier concluded, chuckling.

(Merck's lawyers had asked Higbee for an order to that effect. Juror number 7's father had served in the Egyptian Army and fought in one of the region's wars with Israel.)

As he ate his granola, I asked Lanier how he felt about cross-examining Reicin.

"I guess I look forward to the challenge," Lanier said. "She could be the press secretary for the president [the way she] deflects, dodges, and doesn't answer the question." The president at the time was George W. Bush, and given Lanier's Republican sympathies, I was a little surprised at the analogy.

I asked if he thought he'd beaten Reicin in their previous encounters.

"I won each time," he said, with a smile.

He *had* won the Vioxx cases he'd tried before, but many in his camp thought his duels with *her* had been no better than draws.

Still, by lunchtime, Lanier was sounding grim. Reicin had enjoyed the benefit of a deferential examination by Paul Strain all morning. "The jury is taking notes. I don't know if they're writing grocery lists," Lanier said, striding into the plaintiffs' back room. "We're going to have to *kill* her."

Leone remained sanguine. He, too, had been watching the jurors. "They're not looking at her," he said.

So what, I asked him.

"You're married, right?" Leone said, turning his gaze on me.

We had gone over this ground before. I was, I said.

"When you're angry with your husband, are you *more* likely to look at him?"

Leone had a point.

The jurors passed within a few feet of Reicin in the witness box when they entered the court room. "Every time they come in, they look away," he said.

IT WAS LATE AFTERNOON before Strain announced he had no further questions, and Lanier jumped to his feet.

"May I, Your Honor?" Lanier said, even before Strain had walked back to the defense counsel table.

"You may," she said, and so it began.

The speedy transition was a trademark Lanier move. Its intended audience was, of course, the jury, and its message: battle-readiness. "I've been polite. I've let them have their turn. I haven't interrupted. Now it's my turn," he said later. "And I don't need 15 minutes to gather my notes. If you know what you're doing, you don't need it," he added, in a scornful reference to Paul Strain, who invariably asked for a break to "set up" after Lanier's examinations.

"Good afternoon!" Lanier said to Reicin, cheerily. "I think this is my fourth time to get to ask you questions under oath, isn't it?"

"Um, it may be number five," Reicin replied. (It was.)

"You and I are not strangers, are we?" Lanier said.

"I have met you before," Reicin said, coolly.

I could feel a potent brew of dislike and contempt pass between them.

Draping himself on the lectern that Strain had left behind in his hasty departure from the courtroom well, Lanier leaned toward Reicin. He grinned at her. "Not all of what you do is science, is it?" he said.

"Um, as with any job, there are a variety of things that I do," Reicin said, turning to the jury. "I have some administrative things that I do, but the majority of what I do is scientific."

"You didn't tell the jury about the times you go to Wall Street trying to boost up the Merck stock price, did you," Lanier said, slyly.

"I've dealt with analysts once. And it was not to boost up the stock price, it was to provide scientific information," Reicin said.

Lanier reminded Reicin that in previous testimony she had admitted to more than one meeting with analysts.

Reicin insisted she could remember only one such occasion, then added, "So now I'm remembering, if I'm in a scientific meeting, analysts will come up to me and ask me about data. I consider that a scientific exchange, however."

"I want to show you Exhibit 44," Lanier said eventually.

It was an email to Reicin from one of David Anstice's top lieutenants on Merck's business side, sent two-and-a-half months after Merck received the cardiovascular results of VIGOR, on May 25, 2000. The president of Merck Research Labs, Edward Scolnick, was copied on it.

Alice (sic), *attached are 2 analyst reports which most clearly demonstrate the success of our efforts to defuse the CV* [cardiovascular] *risk issue for Vioxx. You played a major role in making this happen . . . I wanted to personally thank you for all your efforts and the tremendous support you provided for the marketing organization. Regards, Margie.*

A report on the VIGOR study by an analyst at the investment bank, Deutsche Bank Alex. Brown was attached. "Cardiac Events Not an Issue," the report declared, "Maintain BUY Rating."

Lanier put the email on the projector and read it out line by line for the jury, questioning Reicin as he went.

"So you're out there as the defender of the franchise meeting with the stock analysts?" Lanier said.

"No, that's incorrect," Reicin said.

"You're out there and your efforts have been commended to... not just your boss, but your boss's boss's boss, the very top of your company, your efforts to defuse the CV risk issue for Vioxx, right?" Lanier continued, ignoring Reicin's response.

"That is what she wrote," Reicin said this time.

"She said you played a major role in making this happen. That 'this' is defusing the heart attack risk issue for Vioxx. Is that right?"

"Um, she wrote, 'CV risk issue for Vioxx.'" Reicin countered.

"Don't you understand CV risk issue includes heart attacks?" Lanier said sternly.

"It would include heart attacks," Reicin conceded.

Seeger had been wary of coming down too hard on Reicin lest he look like a bully, but Lanier was just this side of rude. He believed that like all women witnesses, Reicin was walking a tightrope of her own. The jury would see her as "witchy" if she came on too strong, and as a "doormat" if she wasn't assertive enough.

"It's very hard to strike the right balance," Lanier said, and he was doing his best to make it harder.

LANIER FOCUSED HIS CROSS-EXAMINATION that afternoon on the 18 days in March 2000 immediately following Merck's receipt of the VIGOR results. In those 18 days, Merck's position on the results went from *private* certainty that Vioxx caused heart attacks to the equal and opposite *public* certainty that Vioxx was benign. Internal documents turned over to the plaintiffs' lawyers provide a window into the internal deliberations that culminated in this radical reassessment of Vioxx's risks. They paint a striking picture of a hasty process that gave short shrift to opposing evidence and opinions, a keen awareness among company scientists of the need to "position" VIGOR's results in ways that protected Vioxx in the marketplace, and a clinical detachment from the implications of the results for real, live, human beings. Lanier had prepared a timeline tracing the company's about-face with excerpts from company documents, as well as graphics and photographs, and he used it to great effect with Reicin.

His timeline began on March 9, 2000, when the president of Merck Research Labs, Edward Scolnick, commented on the VIGOR results in an email the jury had already seen. Scolnick sent the email to Reicin, her boss, Alan Nies, and the study's chief statistician, Deborah Shapiro shortly before midnight on March 9, and he opened by acknowledging the good news in VIGOR—that Vioxx caused fewer gastrointestinal problems than naproxen.

> "To all: I just received and went through the data. Thank you for sending it to me. There is no doubt about the pub [perforations, ulcers, bleeds] data. very very strong. as expected..."

Scolnick went on to discuss VIGOR's cardiovascular results.

> "The CV [cardiovascular] events are clearly there... this is real... It is a shame but it is a low incidence and it is mechanism based as we worried it was."

That is, the potential to damage the heart was intrinsic to the unique way in which Vioxx worked to reduce pain (its so-called mechanism). The very thing that made Vioxx safer for the gut was a danger to the heart, according to Scolnick.

March 9, "real...as we worried," read the first entry on Lanier's timeline, a reference to Scolnick's concern that Vioxx posed a "real" cardiovascular threat to patients.

"Now this is the assessment of Ed Scolnick on March the 9th, right?" Lanier said. Reicin said it was.

"And I think you told this jury yesterday that 'I was concerned. I was worried. And my first reaction to the data was, Oh, My Gosh! Did we inadvertently cause harm, and did Vioxx increase the [heart attack] rate?'" Lanier said, dripping scorn.

"That's correct," Reicin said.

"You [and] the top scientist are thinking on March the 9th, our drug may be killing people?" Lanier continued.

"No, actually, there was no difference in mortality," Reicin said.

(Though more Vioxx subjects died in VIGOR, the difference in the number of deaths between the Vioxx and naproxen groups was not statistically significant.)

"Ma'am, there was a *fivefold* increase in heart attacks," Lanier said.

"That's correct," Reicin replied.

"Are you saying you were thinking, 'oh, my goodness, we might be causing heart attacks,' but it never occurred to you some of those people might die?" Lanier said.

"Um, you're asking me what I thought about. The mortality was similar and the concern was about the increase in cardiovascular events," Reicin said.

"Okay. So your concern wasn't that people will die. Your concern that day was, oh, my goodness, we might be causing heart attacks in people," Lanier said.

"That's correct," Reicin said.

"Did you, uh, stop running the ads?" Lanier asked casually.

"I can't tell you one way or another," Reicin said.

"We've got the book of ads, and I think it's going to reflect that y'all continued your TV ads just exactly as planned," Lanier said.

Dara Hegar had risen to hand Lanier the fat three-ring binder which contained the list of every advertisement Merck had ever run to promote Vioxx.

Reicin was unruffled. "Okay," she said.

"Did you know that?" Lanier demanded.

"Marketing weren't aware of the data at this point in time," Reicin said, still calm.

"So when y'all are thinking we may be causing heart attacks, y'all didn't alert marketing to stop the TV ads or change them, did you?" Lanier said.

"We had to understand the data first," Reicin said. A hint of anger had crept into her voice.

"Excuse me, ma'am. Did you alert marketing to either stop the ads or change the ads?" Lanier asked, again.

"No, we did *not*," Reicin said.

"You didn't tell them, 'Stop the ads until we understand the data, until we understand whether or not we're causing heart attacks.' You didn't tell them that?" Lanier pressed.

"I was not in communication with marketing at all," Reicin replied. "I don't know what Dr. Scolnick did."

As he questioned Reicin, Lanier clicked on his remote to reveal the next slide. It was a still photo of the skater Dorothy Hamill, with the caption, "Ads Still Running." Placed next to Scolnick's assessment that Vioxx's cardiovascular side-effects were "real...as we worried," the Hamill photo took on a chilling cast. (The Hamill commercials were the ones that generated $4 in new prescriptions for each dollar Merck spent on airtime.)

Three days later, an email from Reicin gave the first hint that company scientists were considering a new explanation for the VIGOR results—naproxen was a super-aspirin that prevented heart attacks by blocking platelets and inhibiting blood clots. And, there were more heart attacks on Vioxx than on naproxen because unlike naproxen, Vioxx did not prevent heart attacks. The problem was finding evidence to support the claim of naproxen's protective powers. Reicin sent the email in the wee hours of Monday, March 13, 2000, to Alan Nies, her immediate boss, and Scolnick:

Alan and Ed:
Below is attached the abstract for the only study I could find which assessed the potential cardio-protective effects of an NSAID.
Alise

Though she found no scientific papers showing that naproxen prevented heart attacks, Reicin *had* found a small study involving a different non-steroidal anti-inflammatory drug (NSAID), called flurbiprofen. The study showed that patients on flurbiprofen were far less likely than those on placebo to suffer a second heart attack.

With a click of his remote, Lanier added a second date to his timeline, March 12, and the caption, "Can't find anything on naproxen."

"And on the timeline I put the 12th, but technically it was the 13th, wasn't it?" Lanier said.

"That's correct," Reicin said.

"Because you had been researching all day long, and you hit this at 1:20 in the morning. You had been pulling an all-nighter looking for this, hadn't you?"

"I was working very long hours. I don't know if I stayed up all night that night," Reicin responded.

"Was this a weekend?" Lanier asked.

"It certainly may have been," Reicin said.

"Maybe a Sunday night?" Lanier pressed, with a grin.

The two had sparred over this email in every trial. Both knew full well that it had been sent on a Sunday night.

"Your ads are still running at this point, aren't they? You haven't told anybody..." Lanier said

"I can't tell you one way or the other," Reicin interrupted.

"You had not told anybody, pull the ads," Lanier pressed.

"I personally had not," she said.

Did you tell the FDA, Lanier asked.

Not for another couple of weeks, Reicin said.

Did you send out an overnight letter by Fed-Ex to all the physicians in the country, he asked. It was a reference, as the jury knew, to the letter Merck's marketers sent out to the entire membership of the American Medical Association, after cardiologists Eric Topol and Steven Nissen raised an alarm in 2001 about Vioxx's risks in the AMA's prestigious journal. Did you call the Stanford gastroenterologist James Fries, Lanier asked, referring this time to Merck's attempt to curb the "unbalanced" discussion of Vioxx's risks by one of Fries's researchers, in 2000. Reicin answered each question, "No." Lanier would go through this litany each time he clicked on another date in his timeline. I noticed the policeman, juror number 2, looking grim, as he listened with a palm to his face.

The following day, March 14, 2001, the top brass at Merck Research Labs still seemed to be of the opinion that VIGOR had shown that Vioxx caused heart attacks and other cardiovascular side effects. And they were making plans to change the label to say so.

After a conference call that day, the head of the Worldwide Regulatory Affairs department at Merck, David Blois, emailed Scolnick, to whom he reported, and Reicin, among others.

To all,
Following our phone conversation today, attempted to construct
a "to do" list…I realize this is a daunting list of things we as
a team need to accomplish in a very short time, but here goes."

Number 9 on Blois's list of 15 was "label modifications for the CV [cardiovascular] events." Blois gave the group two weeks to complete the task.

But the winds were shifting and just five days later, on March 19, 2000, the unproven assertion that naproxen prevents heart attacks was gaining favor, as seen in this draft briefing statement for public affairs and investor relations employees:

"If possible we should position things as a 'reduction in events with naproxen vs. rofecoxib [Vioxx],*' rather than 'an increase in CVD* [cardiovascular disease] *events with Vioxx vs. naproxen'"*

The author of the briefing statement, a physician in Merck Research Labs, appeared acutely aware that the findings would hurt Vioxx's position vis-à-vis its main competitor in the painkiller market, Celebrex:

"The implications for the arthritis & analgesia franchise are high—due to differences in study design…there may not be similar findings in the Searle [Celebrex] *studies."*

And, he suggested several additional ways to limit the damage to Vioxx's sales from the VIGOR findings:

"We should (hopefully) position this as applying only to patients with RA [rheumatoid arthritis], *only with the highest dose of Vioxx, and underscore the substantial benefits of Vioxx compared to traditional NSAIDs* [nonsteroidal anti-inflammatory drugs]*."*

(VIGOR was conducted on subjects with rheumatoid arthritis, not the more common osteoarthritis, and VIGOR subjects were given the highest approved dose of 50mg daily.)

Reicin received that memo late Sunday evening, March 19, 2000. By the time she was done, the VIGOR cardiovascular results were all about naproxen. The strikeouts and underlining show her deletions and additions respectively.

> *"There is an approximate 2-fold* ~~increase~~ <u>decrease</u> *in the risk of certain cardiovascular events, including myocardial infarctions and cerebrovascular events in these RA* [rheumatoid arthritis] *patients treated with* ~~VIOXX~~ <u>naproxen</u> *compared to* ~~naproxen~~ <u>VIOXX.</u>*"*

In testimony, Reicin, Scolnick, and other Merck scientists characterized their re-interpretation of the VIGOR results as the product of a deeper and broader analysis of data. They said they looked at a combined analysis of earlier Vioxx studies, as well as data from two ongoing studies that compared Vioxx to a sugar pill. They said neither set of studies showed evidence of the heart problems seen in the VIGOR study. (Documents turned over to the plaintiffs' lawyers and subsequent published analyses of the data do not support those claims.) That led them to believe that the extra heart attacks among Vioxx subjects in VIGOR were a sign, not of Vioxx's problems, but of naproxen's strength in protecting against heart attacks.

On March 27, 2000, the press release made it official. It said the VIGOR study had shown Vioxx was exceptionally safe for the gut, and added that naproxen subjects in the study had "significantly fewer thromboembolic events." While no other study had shown naproxen to have that effect on the heart, the press release said, the finding was "consistent with naproxen's ability to block platelet aggregation." Merck had managed to give Vioxx a clean bill of health.

Lanier had shown that during 18 days of corporate planning and posturing, as executives scrambled to craft their response to the VIGOR results, no one at Merck thought to tell *patients* that they may be at risk of harm every time they took a Vioxx pill for pain.

No one thought to tell them what Reicin said company scientists believed, at least, at first: that there were two possible explanations for the VIGOR results, and that one of those was that Vioxx increased the risk of cardiovascular problems.

"You kept that knowledge in tight, didn't you?" Lanier asked Reicin, as he wrapped up his timeline the next morning,

"No, that's just not true," Reicin said.

"Well, let's see. You're still running your ads, aren't you?" Lanier said.

"We went through this yesterday. I can't say yes or no to that. I don't know," she said.

Lanier was incredulous, as he knew so well how to be.

"You didn't check it out? We have a whole notebook of these," he said. "Did you know that the ads, never for the entire history you run them, make any mention of any concern about heart attacks, not one ad in the entire history that they're on TV?" That, of course, was why he and Leone brought up the ads at every turn, but Reicin wasn't about to let such a blunt statement of a damaging fact stand uncontested.

"I'm not sure that's true," she said.

"Really?" Lanier countered.

"Yes, I'm not sure that's true," Reicin said, again. It was true, and I found it hard to believe that after testifying at so many Vioxx trials, she harbored any doubt that it wasn't.

"Okay, well every ad we have been given..." Lanier began.

Strain jumped to his feet to insist that Lanier was wrong about the ads.

In the melee that followed, Lanier began running through the commercials by their names—"Dog Park," "The Gardner," "Dorothy Hamill,"—and offered to play one. That was the last thing his opponents wanted and Strain asked for a sidebar, where he argued, in vain, that Lanier's request was out of line because Reicin had had nothing to do with advertising.

Behind me, I heard one of Lanier's lawyers mutter, "She's such a liar."

Beside me, Rick Meadow, the head of Lanier's New York office, hadn't taken his eyes off Reicin, who was keeping *her* gaze fixed on the jury. "The jury is not even looking at her," Meadow said, with grim satisfaction. He appeared to be right.

Lanier did get to play a TV ad. In the process, he also got a frankly unbelievable admission from Reicin.

"You understand y'all were running TV advertisements on a daily basis, basically, did you know that?" Lanier said.

Reicin said she didn't.

"When you were at home, did you ever watch them on TV?" he asked.

"I don't a watch a lot of TV," Reicin said.

"That wasn't my question, ma'am," Lanier said. "Did you ever see any of your ads on TV?"

"Maybe once," Reicin said.

Once! I marveled at Reicin's mastery of the courtroom and the process.

Even with Lanier leading the charge, she was holding her ground. With every move, she conveyed the sense that she was trying to explain impossibly complex matters, and that given Lanier's inferior grasp of the subject, her task was an uphill one.

LATER, I WONDERED ABOUT Lanier's decision to spend so much time on Merck's failure to warn consumers during those 18 days in March 2000. After all, with the plaintiffs alleging Merck had hidden Vioxx's risks for years, what did it matter that Merck hadn't pulled its commercials during those 18 days? Why not go after the more substantive point that there wasn't much scientific evidence to back up Merck's claim that naproxen prevented heart attacks? When I put those questions to Lanier, he answered them with this analogy.

"If I have a plate of food, and I say, 'Snigdha, eat it. Oh, by the way, it may be poisoned or maybe not,' would you say, 'Yeah, I'll take my chances and eat it,'" Lanier said, "Or would you say, 'Let me find out first if it's poisoned or not.'" If it's proper to warn a person that the food set before them could hurt them, he demanded, "Why wouldn't you do that with a drug?" He answered the question himself, "It's because Scolnick [the top scientist] thought it was [only hurting] a few people, and it wasn't anyone he knew."

Rather than go after the legitimacy of the analysis or the naproxen theory, Lanier had chosen to accept at face value that there was a period of genuine uncertainty inside Merck about which of the two interpretations of the VIGOR results was correct—was Vioxx causing heart attacks or naproxen preventing them?

If the uncertainty was real, and shared within the company, he was asking, why not at least stop selling Vioxx on TV?

"They did all the research. They knew they were selling four dollars for every dollar they spent on advertising....they should have warned," Lanier said.

Lanier's approach highlighted Reicin's role as a defender of the franchise, and he returned to it after he finished playing the Vioxx commercial and prepared to wrap up his timeline.

"No reference to the heart at all, is there?" Lanier asked Reicin.

"Not in that ad, no," Reicin said.

"And, yet, in 2001, according to your personnel file, one of the things you did was collaborated on marketing strategy and promotional materials," Lanier said, and he showed the jury Reicin's 2001 performance evaluation once again. "Do you see that?"

"I do, but I had nothing to do with TV ads. I never even saw that ad before today," Reicin said.

"The marketing strategy, the promotional materials you coordinated, but not on TV ads?" Lanier pressed.

Reicin said she had sometimes weighed in on promotional materials to doctors, but never on direct-to-consumer advertising.

Maybe so, but she had just confirmed her hyphenated identity, as a marketer-scientist.

MERCK SCIENTISTS WERE FAR from convinced that naproxen was the super-aspirin they had told the world it was. Their own academic consultants were telling them that that there was neither pharmacologic nor epidemiologic evidence to support the theory. Their experts also told them that the pre-VIGOR Vioxx studies, which Merck cited as evidence of Vioxx's safety, were too small to detect Vioxx's problems, if any existed. Scolnick, Reicin, and others inside Merck debated at length the merits of doing a study that directly addressed the question raised by VIGOR—was Vioxx safe for the heart?

"I will tell you my worry quotient is high. I actually am in minor agony...WE WILL NOT KNOW FOR SURE WHAT IS GOING ON UNTIL WE DO THIS STUDY..." Scolnick wrote Reicin on April 12, 2000, two weeks after Merck issued the VIGOR press release.

But there were competing worries that a safety study could backfire. There was the obvious one that the study would corroborate VIGOR's findings. There was a separate concern that the drug to which Vioxx was being compared—Tylenol was one candidate—might turn out to have fewer gastrointestinal side effects and undermine Vioxx's unique claim to gastrointestinal safety. (Reicin raised both issues in a memo to Scolnick a few days later.) And then there was the question of how it would look to doctors, patients, and competitors that Merck thought a cardiovascular safety study was warranted after VIGOR.

"There's no compelling marketing need for such a study. The implied message is not favorable," the marketing division said in a presentation titled "Key Marketing Messages," prepared for a meeting of senior executives in May 2000, a few months after the VIGOR results were released.

A year-and-a-half later, after the Cleveland Clinic cardiologists, Eric Topol and Steven Nissen, issued their call for a safety study, and groups such as the American Heart Association and the Arthritis Foundation followed, at least some in marketing were coming around to a different point of view.

"Handled correctly, there is some positive Pr *(sic)* we can gain from saying we are conducting a study (there are industry examples of other products who benefited in this way)," a senior marketing executive, Wendy Dixon, wrote in a September 17, 2001, email to a colleague. "If we manage the PR well, it could be a positive expression of our confidence in the brand," her colleague responded.

The debate continued two months later, after Merck received the "ugly label" from the FDA. Though Scolnick insisted he would never accept a label that warned of Vioxx's cardiac risks, he was apparently persuaded that they did exist, as suggested by the safety study he soon proposed.

"I think the question we should answer now is NOT whether Vioxx or any Coxib is safe for Cv *(sic)* outcomes," Scolnick wrote to his senior team on November 21, 2001. "I think the question NOW is what is the best antiplatelet regime to use with a Coxib. I think that is THE medical question and if we answer it, the problem will dissipate."

He proposed a study to show that Vioxx combined with aspirin was just as safe for the heart as naproxen. A few months later, Merck signed a preliminary agreement with a Harvard teaching hospital, Brigham and Women's Hospital in Boston, to do a study comparing Vioxx to placebo, but that study was shelved when Merck got the Vioxx label it wanted in April 2002. Merck never did do a study to test if Vioxx could cause heart attacks.

"Some people have to stand up and say what's right."

CHAPTER 9

The Plaintiff's Final Witness

Atlantic City, February 5–7, 2007

LANIER'S FINAL WITNESS WAS a bona fide "get" from the ivy-covered bastions of the medical establishment. Cardiologist Harlan Krumholz was professor of medicine at Yale University, nominee for president of the American Heart Association, and an editor of the pre-eminent cardiology journal in the country. He was even on the short list of "big names" Merck had considered hiring as consultants, back when Vioxx was still on the market. His presence in the courtroom attested to Lanier's persistence, and to how Vioxx was radicalizing at least some among medicine's elite. Krumholz had rebuffed Lanier's overtures a couple of times, but relented when he realized how little he himself had known of Merck's strategies to promote Vioxx and hide its risks before the lawsuits exposed them. There are people who would be alive today if Merck had told the truth, he thought, and he told Lanier he would testify. Krumholz's maiden appearance had been in Lanier's earlier Vioxx trial before Judge Higbee. He took the stand for a second time a few moments after Reicin left.

I felt the tension in the courtroom ebb as Krumholz was sworn in. Reicin's appearance had been filled with angry drama. Krumholz's arrival promised at least a brief respite. He was a Midwesterner by birth, and in contrast to Reicin, who was a controlled, tightly-wound presence, Krumholz projected solidness and calm. At 48, his temples were beginning to gray. The crown of his head was balding. But his face was still youthful, and he was trim.

Lanier launched the proceedings with a small plastic model of the heart, which he carried to the judge's bench.

"I'd ask that the witness be allowed to get close enough to the jury to show them this as he explains the heart," Lanier said to the judge.

"That's fine," Higbee said. "You can step down, Doctor."

Krumholz dismounted and walked to the jury box a few paces away. There he came to a stop and stood before the jurors, plastic heart in hand. Scarcely a foot separated him from those in the front row. They could see he was a little nervous.

"So I'm enthusiastic about the heart. I'm a cardiologist," Krumholz began, smiling sheepishly, as if to apologize for his enthusiasm. "It is a remarkable muscle."

He held up the model heart, took it apart to show off its different parts, and walked the length of the jury box so all the jurors could see it. His short journey, from witness to jury box, and the plastic heart in his hands had achieved a subtle, yet significant, shift in Krumholz's courtroom identity. He had gone from partisan witness to dispassionate teacher.

Lanier had undergone his own (temporary) transformation—from hotshot lawyer to eager pupil and teacher's aide. He stood by the double-wide tablet, with red, blue, and black markers at the ready. When Krumholz described the heart's four chambers, Lanier drew them on his tablet. When Krumholz said what the chambers were called, Lanier painstakingly wrote out the names, sounding them out as he did— "au-ri-cle," "ven-tri-cle." You'd think he'd never heard the terms before.

The dance between Krumholz and Lanier was unrehearsed, but its message was calculated. Krumholz was his own man. *He* was calling the shots, and his testimony to the jury would be guided by his expertise, not tailored to Lanier's convenience. As if to underline Krumholz's control of the proceedings, Lanier returned to his table at one point and sat back in his chair. For a few minutes, Krumholz stood alone in the courtroom well speaking to the jurors, who appeared as engrossed in the lesson as their teacher.

"You had a first," Dara Hegar told Krumholz afterwards. "Juror number 1 finally smiled."

Juror number 1 was the elderly, taciturn forewoman of the jury. I hadn't known she *could* smile. That evening, Leone reported his shadow jurors had loved Krumholz's lesson. They gave him a 9.2 (out of a possible 10). When Krumholz protested that wasn't good enough, Lanier comforted him. Why, Reicin had gotten a 4.2 last week, he said, and "a 9 in the late afternoon, it's like a 10 or 11." The jury was bored. You educated them a bit, he said.

The assessments of his shadow (or gallery) jurors were Leone's primary tool for taking the pulse of the trial. He received the gallery reports, as they were called, around 8 o'clock every evening, and he read them in the privacy of his room, where Lanier and Hegar often joined him. When others on the trial team got glimpses, it was only under Leone's watchful eye. Lanier informed me early on that Leone had insisted the reports remain off-limits to me. Occasionally, Lanier tried to get around his promise to Leone by reading snippets out loud in my presence. Or he weaved them into conversation, as he had done that evening. Mostly, I surmised the tenor and content of the nightly gallery reports from Leone's comments to Lanier each morning on which issues to emphasize with the witness that day.

IT WAS TWO WEEKS into the trial, and Lanier had thoroughly debunked Merck's claim that there had been no sign that Vioxx was risky until the end of its market life. But he thought the plaintiffs had to do more to win. They had to show the jury *how* Vioxx acted in the body to cause heart attacks. The scientific thinking on that question was still evolving, but the consensus view was that Vioxx did so by disrupting the balance between clot-promoting and clot-busting agents in the blood. Lanier had already introduced the concept to the jury with the copper scales from eBay and the plastic toys from a party supply store near his house. Krumholz would put meat on those bones, and add his imprimatur to the theory in the process.

Krumholz returned to his post in front of the jury box the next morning, armed again with the plastic heart. Lanier had positioned the old-fashioned scales and party toys at the ready on a small table close by.

"Refresh our memory on what a heart attack is," Lanier told Krumholz.

Krumholz smiled and reminded the jury that a heart attack causes heart muscle to die. It happens when plaque deposits inside the coronary arteries crack open, and a blood clot forms at the site and grows large enough to obstruct the flow of blood to the heart. He described the plaque deposits as "bumps and lumps" in the vessel walls.

"We think that these bumps and lumps actually crack and fracture a lot, and heart attacks don't occur," Krumholz said.

"Why?" asked Lanier.

"Because...as that blood clot starts to form, there are things in the body that say, 'Ooh, we should form a blood clot here,'" Krumholz said, "and other parts of the body that sort of say, 'Keep the blood going. Keep it going.'"

Krumholz was referring, as the jury knew, to the signals that the anti- and pro-clotting molecules, thromboxane and prostacyclin, send to platelets in the blood, and he elaborated with the help of Lanier's scales and the collection of green and red party toys piled in it. He turned first to the green party toys that denoted prostacyclin.

"Prostacyclin is kind of like soft music," Krumholz said. It calms the platelets that rush to the site of the cracking plaque and prepare to form a blood clot. It tells the platelets, "This isn't life-threatening... Keep going. Relax," Krumholz said, and turned next to the red party toys in the other pan.

"Thromboxane is the bugle saying, 'We got a problem, platelets, wake up! We need you to spring into action. Find out where to go, and form a clot,'" he said.

When the prostacyclin and thromboxane are in balance, the blood clots form where the body needs them to patch up tears and injuries, but not in places—such as the arteries that feed the heart— where they can cause a heart attack.

"It's a cool system, when it works right," Krumholz said. But when you tilt the balance, he said, removing a few of the green party toys from prostacyclin pan of the scale, you're changing the dynamic and making clots more likely.

"Now, that doesn't mean every minute you're going to clot. Not at all... When a clot starts to form, sometimes you still may be able to break up the clot," Krumholz said, "but you're tilting the balance."

Merck had known that Vioxx may have the power to tilt that balance and cause heart attacks at least since 1997, two years before it started selling Vioxx. But VIGOR was the first study large enough to be able to spot that effect, Krumholz said.

"Dr. Reicin testified in this case that, in her opinion—Ed Scolnick, but also herself—when she saw [the VIGOR results], her first reaction was, 'Oh, my goodness! We're doing harm. We're causing heart attacks,'" Lanier said. "If a drug company's people truly think their drug is causing heart attacks and doing harm, do they continue business as normal, or should they say stop and do an investigation?" he asked Krumholz.

"I think it is fairly obvious that if you get that kind of result and you are aiming to have 20 million people on the medication, [including]...many people who have risk of heart disease, that...your first assumption has to be, What have we potentially caused?" Krumholz said.

The evidence from VIGOR was not definitive, he continued. "But...yeah, I'm worried, because I had a plausible mechanism...I've got to prove that this *isn't* a problem, or I've got to slow down the train here, because this could be an issue."

Krumholz had neatly reinforced the potential significance of the VIGOR findings by placing them in the context of what Merck scientists had known of Vioxx's biological mechanism at the time. The disconnect between Vioxx's potential for harm and Merck's response to VIGOR now looked even starker. It was just what Lanier had wanted.

IN THE AFTERMATH OF the VIGOR study, two large Vioxx studies among elderly subjects with Alzheimer's disease (and those likely to develop it) emerged as a centerpiece of Merck's efforts to prove Vioxx was safe for the heart. The company claimed the studies showed that Vioxx was safer even than placebo. According to Krumholz, they showed the exact opposite.

"I know it's [Lanier's] case," Krumholz had said to the other lawyers on Sunday, as Lanier was flying back from his weekend in Houston. But "there are several things that are nonnegotiable to me," and bringing to light the truth on those Alzheimer's studies was one of the studies. He and his researchers had spent months making sense of them. "It's what [Merck] did most wrong," he said. "It's the lynchpin of how we're going to hang them."

The Alzheimer's studies were not yet complete when Merck scientists received the VIGOR results, in March 2000. Merck took an

advance look at the incidence of heart problems in the Alzheimer's studies in September 2000. It found there had been fewer heart attacks and
strokes on Vioxx than on placebo, but many more deaths. Thirty Vioxx
subjects had died, compared to 10 on placebo. Merck scientists did not
disclose the deaths to the FDA's Arthritis Advisory Committee, when
it met in February 2001 to evaluate the latest data on Vioxx's risks and
benefits. They gave only the favorable data on heart attacks and strokes.

Just weeks later, Merck scientists learned of more deaths in the
continuing study. Negotiations with the FDA over changes to the
Vioxx label loomed on the horizon.

"At this delicate time, how should we handle the data?" Reicin's
boss, Alan Nies, wrote on March 22, 2001, in an email to other
senior scientists.

They "handled" the data by sitting on it some more.

The following month, a rigorous statistical analysis of the latest
data from the Alzheimer's studies showed the risk of death to be three
times as high on Vioxx as on placebo. It also showed that the odds
were one in a thousand that the excess deaths in the Vioxx group were
unrelated to the drug. Once again Merck painted a much different
picture for the FDA, in a Vioxx "safety update report" in July 2001.
As it had at the advisory committee meeting, Merck reported there
had been fewer cardiovascular events on Vioxx than on placebo in the
studies. For the first time, it told the FDA that deaths on Vioxx had
exceeded those on placebo. But it gave the FDA different numbers
than those it had used in its internal analysis, with the result that
the difference in mortality between the two groups was less striking. (The report to the FDA does not say how Merck calculated that
death data, but the company appears to have used a less comprehen-
sive counting method than the one specified in the trials' rules and
used in its internal report.) Also missing from the FDA report was
the statistical analysis that established that more Vioxx subjects were

dying in the studies, not by chance but because of the drug. Instead, in page after page of tables and analyses, the company argued there was no pattern to the deaths, attributing them to causes as various as trauma, accidents, and pneumonia, in addition to heart attacks and strokes. The report concluded: "Overall review of the deaths does not identify a…likely relationship to rofecoxib."

A hush fell over Lanier's room Sunday night as Krumholz recited from memory death counts, dates, and the results of statistical analyses.

"You know this stuff cold, don't you," Lanier said admiringly.

Leone knew the plaintiffs could make all kinds of hay with the Alzheimer's saga.

"Oh, man. They were treating 'em like guinea pigs," he chuckled, when Krumholz explained that Merck had allowed the trials to continue despite the imbalance in deaths between the Vioxx and placebo groups. "You know how mad people can get" at that, he said, picturing the jury's reaction.

"Their [Merck's] claim is that they gave everything to the FDA. But they didn't give this," Leone said at another point. "That would be a great thing to show, Mark."

For all the Vioxx cases that had come to trial thus far, the story of the Alzheimer's trials had yet to be fully told.

By the next evening, however, Lanier was having second thoughts about spending time on it with the jury. He feared it was too complicated and the jury would not follow it. (Krumholz is used to talking to kids who get into Yale medical school, Lanier had complained the week before. He wanted Krumholz to be "idiot simple.")

Tell the "kiddy version" of the Alzheimer's story, he said to Krumholz. Like children's editions of literary classics, he said. Like Robert Louis Stevenson's *Kidnapped,* he added helpfully.

What am I even doing testifying if I can't get this story out, Krumholz thought. Merck's manipulation of science in the

Alzheimer's trials went to the heart of everything that was rotten about Vioxx and of why he had agreed to testify in the Vioxx cases. He pushed back.

"Some people have to stand up and say what's right," he said later. "I've got some capital. I'm a tenured professor and I have a reputation. If *I* can't do this, then I don't know who is going to do it."

In the end, the two men struck an uneasy compromise. Krumholz explained the broad outlines of the story. His hurried account came at the close of Lanier's direct exam.

"EXPLAIN TO US, WHEN you dig down deep into the Alzheimer's data, first of all, does it really establish that Vioxx is safe?" Lanier said to Krumholz.

"I don't think it does," Krumholz said. "Let me say it more strongly. It does not."

The Vioxx groups in the Alzheimer's studies had fewer heart attacks than those given placebo, and Krumholz's first task was to explain why those numbers *could not* accurately reflect the cardiovascular risks Vioxx posed to subjects in those studies.

Doctors need two things to diagnose a heart attack, he said. They need to know that the patient is having (or has had) the symptoms of a heart attack. Then they need to run tests to make the definitive diagnosis. The subjects in these studies had Alzheimer's or the cognitive problems that precede the disease. They could not have been relied upon to remember or describe their symptoms accurately, Krumholz said, and they were unlikely to have received the same level of testing and care as those without the disease.

"I'll tell you honestly, when an Alzheimer's patient comes to the hospital, sometimes, even often," Krumholz said, "[You] do what you can to make them comfortable, but not necessarily subject them to a lot of tests and procedures."

Many heart attacks in these studies would have gone uncounted, he said.

"If you can't really look accurately at…the heart attack lists," Lanier interjected, "what do you look at?"

"So in these patients, I felt there was only one thing you could truly rely on," Krumholz said. "That's if they survived, [or] whether they died, because that was the only thing I could be certain had happened."

In other words, you had to count the bodies for a true measure of Vioxx's cardiovascular effects in the Alzheimer's studies.

Merck scientists understood this, and had written out a detailed plan to analyze the deaths before the studies began. The plan—which they proceeded to ignore—said all deaths in the trial would be counted, no matter their apparent cause, even if subjects had stopped taking the medication and dropped out of the trial before they died. (Those are the standard methods to measure cardiovascular effects in a trial.) Krumholz told the jury those were the counts he went to next.

"What did you find?" Lanier asked.

There were three times as many deaths in the Vioxx group as on placebo, Krumholz said.

The court reporter, Regina Tell, bit her lip as she typed in Krumholz's testimony, and her usually impervious face registered shock. The Alzheimer's studies had not shown Vioxx was safer for the heart than placebo, after all. Far from it.

Lanier repeated his question. Krumholz gave the same answer.

Did Merck scientists tell the FDA, Lanier asked. They did not, Krumholz replied. They told the FDA advisory committee in February 2001 that the cardiovascular data from the Alzheimer's trials was "reassuring." Had they told them about the deaths, Krumholz said, the FDA advisors would have known to go digging deeper and reached very different conclusions.

There was much, much more of the Alzheimer's story to tell. Unfortunately, Lanier had spent all the time he had allotted to it.

"You have thirty seconds to wrap up the Alzheimer's story," he told Krumholz.

Krumholz resisted. He wanted to tell the jury more.

"I have to show this Bain memo," he said, referring to a memo prepared by the head of Merck's biostatistics unit, Raymond Bain.

Lanier looked a little put out, but did as Krumholz requested.

The memo, dated October 31, 2001, laid out in precise and elegant detail how Vioxx affected the odds of death in the Alzheimer's studies. It showed the risk of death to be almost five times as high on Vioxx as on placebo in one study, and two-and-a-half times as high in a second study. A third Alzheimer's study, which had been terminated early, did not yield enough data for the calculation.

Together, the three studies showed the risk of death on Vioxx was 2.56 times as high as on placebo. Tests showed a high degree of statistical certainty about these results.

"Bottom line, was Alzheimer's reassuring, if you dig down deep and really look?" Lanier asked.

"Not reassuring, and that analysis was never shown. Never shown," Krumholz said somberly, and Lanier moved on to a different subject. A short while later he wrapped up his direct exam.

CROSS-EXAMINATIONS ARE MEANT TO humiliate and intimidate, and Krumholz had been dreading his. The plaintiffs' lawyers showered Krumholz with critiques and advice, beginning on Sunday when he arrived in Atlantic City. They said his body language was "defensive and hesitant" under hostile questioning. Never let them see you sweat, they counseled. They offered Alise Reicin as a model. "It's all how you look," they said.

They mimicked Reicin when she was cornered: "Yes, Mr. Lanier," they said, their smiles saccharine sweet.

That was Sunday afternoon. Sunday evening, Leone got to Atlantic City. He was the team's expert on preparing witnesses for the courtroom.

"You can't be cocky," he told Krumholz. "They'll come after you like banshees." He imitated a cat hissing and clawing, to be sure Krumholz got the message.

"Who wants to cross?" Lanier asked his team the next night.

Many of them did. They were lawyers, after all, and they relished the idea of demolishing a witness, even if in sport. They threw out their questions staccato style, and Krumholz's answers rarely satisfied.

"Nonresponsive," they cried, and interrupted him repeatedly.

Krumholz rubbed his eyes. It was almost 10 P.M. He looked a bit rattled.

The master-cross examiner came to Krumholz's rescue.

"Isn't it true you killed your wife?" Lanier said, facing Krumholz. Lanier answered his own question. "Absolutely," he said. He was showing Krumholz how it was done. "Don't be evasive," he said. "Go slow."

Leone's advice was more specific. It had to do with Diane Sullivan.

"Don't let her get you mad," Leone warned. "You want to stay nice, no matter how nasty she gets."

The next day, Sullivan did not disappoint.

"I'm not sure where to begin," she said to Krumholz when she took the floor. "I guess we'll begin close to where you left off in talking about the Alzheimer's studies. Do you remember your testimony about that recently?"

"Yes, I remember that testimony," Krumholz said.

Aren't you cherry-picking by only talking about the Alzheimer's studies, she asked. Isn't it true that there were fewer deaths on Vioxx than on placebo in another group of Vioxx studies—those done on subject with osteoarthritis? Krumholz explained why the arthritis studies, in which deaths on placebo did outnumber those on Vioxx, could not be interpreted to mean that Vioxx was safe. The studies were too small and too short to differentiate between Vioxx and placebo, he said. The number of deaths in those studies signified nothing, he said. Sullivan ignored his answer, and repeated her question in a slightly different form. Krumholz thought Sullivan was trying to trap him into contradicting himself. He concentrated as hard as he could and calmly repeated himself.

Eventually, Sullivan flitted to a new line of attack.

Many of the Vioxx subjects who died in the Alzheimer's studies died from causes such as car accidents, electrocutions, head trauma, and pneumonia, Sullivan said. Nobody has published in the scientific literature that Vioxx causes car accidents and electrocutions, have they, Sullivan asked. Other scientists hadn't seen the data he had, Krumholz said stolidly. He explained again why it was important to count all deaths in the Alzheimer's studies, no matter their apparent cause.

No scientist has published a peer-reviewed paper saying the deaths were related to Vioxx, Sullivan persisted.

"People can't publish what they don't have access to," Krumholz said. "You're right, no one has published that."

In an appeal to the jury's lay sensibilities, Sullivan was implicitly arguing that a death that *looked* unconnected to Vioxx could not properly be counted in an assessment of the drug's safety. She was within her rights to make that argument. But then Sullivan overreached. She said the FDA agreed with her.

"Dr. Krumholz, you know that the FDA took a look at this data and said electric shock, head trauma, car accidents, there's no pattern here, this is not drug-related?" Sullivan asked.

"Show him the document where the FDA said that," Higbee interjected.

A few minutes later, Sullivan produced an FDA report on the Alzheimer's trials. The only problem was that it didn't say what she claimed it said. Higbee sent the jury out of the courtroom and scolded Sullivan for breaking what she called a cardinal rule of cross-examination.

"It is unfair to say to a witness who has reviewed thousands...of pages of documents, 'isn't it true the FDA said XYZ' when, in fact, you have nothing that suggests that," Higbee said.

In fact, the FDA document backed up Krumholz's point. It noted that an FDA reviewer had asked Merck for additional analyses of the Alzheimer's trials, but the request was "pending." That was as of December 2004, three months after Merck stopped selling Vioxx. Incredibly, Sullivan told Higbee Merck hadn't turned over the information, because the company was still, three years later, collecting data from the studies and analyzing it.

That night Leone told Krumholz the shadow jury had rated his performance an 8 (out of 10). No one gets such a high rating on cross-examination, Leone told him. You did really well, he said.

Sullivan attacked harder the next day. Krumholz remained polite. It was his Ohio upbringing, he said. People there were more polite than on the East Coast. But, he made no bones about what he thought of her tactics.

When Sullivan suggested Krumholz had misrepresented the findings of Vioxx studies, Krumholz challenged her. "If you can find someone to discredit me, bring them in here. Let them go through the data," he said. "I'd like to go over the data. Can we go over the data?" he asked Sullivan, again and again.

When Sullivan repeated a question for the umpteenth time, Krumholz responded, "If you've been listening to what I've been saying, ma'am...."

When she misrepresented his testimony, he responded simply, "I think you know I didn't say that."

Before she was done, Sullivan managed to provoke Higbee again, this time for attempting to alert the jury to an FDA memo that Higbee had expressly ruled out of bounds. As she had the day before, Higbee sent the jury out of the courtroom.

"You can ignore the last statement of counsel," she told jurors before they filed out. "It was completely improper."

Like Lanier, Sullivan understood that the jury would be more likely to find in favor of the plaintiffs if the results of the clinical trials were backed up by a plausible theory of *how* Vioxx caused heart attacks. The FDA memo she had referred to cast doubt on the so-called COX-2 hypothesis that held Vioxx caused heart attacks by disrupting the balance of clot-promoting and clot-inhibiting molecules in the body. Higbee had kept the memo out of the trial because she (and others) felt it offered scant scientific evidence for its conclusions.

At sidebar, Sullivan insisted she hadn't violated the judge's ruling.

"Miss Sullivan, Miss Sullivan," said Higbee, interrupting her. "Miss Sullivan, you are a very skillful, very bright lawyer. You purposely said in front of the jury—implied in front of the jury—that you had an FDA memo that agreed with [your position]."

"I'm sorry, Your Honor," Sullivan said. Higbee wasn't done.

"We have talked about this FDA report not once or twice or something you could forget about. Every trial we have spent two or three hours on this particular memo. There have been briefs on it, motions on it, discussions on it, hearings on it, and I have ruled up to now that the memo shouldn't be mentioned or produced in front of the jury. I'm finding you in contempt of court for that statement to the jury, and I'm fining you personally $1,000. And when you come back, I'm going to tell the jury it was totally improper and they should ignore it."

The court reporter captured Sullivan's unrepentant closing words at the sidebar. They concerned the disputed memo.

"I guess I can't use it," she remarked. She was smiling as she returned to her seat.

Over lunch, Lanier and Hegar joked how Sullivan would have been in jail for such conduct in a Texas court. Paul Strain would have been ordered to take over. Then they laughed. Except Paul Strain would be in jail too, they said.

(Higbee backtracked on the punishment later. She said that while she, Higbee, had interpreted Sullivan's question as an effort to tell the jury about the controversial FDA memo, the jury was unlikely to have understood Sullivan's message.)

By 4 P.M. it was over. Krumholz sat in the back of the court room, scrolling through his BlackBerry, while the lawyers milled about.

"This could be my swan song," he said, "These people are making fun of her but she's good. She's shameless. I can see why my colleagues don't testify. It's hard to go chest-to-chest with her," he said.

Krumholz hadn't *looked* like he was suffering, but the experience had been "extraordinarily intense," he said later.

Sullivan is "trying to undermine you and discredit you. You're bracing yourself for an attack and also for mental tricks," he said. "You're expecting [her] to get you into a string of logic that makes you contradict yourself. You have to really concentrate."

Krumholz had been Lanier's last witness, and the next day Lanier rested his case. It was a high note on which to end. The shadow jury showed he was winning, and by a wide margin.

"I've never been so far ahead," he told Krumholz gleefully.

He may have been counting his chickens before they were hatched. It was now Sullivan's turn to put on Merck's case.

"Never get a verdict, if you think things aren't going well."

CHAPTER 10

Merck's Defense

Atlantic City, February 22–28, 2007

STRIPPED TO ITS CORE, Merck's defense rested on two pillars.

The first was the scientifically dubious proposition that there was no evidence Vioxx could cause heart attacks. Neither VIGOR, nor any trial after that, including the one that led Merck to stop selling Vioxx in 2004, had shown Vioxx was risky, according to Merck's lawyers.

The second pillar was that every aspect of Merck's research and marketing of Vioxx had been done with the knowledge and express permission of the Food and Drug Administration. The FDA had vouched for Vioxx's safety by approving Merck's label, not once or twice, but on four separate occasions. If its federal regulator had believed Vioxx carried risks that Merck hadn't disclosed, that argument went, it could have compelled Merck to disclose them. It didn't, which meant that Merck's actions were everything they should have been. There had been no "failure to warn" of Vioxx's risks, as the plaintiffs alleged. Sullivan presented Merck's case through three scientists and through a former FDA official, Lisa Rarick, who now served as an expert witness for Merck in its Vioxx cases. Higbee had been reluctant to let Rarick testify, because she considered Merck's

FDA defense misleading. But after weeks of sidebars, motions, and briefs, Merck's lawyers prevailed, and Rarick took the stand.

Lisa Rarick had joined the FDA in the late 1980s as a medical officer—the front-line rank and file position in the drug approval process—after completing her training as an obstetrician-gynecologist at Georgetown University in Washington. She had risen through the ranks for 15 years, and by the time she left, in 2003, she worked in the office of the FDA commissioner.

Afterwards, Rarick parlayed her years in the government into a lucrative consulting career, which included testifying for drug companies in product liability lawsuits. She had earned close to $300,000 for her testimony in four previous Vioxx trials. The Merck lawyers claimed the money did not influence her opinions because she didn't need it. Diane Sullivan was itching to tell the jury that Rarick had married into the fortune of the family that founded Marshall Field, the famed Chicago department store, but Higbee wouldn't let her.

"She's the only person in the courtroom richer than Mark Lanier," another Merck lawyer sniffed at sidebar. (Seeger was said to be richer than Lanier, actually.)

The 47-year-old Rarick dressed for her first day in court in a black suit, a white shirt with its top buttons undone, and a slim scarf around her neck that evoked a man's tie.

Sullivan began her direct exam of Rarick with the document which had earned her the contempt-of-court citation and $1,000 fine from the judge when Harlan Krumholz was on the stand. (Higbee had relented on that issue as well, and the jury would see the document for the first time that day.) It was a memo issued by the FDA in April 2005, some six months after Merck had withdrawn Vioxx. It contained the FDA's official pronouncements on the cardiovascular risks of Vioxx and two other two COX-2 painkillers, and it appeared to have been written with an eye to giving the FDA bureaucratic cover from withering criticism of its role in the Vioxx debacle by Congress, prominent scientists, and the media. In the process, the memo cast a rosy glow on Merck's actions as well.

"I'm going to start at the end, if we could, Dr. Rarick, and we'll go back to the beginning," Sullivan said. "The jury heard a day or two ago about a 2005 advisory committee that related to COX-2s and other pain relievers."

"Yes, there was a February 2005 advisory committee that the FDA held to discuss all those nonsteroidal anti-inflammatory drugs [NSAIDS]," Rarick responded.

And the jury heard from the plaintiffs that there was a vote at that advisory committee, 32 to 0, that Vioxx increased cardiovascular events," Sullivan said.

"Correct," Rarick said.

The advisory committee had also voted unanimously that the other two COX-2 painkillers, Celebrex and Bextra, which were manufactured by Pfizer, increased the risk of cardiovascular events.

"And, Dr. Rarick, tell the jury how it works," Sullivan continued, "the advisory committee, the outside experts meet and give recommendations to the FDA?"

"Exactly," Rarick said. "And then the FDA is charged with saying what they're going to do with those recommendations."

"And the jury hasn't seen the FDA's conclusions in 2005 yet, and we would like to put it on the screen and talk to them about it," Sullivan continued.

"No objection, Judge," Lanier chirruped, as Sullivan offered the document into evidence and projected it on the screen.

"Dr. Rarick, you're familiar with this document?" Sullivan asked.

"Yes, I am," Rarick said.

"And the FDA called it a decision memo?" Sullivan said.

"Exactly," Rarick said.

The FDA memo opened with the assertion that the three COX-2 painkillers—Vioxx, Celebrex, and Bextra—were "associated with an increased risk of serious cardiovascular adverse events compared to placebo." The jury could not have anticipated what came next. According to the memo, the risks of the COX-2 selective painkillers were "indistinguishable" from those of the older nonsteroidal anti-inflammatory drugs. You could see why Sullivan had fought so hard to show the memo to the jury.

In one fell swoop, the memo bolstered Merck's position that Vioxx's risks were garden-variety and had merited no special warning to doctors and patients. And it left the plaintiffs without the thing Lanier considered crucial to a favorable jury verdict—a biologically plausible "mechanism" that explained how Vioxx caused heart attacks.

Lanier had argued that Vioxx's cardiovascular risks flowed from a property unique to Vioxx (and the other COX-2 painkillers) of blocking the COX-2 enzyme, which was associated with pain and inflammation, but not the stomach-protecting COX-1 enzyme. He said that by doing so Vioxx upset the balance between clot-promoting and clot-busting molecules, and increased the chances that the routine cracking of plaque deposits in the coronary arteries would be followed by the formation of blood clots and heart attacks. But if the FDA was right and older painkillers, which blocked both COX-1 and COX-2 enzymes, were just as risky, Vioxx's property of selectively blocking the COX-2 enzyme was irrelevant to its cardiovascular risks, and the plaintiffs were left without support for their explanation of how Vioxx caused heart attacks.

Many scientists outside the FDA said the memo's conclusions were just wrong, as was the FDA's decision that the only COX-2 left on the market, Celebrex, and older NSAIDs carry the same new warning about cardiovascular side effects. The chairman of the FDA advisory committee, pharmacologist Alastair J. J. Wood of Vanderbilt

University Medical School, said "there was clear evidence" that Celebrex, the only COX-2 painkiller still on the market, was riskier than the older painkillers.

Higbee said she had kept the memo out of evidence thus far because the FDA had provided little scientific data to back up its conclusion that all the NSAIDs posed similar cardiovascular risks. The FDA itself acknowledged that its position was based on a paucity of evidence. (The memo said results of trials comparing the older painkillers to the COX-2 drugs were inconsistent, and, there weren't enough long-term safety trials comparing the older painkillers to placebo to settle the question.)

"It's just always appeared to me that this paper goes on for about 10 pages saying 'nothing is that clear…, we're not sure, we don't know,' and then says, 'let's put a black box on all of them,' " Higbee had explained in one of many sidebars, in which Merck's lawyers argued for the memo.

She gave in eventually after the plaintiffs' lawyers pressed her to let in the advisory committee's vote affirming Vioxx's cardiovascular risks. They wanted to use it to rebut Merck's expert witnesses who insisted there was no scientific evidence that Vioxx was risky. Higbee ruled that if the plaintiffs' lawyers told the jury about the vote, Merck would get to tell the jury about the FDA's memo.

"Judge, we're taking the deal," Chris Seeger had joked.

"It is not a deal," Higbee responded, before reconsidering. "It is. I guess it is."

The FDA had also used the memo to affirm that its previous assessments of Vioxx's risks had been correct. According to the FDA memo, Vioxx's cardiovascular risks became evident only after the cancer prevention study that led Merck to withdraw it. No previous Vioxx study, including VIGOR and the studies in Alzheimer's patients, had signaled the risks, the FDA said. It seemed Merck could count on the FDA's protection in Vioxx's afterlife as much as it had during the drug's lucrative market life.

THE HISTORY OF FDA regulation of Vioxx was a history of missed opportunities. There is ample documentary evidence that FDA scientists understood VIGOR to be a signal of Vioxx's cardiovascular risks. They knew that interpretation to be consistent with the results of other sizeable Vioxx studies. But instead of sharing that assessment with doctors and patients, the FDA hid behind a veil of scientific uncertainty. The Vioxx label it approved in 2002 said the evidence on Vioxx's cardiovascular risks was mixed, and the meaning of the evidence was "unknown."

For doctors it was as good as an "all clear" signal to prescribe Vioxx freely. Merck was bombarding them with sales pitches that said naproxen was the reason for the heart attacks in VIGOR and Vioxx was benign. Patients asked for it by name. If the FDA said the safety evidence was murky, who were doctors to say otherwise?

But no matter how you interpreted the VIGOR study, it argued against using Vioxx, according to Alastair J.J. Wood, the pharmacologist who chaired the FDA's 2005 advisory committee on the COX-2 drugs.

"I don't think it matter very much whether naproxen was protective or Vioxx was toxic. The whole indication for Vioxx—the whole reason to give COX-2 inhibitors—was the potential for new safety," Wood explained.

Clinical trials had found no evidence that Vioxx was any better at fighting pain than the older drugs to which it was compared, he said. So when VIGOR showed there were half as many cardiovascular problems on naproxen as on Vioxx, Wood said, the logical choice was to prescribe naproxen over Vioxx. As to Vioxx's superior gastrointestinal safety, you could get the same benefit in other ways.

"We knew by that time that you could reduce the risk of gastric events [on naproxen and other NSAIDs] with proton-pump inhibitors," Wood said.

"I executed on that in my life," Wood said. "My wife had a hip replacement. I made sure she wasn't on Vioxx in the days leading up to it. My own view was that if she had a heart attack, it was less recoverable than a gastrointestinal bleed."

The FDA had, in effect, advised doctors to expose their patients to the risk of heart attacks and other cardiovascular problems on Vioxx for no net advantage in pain relief or gastrointestinal safety, and the FDA's scientists understood that. The lead scientist charged with reviewing the data on Vioxx had earlier concluded, "There was no overall safety advantage for [Vioxx] when compared to naproxen" in VIGOR, and recommended that the FDA "deemphasize the safety advantages" of Vioxx in the label.

To the extent that the label advised doctors to be cautious in prescribing Vioxx, it was only in patients who had already suffered heart attacks.

Wood called that "statistical nonsense." Among low-risk patients, heart attacks would be rarer and thus harder to detect, he said, but "for the guy who got it, it would be just as devastating."

Vioxx could not have become a multi-billion dollar drug, and caused tens of thousands of heart attacks and deaths, without the FDA's help.

Despite years of legal discovery at Merck and the FDA, it is still not known precisely why the FDA abandoned its original assessment of Vioxx's risks to sign off on the weak amendments that Merck favored in April 2002. One part of the answer surely is that the FDA did not have the legal authority to force Merck to issue a clearer warning of Vioxx's risks, short of ordering Vioxx off the market, an action that was unlikely to withstand legal challenge by Merck.

IN SEPTEMBER 2001, WHEN Mike Humeston had his heart attack, Merck had been in possession of the VIGOR results for 18 months, but the Vioxx label contained no mention of the cardiovascular side effects seen in VIGOR. (That was the basis of the Humestons's "failure to warn" claim against Merck.) Merck's two-pronged defense was that, first, the VIGOR study had not shown that Vioxx could cause heart attacks, so Merck had no reason to warn of Vioxx's risks; and second, that its hands were tied by the FDA as far as what it could say. According to this line of reasoning, the Vioxx label hadn't been changed as of Mike Humeston's heart attack, because the company was still waiting to hear back from the FDA on the proposed labels it had submitted.

The plaintiffs responded that Vioxx was Merck's product, and under federal law, it was Merck's responsibility, not the FDA's, to make sure the Vioxx label accurately reflected Vioxx's risks. Higbee agreed. Her reading of the law (confirmed by the U.S. Supreme Court in an unrelated case in 2009) was that the FDA exercised ultimate power over the description of a drug's risks and benefits in the drug label *before* the drug was marketed—it could withhold permission to sell the drug if it did not approve of the label. But after the drug was on the market, the FDA's power over the label was limited. It retained control over whether a drug company could claim new uses or benefits for the drug, and over how those were described on the label. But the FDA no longer had the authority to tell a company when or how to disclose the drug's risks on the label. The FDA's only recourse if it disapproved of the company's disclosures was the extreme one of declaring the drug "misbranded" and ordering it off the market. And it had to be prepared to defend its action in federal court, if the drug company sued.

By the time of Brian Hermans's heart attack in September 2002, the Vioxx label did include the VIGOR results, but it did not clearly warn of Vioxx's cardiovascular risks. Notwithstanding the fact that the FDA had signed off on those changes, Higbee's ruling still applied—the label's shortcomings were Merck's responsibility, even if the changes were approved by the FDA.

Higbee suspected Merck would use Rarick's testimony to present its own, more sweeping interpretation of the FDA's powers over the drug label, despite her ruling, and she warned the company's lawyers not to do that.

"If you put a witness on the stand to say that, I'm going to wind up telling the jury that what the witness said isn't true, and that, in fact, the law says something different," she told Merck's lawyers. "I don't want to be forced into doing that."

But Sullivan had made an end run around Higbee's rulings before, and she did so again. She made her move in the late afternoon of Rarick's first day on the stand, after Rarick's extensive and glowing testimony about Merck's early Vioxx research and its culmination, in 1999, in the FDA's approval of Vioxx.

"And Dr. Rarick, as part of the FDA's approval of Vioxx in May of 1999, did the FDA also have to approve labeling for the medicine?" Sullivan asked.

"Yes," Rarick said.

"Can you tell the jury how that works?" Sullivan said

Rarick said companies were required to submit a proposed label for review by FDA scientists. The company and the FDA then discussed any changes that needed to be made. "And then, at the time of approval, the FDA has to say here's what your final label looks like," she concluded.

"Okay, and Dr. Rarick, can companies say anything they want in their label or do they need, ultimately, to get FDA approval?"

"Um, they draft a proposed label, as I described…But yes, it is ultimately, up to the FDA to approve the label that's put on the product."

"Dr. Rarick, does the FDA have the *final* say as to what language is used in a company's label for its medicine?" Sullivan asked.

"Yes. Final say, about format, content, language, yes," Rarick said.

"So, when we're talking about risks or warnings or precautions for a medicine, is it true that the FDA is the *ultimate* decider, has the final say on the language used in the labeling?" Sullivan asked.

"Yes," Rarick said.

Seeger stood up to object.

"I think counsel is really getting close to a treacherous territory in suggesting that the FDA is the final arbiter on the label," he said at sidebar.

"It ultimately has to be approved by the FDA. That's the instruction. That's the regulations," Sullivan said.

"That's not true. That's not the law," Seeger said. "She continues to go back to this despite your ruling," Seeger complained to Higbee.

"All right, the jury can go out," Higbee said. It would be the next morning before they returned.

Sullivan said her questions had been about the FDA's powers over the label before a drug was approved. The plaintiffs' lawyers said the questions had started out that way, but veered into the forbidden core of Merck's defense—that the FDA bore ultimate responsibility for what the post-VIGOR label said. They wanted Higbee to tell the jury that Rarick's testimony had been wrong, and to instruct them on what the law really said. Higbee was leaning that way herself.

"There was not an attempt to mislead, Your Honor," said Hope Freiwald.

"Oh, but they were warned, Judge," Seeger said.

"Can I finish?" said Sullivan, jumping in.

Seeger ignored her. The lawyers talked over each other all the time and the court reporter's sidebar transcripts were littered with half-finished sentences. "I want to be sure I am heard on this," Seeger insisted. "You guys have flirted with this line since the trial started. The judge's rulings are clear. Yesterday in her chambers she said, 'I'm warning you, if you go there, I'm going to instruct the jury.' What did you do? You went there," Seeger said.

"Do you feel better now?" Freiwald said to Seeger after he was done. "Good. I'm glad you feel better."

"Thank you very much," Seeger said.

"That's what it's all about," said Freiwald, herself one of the most persistent voices at sidebar.

"I feel better," Seeger said.

"Good. Good," Freiwald said, again.

They went over all the same ground again the next morning.

"We have a skunk in the jury, and there's only one way to clean that smell out, and that's with your instruction," Seeger said.

Higbee did give the jury an instruction before Sullivan returned to her direct examination.

"I just wanted to clarify one point for you now, so there's not any confusion in your mind as you're listening to the testimony," she said. "Regardless of what the FDA did or did not approve, it is the drug manufacturer, and in this case, that's Merck, that has the duty to take reasonable steps to adequately warn about known or knowable risks, and it is you, the jury, who has to ultimately decide whether Merck should have known or did know about the alleged risks of Vioxx at specific times, and whether they adequately warned of these risks at those times."

Higbee's even tone betrayed nothing of the passions this issue had aroused on all sides since the jury had last been in the courtroom—and not just among the lawyers. The judge was upset as well. She had been careful not to couch her instruction to the jury as a correction of Rarick's testimony. But she vowed she wouldn't be as circumspect the next time.

"If I hear her say something that's absolutely a misstatement of the law, there will be a correction right at that time. I'm telling you that right now," she told the Merck lawyers.

That afternoon, with eight minutes to go before court recessed for the weekend, Sullivan passed the witness. Lanier used the time to trigger a second instruction from Higbee on the issue, after Rarick refused to concede that Merck hadn't needed the FDA's permission to warn patients about the risk of heart attack after VIGOR. Higbee obliged.

"The FDA has regulations which specifically say that if, in fact, there's a reasonable association between a drug and a serious risk of harm, the company can, without FDA approval, change their label. Only as to warnings. They cannot change it for benefits," Higbee said.

A stray remark by Sullivan at the judge's bench a few minutes later suggested why Sullivan and her witness were continuing to flout Higbee's ruling on the limits of the FDA's powers.

"The issue is as clear as it ever is going to be for the Appellate Division," Sullivan was recorded as saying.

Higbee's interpretation of the FDA's authority over the drug label would certainly figure in Merck's appeal, if it lost the cases. But Merck's lawyers had already created a solid record of their objections to Higbee's ruling, and the company's position did not need the clarification Sullivan claimed to be providing. Jerry Kristal, the veteran Weitz & Luxenberg plaintiffs' lawyer, thought Sullivan had other reasons for violating Higbee's ruling repeatedly.

"Sometimes lawyers 'judge-bait,' hoping a juror or two somehow becomes sympathetic toward them because they think the judge is being unfair or is beating them up. Sometimes lawyers think the mere repetition of something makes it sound correct. Maybe it was a 'stage-whispered' veiled threat," Kristal said. "Maybe she just couldn't help herself. Zealots sometimes lose the big picture. Who knows?"

Higbee took note of Sullivan's remark in a tense exchange when court resumed on Monday.

I GOT THE CHANCE to observe Carol Higbee at close quarters once during the trial, and only briefly, as the lawyers argued motions in a conference room down the hall from her chambers. Two things stood out in my mind afterwards. The first was how much firmer she was with the Merck lawyers in that setting. She disposed of their objections quickly, instead of letting them hold forth at length. The second was her physical presence. From where I sat in the courtroom gallery, Higbee was a rotund, disembodied head, usually bent over in concentration, and her body was hidden behind the massive judge's bench. In the conference room that day, Higbee had dispensed with the black judicial robe she wore to the courtroom, and her bulky body, clothed in a cheerful pink paisley dress, had a surprisingly powerful presence of its own. Her face was expressive up close. It was the face of an intelligent woman, and I finally understood why the plaintiffs' lawyers believed that Higbee's bland indifference to the contempt with which Merck's lawyers treated her was a strategic façade.

As the Vioxx mass tort judge in New Jersey, Higbee had more Vioxx cases in her docket than any other judge in the country. She had made it her business to understand the complexities of the underlying science, and was arguably a little too well-informed from the standpoint of a company whose defense rested heavily on scientific sleights of hand. The plaintiffs' lawyers believed Merck's team was trying to have Higbee taken off the Vioxx cases by provoking her into a display of anger that Merck could cite as evidence of her bias.

Many incidents during the trial lent credence to that theory. One occurred during Lanier's cross-examination of Rarick when, in a rare slip, Higbee lost her patience with Merck's lawyers in the jury's presence. Lanier was questioning Rarick about the long lags between the completion of many of Merck's studies and the submission of the studies' results to the FDA, using a list of studies and the dates of their completion and submission to the FDA. Merck had prepared the list in response to a Congressional request after Vioxx was withdrawn. Rarick insisted she couldn't be sure the list was accurate, or complete. Lanier thought she was stalling, and so apparently did Higbee.

"Your Honor, I ask that the witness be instructed when and where this was prepared for, so she understands the significance and gravity of Merck not doing it properly," Lanier said.

Strain shot up. "There's no gravity. There's no significance. That's absolutely improper. Absolutely improper."

"Well, it's your document and now she is suggesting it may not be complete," Higbee said.

"This is just not right. We're getting the misimpression to the jury," Strain said.

Higbee rolled her eyes. "We can take a recess, and you can produce, because I have asked Merck to do this before, a list of all studies and when they were submitted to the FDA. The bottom line is, if you have a different list than this, I want to see it," she said.

The jurors were on their feet and ready to leave, but Strain apparently felt he could not let Higbee's rebuke go unanswered. "Whatever Your Honor has asked Merck to submit, Merck has," he said.

"I thought you had. Let's see," Higbee replied.

It was a particularly damaging exchange for Merck, because Higbee's comment echoed the plaintiffs' allegations that Merck had hidden pertinent information about Vioxx's risks from the FDA, from doctors and patients, and now from juries. And the sidebar that followed was bitter. In my notes from that afternoon, I found this: "I'm waiting for a fistfight to break out," I wrote. "No kidding."

Hope Freiwald complained that Higbee held Merck and the plaintiffs to different standards.

"The fact is that the flash points with plaintiffs are not what they are when it comes to Merck. Frankly, Your Honor, I think it is highly prejudicial that the witness appeared to be, and Merck's counsel appeared to be, scolded in front of the jury," she said.

"Counsel, would you stop fighting and just go get the document," Higbee finally said to Freiwald.

"I'm afraid I need to make a motion, if I may," Strain said, when he and Freiwald returned to the judge's bench after a break. "I believe that the words of the Court in front of the jury and the vehemence with which you have said them have cast us in a very harmful and prejudicial light, and I move for a mistrial on that basis, Your Honor," he said.

"And, Your Honor, if I may add," Freiwald began, "the prejudice was compounded by the fact that Your Honor has already instructed the jury three times yesterday while this witness was testifying, suggesting that she was mischaracterizing the law, the implication that she was not being candid. Cumulatively, I think there is just irreparable prejudice in the minds of the jury, and I think that is part of the context of this motion, as well. I don't think that it, frankly, can be cured."

Freiwald and Strain had spoken in low voices. And Higbee's face had remained expressionless, as she listened. Yet something of the high drama of the moment came through. I remember watching the three of them, not entirely sure of what was being said but riveted by the scene.

"Miss Freiwald, I have been restrained in front of this jury. There are so many times where I could have reprimanded counsel in front of the jury and didn't. I have bent over backwards not to say things, but there are times when I am compelled to say things in front of the jury. Those rulings on the evidence on the regulations were things that I told you over and over I was going to tell the jury if you put her on the stand and had her say what she said," Higbee said. "And after I did it, Miss Sullivan says on the record, 'Now I've got an appealable issue.' I understand exactly where you're coming from. It is on the record. You've got another appealable issue. Now, please be seated."

Sullivan, whose provocations Higbee was mostly referring to, listened from afar.

"They're desperate," court reporter Regina Tell would say later. They'll do anything to save their case, she said.

"Never get a verdict, if you think things aren't going well," Kristal said. "That's Diane Sullivan's ultimate goal."

The next day, Higbee would be forced to instruct the jury again on the FDA regulations, in response to Rarick's testimony.

"We're okay. We're okay. They're pissing her off like you wouldn't believe," Seeger said in the plaintiffs' back room. "And we're helping them to the grave."

FOR FIVE WEEKS, LANIER had shown the jury document after document on Merck's deceptive marketing of Vioxx and manipulation of clinical trials, and on the scientific analyses it should have submitted to the FDA but didn't. Rarick had testified, in effect, as a character witness for Merck. They were an ethical company, she said, and they'd done everything by the book. And because of her long association with the FDA, the implication of her testimony was that the FDA thought so too.

Lanier attacked Rarick's testimony on several fronts. The first was that Rarick was in court as a mercenary, not a government representative.

"Ma'am, let's be clear about a couple of things first out," Lanier said, as he launched into his 8-minute cross-examination on Friday afternoon, before court recessed for the weekend.

"Sure," Rarick responded.

"You are not here speaking for the FDA, are you?" he said.

"No, I am not," Rarick said.

"You don't work for the FDA?" Lanier repeated.

"Correct," she said.

"You haven't worked there for years?" Lanier said.

"I haven't worked there for three-and-a-half years," Rarick said.

"The people paying you thousands of dollars a day to sit here and give this testimony is Merck, right?" Lanier went on.

"Correct," Rarick said.

And Lanier attacked the FDA itself, saying it wasn't the all-knowing, all-seeing regulator Rarick claimed it was, but an agency with many troubles of its own. By using the controversial 2005 FDA memo, the defense had opened the door to a report on the FDA issued the following year by the Institute of Medicine (the health arm of the National Academy of Sciences). The report was critical of the FDA and said, among other things, that its culture needed to be changed to bring about a more credible approach to drug safety. Lanier questioned Rarick about the report, who said she disagreed with its findings.

He used the words of Merck's top scientist, Edward Scolnick, to argue that Merck understood the FDA was a weak regulator and took advantage of its weaknesses. In emails, Scolnick had called the FDA's scientists "Grade D high school students," and described its review system as an "anachronism because they cannot possibly keep up with science given their hiring constraints." Rarick brushed off Scolnick's insults, insisting that both he and Merck had always behaved "appropriately and professionally with the FDA."

Rarick was the last witness to testify before the jury began its deliberations, and the plaintiffs' lawyers agreed she had been good.

"Nothing bothered her. Not a single thing," said Moshe Horn, one of Chris Seeger's lawyers. "She's smart and tough."

Sullivan was resting her case on its strongest evidence—the FDA's imprimatur on Merck's assessments of Vioxx's risks while Vioxx was on the market and after, and on how those risks were disclosed to doctors and patients in the Vioxx labels. Lanier had countered that the FDA's support signified less than Sullivan was suggesting. He said the FDA had neither the means nor the political clout to stand up to drug companies and that Merck had withheld information the agency had sought on Vioxx's risks. He had argued the law itself recognized the limits of the FDA's backing by giving Merck, not the FDA, ultimate responsibility over its product's label.

The jury would have to sort out for itself what deference the FDA's support deserved.

"Whatever happens, they know they've been in a fight."

CHAPTER 11

Closing Arguments

Atlantic City, February 28–March 1, 2007

As if more evidence were needed that relations between the two sides had frayed dangerously thin, it came at the conclusion of Lisa Rarick's testimony, when Paul Strain and Bob Leone exchanged words, and Strain invited Leone "to take it outside." To be fair, Strain had his reasons. And Leone felt he had his.

The day before, Judge Higbee had announced that closing arguments would take place immediately after Rarick's testimony. The trial, which was in its fifth week, was behind schedule, and Higbee was impatient to wrap up the first phase. Merck's lawyers hated the plan. By the time Rarick was done, there would likely be time only for Sullivan to present her argument. (The plaintiffs had the burden of proof, so Lanier would get the last word.) It wasn't fair, Sullivan said, that Lanier would have all night to go over her closing argument before making his. Sullivan, Strain, and Hope Freiwald argued the point with Higbee ad nauseum. But the judge held firm, and at 3:30 on the afternoon of February 28, the jury was seated, the courtroom was hushed, and Diane Sullivan had the floor. She was about to begin her closing argument when Higbee relented.

"Counsel can approach one more time," she said. "Sorry, ladies and gentleman, this time this is my indecisiveness that is causing the issue," she told the jury.

"I don't know why I bend over backwards to be fair to you people," she told Sullivan at the bench. "You never ever acknowledge that I'm fair to you. But I'm not going to make you do it,"

"She was crying, Dara," Higbee told Hegar in an aside at the bench a little later, as lawyers from both sides milled about. "I couldn't make her do it."

"You can't see it from where you are, but Diane was white. She looked like she was going to vomit." Regina Tell, the court reporter, said the next morning.

The jury had left and the courtroom was emptying out when Leone and Strain crossed paths.

"You couldn't do it. You couldn't do it," Leone taunted, and he flapped his shoulders and clucked like a chicken at Strain.

"You want to take it outside?" Strain asked.

Leone clucked some more and Strain repeated his invitation.

The standoff ended only when Lanier pulled Leone aside and the two raced out of the courthouse, laughing. Their exit had the feel of a getaway—they half thought Strain might complain to Higbee.

"What was Strain going to say? 'Your Honor, he clucked at me like a chicken?'" Hegar joked, as Lanier and Leone told the story to an appreciative audience that evening.

"I would say, 'if the feather fits...'" Leone responded.

For weeks, I had anticipated (and guiltily hoped for) such an altercation. But I hadn't picked the two white-haired men in the bunch as the likely combatants. Still, Strain was always pugnacious. And Leone's outburst also was in character.

One time, the story went, Leone was so disgusted that he put a hex on a defense lawyer, his children, and his grandchildren. He reconsidered overnight and returned the next day to take it off the children and grandchildren.

"Whatever happens, they know they've been in a fight," Leone said to Chris Seeger, as the group gathered before court in Lanier's suite the next morning.

"They've got some battle scars," Seeger agreed. "They've got to have spent over $15 million of lawyers' time" in this trial, he said.

As heated as the Leone-Strain encounter had been, it was nothing compared to the afternoon two weeks earlier when Merck accused Lanier of communicating with the jury as Strain questioned a witness. The witness was a Merck scientist named Briggs Morrison, who, like Reicin, had testified in previous Vioxx trials.

Lanier's alleged infraction occurred as Strain was questioning Morrison on the dominant theory of how Vioxx causes heart attacks. After answering Strain's questions, Morrison looked over at the plaintiffs' counsel table and casually addressed Lanier, who had pressed him on the same issue during the cross-examination..

"That's what I was talking to you [about] earlier," Morrison said to Lanier.

Lanier was incapable of letting a remark like that go unanswered, and during a brief pause in which Strain had his back turned to Morrison and the jury, Lanier waved a document in Morrison's direction, as if to refute him. (It was a research paper by Morrison that the two had also discussed earlier.)

"Our concern, Your Honor," Strain said, the next afternoon, "is we believe that [he] was not only communicating with Dr. Morrison, but due to Mr. Lanier's proximity to the jury he was effectively communicating with the jury."

"That's outrageous," said Seeger, who sat next to Lanier at the counsel table. "He did not address the jury." Morrison had initiated the interaction, Seeger said. "I mean, Morrison was looking at Mark the whole time. He would answer your question and give Mark a little grin..."

Strain said he hadn't *seen* Lanier interacting with the jury, but other Merck lawyers had. And, he said, Court TV's webcast had captured the incident.

"You saw this on the tape?" Higbee said.

"I saw it myself. I was sitting right in the middle," interjected Hope Freiwald.

"And you didn't raise it at the time?" Higbee asked.

"I was in the second row yesterday, Judge. I wasn't right behind counsel table," Freiwald replied. "I didn't want to jump up."

"They had no qualms about approaching the bench on the most mundane of matters," Lanier countered. "So I would think [for] something they considered this important they would have no qualms of bringing it to you."

According to the plaintiffs' lawyers, Lanier had not been trying to communicate with the jury, (and there was nothing on the Court TV webcast to suggest he had.) He *had* had an animated nonverbal exchange with a witness. It was a breach of courtroom protocol, but an unremarkable one in the freewheeling atmosphere of a trial in which one opposing counsel, Paul Strain, kept up a steady patter of objections and addendums to Lanier's questions, and the other, Diane Sullivan ignored the judge's rulings as and when it suited her.

Lanier made that point forcefully.

"It pales in comparison to the verbal communications being done by the Merck lawyers on a daily basis," he said, "when they call out exhibits and they tell you to change and to show something else. 'Show the rest of the sentence.' 'Show the other paragraph.' They are not only communicating to the witnesses verbally, they're communicating to the jury."

Seeger threw in another complaint. He directed it at Hope Freiwald.

"It doesn't even come close [to] what my client has had to go through sitting next to you," Seeger said to Freiwald, "because Mike Humeston hears you constantly make comments about Mark being a liar, and if you want I'll put him on the stand and let him tell the Court."

("It was a drumbeat of that crap," Mike Humeston said later. "I think they were trying to intimidate us.")

"It is true," Leone said, leaping in to the fray.

"That is just completely inappropriate and completely untrue," said Freiwald, outraged.

"You want to ask Mike?" Seeger challenged Freiwald. "He is in the courtroom."

But Merck's lawyers weren't about to back down.

"I don't want to get into a spitting contest with you over who does it more or doesn't, and I really take offense at Chris's comments," Freiwald said.

"And I'm offended that you do that around my client," Seeger said.

"She talks out loud enough for the client to hear," said Leone, jumping in again.

"Will you stop?" Freiwald said.

"You talk loud enough for the client to hear," Leone said, undaunted. He rarely spoke at sidebars, preferring to listen from a distance. Now he barked at Freiwald, "Why are you interrupting?"

"I talk to my colleagues, and if your shadow jurors or your clients are too close and hear that I certainly don't intend for that to happen," Freiwald said.

"You have a young kid who lost his father," said Seeger, referring to Kyle Hermans. "You may not respect that, but [he doesn't] need to hear you say, 'Mark Lanier is a liar.'"

"Will you stop?" Freiwald said.

"He got so upset one day in court that he had to leave the courtroom because of it," Lanier added.

"I take exception to that. I don't think it is true," Freiwald said.

"She does it on purpose," Leone said, darkly.

"His daddy is dead, Hope," Lanier said.

"Mark, stop it," Freiwald said.

It was three against one, but if anyone could take it, the redoubtable Hope Freiwald could. I had never seen her back away from a fight.

David Buchanan kept his cool (as he usually did), and steered the proceedings back to the devious game he thought Merck was playing—of laying down a record against Lanier, for use with appellate judges and with judges in future Vioxx cases.

"Your Honor, there is a process to deal with these issues in real time. They have lots of lawyers in the room. They have lots of lawyers watching things remotely. Even if they miss it in the minute they can come to the bench by sidebar," Buchanan said. "If there are real issues they're concerned about in this trial they should be raised while the issue can be dealt with at that moment, not the next day after somebody has watched tape, after somebody has read the transcript to, frankly, sully somebody's reputation before this court or another court."

Higbee's response, which came when court reconvened after a long weekend, disappointed the plaintiffs. She said she did not believe that the jury had understood Lanier's exchange with Morrison. Morrison may even have initiated the exchange, she acknowledged. But she reprimanded Lanier nonetheless.

"The interaction with the witness was not professional, not right, and shouldn't have happened," Higbee said. "It was a serious infraction."

"Both sides have pushed the limits in this trial as much as you can push. And I'm tired of it," Higbee said. "And I said it about a week ago, and I am saying it again. It has got to stop today." She declared she would sanction whoever broke the rules again.

"I don't want to treat you like children. You're not children," she said. "But let's try to keep the level up."

Lanier could hardly believe Higbee had said his behavior was no different from Sullivan's and Strain's.

"I treat her with respect," he said, indignantly.

He said Merck's lawyers were hoping to keep him from trying more Vioxx cases, and he was worried Higbee's reprimand would help that effort by tarnishing his image.

Most of all, I think, Lanier was hurt. He was used to being Higbee's favorite, and it threw him off kilter to fall out of her favor. He pouted for a day, sitting out sidebars, and hoped Higbee had noticed. By the next morning, he was on the mend.

I HAD HAD MY own experience of feeling maligned by Merck's lawyers that same week, when Hope Freiwald complained to the judge that I hadn't identified myself as a reporter before talking to a Merck witness. Icy weather kept me in Washington and away from the trial for a day or two after the alleged incident took place. Freiwald waited until I returned before lodging her complaint in a morning sidebar.

"I think it is inappropriate for somebody who has that kind of access with the plaintiffs and has been spending that kind of time with the plaintiffs to come up to our Merck witnesses just independently," Freiwald told Higbee.

She wanted Higbee to order the plaintiffs' lawyers to keep me away from Merck's witnesses. Sensibly, Higbee declined.

"I don't think I can order her not to contact witnesses," Higbee said, "and therefore I can't order somebody else to tell her not to approach witnesses."

In the trial's paranoid environment, perhaps it was inevitable that Freiwald would regard my overtures with suspicion. But unless her witness had lied to her, Freiwald knew I had made no pretense of being anything but a reporter. She also knew that my brief conversation with her witness had been innocuous. She said as much when we talked later. Yet she chose to present it in the worst possible light to the judge. It may have been business as usual for her, but it left a bad taste in my mouth. Lanier suggested I set the record straight. Next day, on the drive to court, I wrote out a statement describing my interaction with the witness. I watched from my seat in the courtroom gallery as Lanier stood at the judge's bench to read it at the morning's first sidebar.

"I spoke to Miss Prakash and she takes strong exception to Miss Freiwald's statement," Lanier read. "Miss Prakash takes her professional ethics as seriously as we're sure Miss Freiwald [takes hers] and wants the record to reflect that she conducted herself properly and professionally and fully disclosed her identity."

Leone, who had also been listening to the sidebar, strolled over to my seat a few minutes later. He handed me a piece of yellow, ruled paper. From its irregular edges, I surmised he had torn it hastily off a writing pad.

"Little Lies, Lies and Outrageous Lies: the Merck Story," by Snigdhah *(sic)* Prakash," Leone had written. "Prologue: One might think it odd, or perhaps strange to refer to lies three times in the title of one book about a Pharma company. But I experienced the lies of Merck first hand on February 15, 2007, in Atlantic City, New Jersey. It was another one of those Vioxx trials, one dead, one wounded. I had just walked into the courtroom…"

I burst out laughing when I read the note. Leone looked pleased and laughed too. When I looked up, Freiwald was glaring at me. She was right. We were laughing at her.

I had just had a little taste of what lawyers on both sides went through every day. This was war, and they were taking no prisoners.

I WASN'T THE PARTISAN that Freiwald had insinuated I was. But I did have a point of view on the questions before the jury, and it was not the one Freiwald was hired to espouse. My opinions were shaped by years of reporting on the Vioxx saga, and sadly, the evidence presented at trial only strengthened my misgivings about Merck's conduct. Well before I got to Atlantic City, and long after, I struggled to reconcile Merck's claim that its scientists had not known of Vioxx's risks until just before Merck withdrew the drug with all the documentary evidence that showed otherwise. I wondered why the company's scientists had gone to such lengths to massage the results of their clinical trials, if they were so sure Vioxx was benign. Why had they withheld information from the FDA and the scientific community? Why had they fretted about Vioxx's potential risks privately but never done a safety study to settle the matter directly? And most troubling of all, why had they not factored in the potential cost in human lives?

I asked many scientists with experience in weighing complex medical data how they made sense of these contradictions. Could Merck's scientists have truly believed that Vioxx was safe? Some, such as the well-known pharmacologist Alastair Wood, said, essentially, "yes, and no."

"We all rationalize what we see and what we don't," said Wood, who chaired the FDA committee on COX-2 painkillers after Vioxx's withdrawal. "Also, in group-think settings, it's awfully hard to be the person who says, 'Wait a minute!' Who wants to be that person?" he said.

Others, such as Catherine DeAngelis, editor-in-chief of the *Journal of the American Medical Association,* were more cynical.

"Marketing, marketing, marketing," DeAngelis said. "Anytime you mix up sales with science, you have problems. Who cares if a hundred patients a month die?"

As it happens, Merck's own history provided a very different model of how to handle uncertainties about a drug's risks. In 1980, Merck and the Japanese company Sankyo were racing to develop the first statin drug when Merck's scientists learned that Sankyo had halted testing of its drug candidate. It was rumored that Sankyo's drug had caused tumors. Merck's molecule was chemically related to Sankyo's, and though early studies had not pointed to safety problems, it was impossible to rule out that possibility. In his book *Medicine, Science and Merck,* Roy Vagelos, who was then head of Merck's research labs, described how and why he decided that Merck should halt tests of its statin candidate as well.

"Although our group of senior executives had talked through all the nuances, my personal decision about the trials had been instantaneous," Vagelos wrote. "We couldn't allow anyone to use our compound if there was the slightest possibility it might be carcinogenic. Even an unsubstantiated rumor was a sufficient basis for making that decision."

When we met in 2009, I asked Vagelos whether he would have decided differently if he could have been sure that Merck's drug posed only a small risk of cancer. I was thinking, of course, of what Ed Scolnick wrote to his scientists on first learning of the heart attacks in VIGOR: "The CV [cardiovascular] events are clearly there... It is a shame but it is a low incidence."

Vagelos's answer stayed with me: "There is no such thing as a little cancer when it's your own," he said.

He reminded me that at the time, Merck had no evidence the drug worked. "It was unacceptable to put *one* person at risk when we didn't know what the drug did," he said.

The decision to expose patients to risk always hinges on balancing benefit to risk, he said. If the benefits are great, such as with HIV drugs, "you can take some risks...and you tell the doctor and the patients, and they can decide if they want to stay alive and risk the side effects of our drugs," he said.

It took two years of safety testing, but Merck eventually resumed work on its compound, which went on to become the world's first statin, Mevacor. What if there hadn't been a happy ending and Merck had lost the statin race, I asked Vagelos, how would he have felt about his decision to suspend testing of a compound that turned out to be safe after all?

"I've never regretted a decision I've made as a doctor or as a scientist, because it's always based on the best information and I'm willing to live with the consequences," Vagelos told me. "In a sense, you're betting your own future when you're willing to live with something that isn't clear. I can't believe that you could win long-term if you fudge something. You'll always be found out."

SULLIVAN AND LANIER DID finally deliver their closing arguments, the day after Leone did his chicken imitation for Strain, and their presentations matched their courtroom personas. Sullivan's was cool and calculated. Her slides were crammed with hard-to-read text—from the Vioxx label, from FDA documents, and from testimony. She had an impressive collection of charts on oversized poster boards covered with yet more text. Maybe it was the poster boards—I found myself thinking of Soviet-era bureaucrats earnestly extolling the virtues of a state-controlled economy. As was his practice, Lanier had organized his closing around a motif, and used a bunch of unlikely images, from black dogs to jukeboxes, to make his points. The overall effect was part Madison Avenue and part Southern country—exuberant and entertaining.

The two lawyers had very different tasks to accomplish in their closing arguments. Over the previous five weeks, Lanier had laid out a densely textured tale of scientific manipulation, slick marketing, and inept government regulation to explain how Merck had been able to hide Vioxx's risks and make billions on the drug. This was his last chance to make sure the jury understood and remembered the high points of the story. Sullivan's task was narrower. The jury could find for Merck if she successfully created enough doubt about *any* of the building blocks of Lanier's argument—the questionable research, deceptive marketing or inept regulation of Vioxx.

The first question before the jury was whether Merck warned physicians about the "known and knowable risks" of cardiovascular events on Vioxx before Mike Humeston and Brian Hermans suffered their heart attacks. To get the jury to answer yes to that question, Lanier would have to persuade the jury that he had proven: first, that Vioxx was risky; second, that Merck knew, or should have known, of those risks; and third, that Merck had not warned Humeston's doctor before September 2001, and Hermans's doctor before September 2002, when the men had their heart attacks.

Merck's position was that Vioxx's alleged cardiovascular side effects did not exist, and that it had given doctors adequate warning of any and all risks at all times. But the jury could find for Merck even if it did not subscribe to every part of Merck's defense.

For example, the jury could find for Merck even if it agreed with the plaintiffs that Vioxx *did* cause heart attacks, if it was also persuaded that Vioxx's risks weren't known or knowable in 2001 and 2002. Equally, it could find for Merck even if it believed that Vioxx's risks were (real and) known or knowable in 2001 and 2002, and that Merck, while denying the risks, had nonetheless faithfully represented the underlying scientific evidence and given doctors enough information to make sound prescribing decisions. Sullivan took the smorgasbord approach in her closing statement and presented a variety of defenses, leaving jurors free to choose the ones they liked best. It was a well-rehearsed and methodical presentation.

She began with the first of the heart attacks at issue in the trial—that of Mike Humeston. It occurred in September 2001, after Merck had completed the VIGOR study but before it changed the Vioxx label to include the study's cardiovascular results. Defending against Humeston's claim, Sullivan repeated Merck's belief that there were more heart attacks on Vioxx than on naproxen in VIGOR because naproxen *prevented* heart attacks. (And Merck, therefore, had no reason to warn that Vioxx was risky.) Regardless, she said, Merck had told doctors about the higher heart-attack rate on Vioxx well before Humeston's heart attack by publishing the VIGOR study's results in a prominent medical journal in November 2000. She also cleverly suggested, but left unsaid, the argument that the judge had struck down many times during Lisa Rarick's testimony—that the Vioxx label did not include the VIGOR results when Mike Humeston had his heart attack because the FDA had failed to clear the changes Merck wanted to make. She said Merck had proposed an amended label that included the VIGOR results to the FDA as early as June 2000 but didn't receive a response until October 2001, one month after Humeston's heart attack.

"For Mr. Hermans, I submit to you, it is even clearer," Sullivan told the jury, because the label had been amended five months before Brian Hermans's heart attack, in September 2002.

Sullivan dismissed the plaintiffs' charge that the label, as amended by Merck, failed to warn that Vioxx could cause heart attacks. The plaintiffs had compared it unfavorably to the alternative proposed by the FDA because the precautionary information was less prominently displayed and caution was advised in a much smaller group of patients than in the FDA label. But the Warnings and Precautions sections were right next to each other, Sullivan said, and held up a copy of the label in her hands to show the jury. The FDA had since combined the two sections because doctors didn't find the distinction to be meaningful, she said.

The plaintiffs also faulted Merck for obscuring the implications of the VIGOR heart attacks with incomplete and misleading data from the Alzheimer's studies. Sullivan countered that the 2002 label reflected what was known at the time.

"That's what the FDA scientists and the outside advisory committee and the scientists at Merck believed was the state of the science in 2002," she said.

Sullivan emphasized Merck's efforts to disseminate the new prescribing information. She said every doctor in the country who had ever prescribed Vioxx got a copy of the new label, with the changes highlighted in yellow. Merck sent out millions of patient information sheets that doctors could give with prescriptions. She reminded the jury that Lisa Rarick had testified that in her 15 years at the FDA, she had never before seen a company go to such lengths to publicize changes to its drug label. It was one of 14 times Sullivan mentioned Rarick by name that morning.

"So, where was the heart attack information buried, ladies and gentlemen?" Sullivan asked. "It was buried in medical journals all over the country. It was buried in the neon-yellow highlights in the patient information package. It was buried in letters that went to every doctor in the country who had ever prescribed Vioxx."

And Sullivan reminded the jury that after the label was amended in 2002, the FDA had approved Vioxx for new uses two more times, in March and in August of 2004.

"They had the absolute authority to say, 'Well, Merck, we want you to say something different in your label. We want you to say that Vioxx increases the risk of heart attack or causes heart attacks.'

But they didn't do that because the evidence didn't support that," Sullivan said. Instead, the FDA stuck to the label it had approved in 2002, she said.

Sullivan closed on a theme she had struck many times during the trial—that Merck was a high-minded and ethical company. She asked jurors to judge Merck by its scientists—people like Alise Reicin and Briggs Morrison (the other Merck scientist who had testified during the trial). They were top researchers in the country, she said. Was it credible that they would do the kinds of things they were being accused of doing, Sullivan asked. Leone would say later that day that he thought it incredible Sullivan had called Morrison and Reicin "top researchers in the country."

"I kept thinking, 'which country?' " he said.

"I think she did a fine job defending Merck's position," Lanier said. He quickly added, "I don't really remember anything" of what she said.

AFTER A SHORT BREAK for the jury to stretch its legs, it was Lanier's turn. Standing about six feet away from the jury box, he began by unveiling the theme of his closing argument.

"Now, I don't know how many of y'all put puzzles together. My family, we've got some littler kids, they do puzzles," he said. "This is not a tough puzzle. This is a pretty simple puzzle. This is an age 3 to 6 puzzle." The jury laughed. As Lanier spoke, the cragged outlines of puzzle pieces floated over the words and symbols already on the screen behind him—"Be the Power," "naproxen defense," "Reicin," and "$$$".

You have to start by sorting through the pieces, Lanier said, and over the next hour, he walked the jury through them. There were the sales tools that Merck used to train its sales representatives to reassure doctors Vioxx was safe, such as Dodge Ball, Be the Power, and the

CV card. There were the exhibits he'd used to pillory Anstice, such as the 2001 FDA warning letter, which described Merck's marketing practices as false and misleading. There was the graph of financial projections, also from 2001, which contained Merck's estimate that it would lose a billion dollars in sales if the information about heart attacks was moved from the "bug-bite bucket" to the Warnings section of the Vioxx label.

There were snatches of emails showing that Merck's internal understanding of Vioxx's risks and VIGOR was quite different from what its scientists were telling the world: "it is mechanism-based" and "it is real" (in which Merck's top scientist explained that there were more heart attacks on Vioxx in VIGOR because of how Vioxx worked, and his belief that the heart attacks were, indeed, caused by Vioxx.)

Put those together with what Merck said about the FDA, Lanier said, and he showed more emails, also written by the top scientist, describing the FDA and its scientists: "they are bastards," "weak and dysfunctional." One slide depicted the relationship between Merck and the FDA as an arm-wrestling contest—the muscular, well-developed arm was tattooed "Merck," and the skinny one bore the letters "FDA."

"That is *not* a fair fight," Lanier declared.

The plaintiffs' primary claim—the one that could yield big money damages—arose from Merck's alleged "failure to warn" doctors about Vioxx's risks. They had a second claim, under New Jersey's Consumer Fraud Act, alleging Merck had misrepresented Vioxx's risks in its advertising. That claim covered Merck's disclosures to doctors and *patients*.

It was why Lanier had been allowed to play Vioxx commercials (which were, arguably, directed only at consumers, not doctors) during the trial. He played two during his closing argument, including the one with Olympic ice skater Dorothy Hamill. That was the commercial Merck marketers had estimated brought in $4 in prescriptions for every $1 spent on airtime.

"Would you listen for them to give even the most remote warning about a heart attack?" Lanier said, and answered the question himself after the commercial. "It is not there. It is not there, ladies and gentlemen. There's no warning.... That ad is running till they pull the drug."

The plaintiffs had an exceptionally distinguished group of academic physicians on their side, and Lanier summoned their testimony one last time. He reminded the jury that Harlan Krumholz had told them there was "no question" in his mind that "Vioxx was a significant contributing factor to heart attacks in people who are exposed to it." Cardiologist Eric Topol, who had been the first to warn of Vioxx's risks, had testified that multiple studies had confirmed Vioxx's risks. And Jerry Avorn of Harvard University had testified that Merck hadn't warned of Vioxx's risks in its old label or the amended one. The amended label advised caution in using Vioxx with people who had already had a heart attack. Lanier reminded the jury that Avorn had told them the data showed Vioxx was risky even for patients *without* a history of heart attacks.

"The warning [Merck] gave was totally inadequate. In fact it was an anti-warning. The label change in April [2002]—that doesn't make any difference. That makes it even worse," Lanier said. "They misled before. They misled after. The new label itself misleads. It is certainly not a warning. Never was. Never was. Never was. And that's a crying shame."

Lanier's final slide showed the completed puzzle. It was a human heart and it bore the caption "88,000 to 140,000 extra heart attacks in America." That was Vioxx's toll over five-and-a-half years, according to a scientist at the FDA.

It had been a polished performance, often hilarious and yet solemn. The death of Brian Hermans—"Kyle's daddy," as Lanier called him at one point—had hovered over the courtroom from the first moments of his closing, when Lanier had expressed the gratitude of the Humestons and of "Kyle and his family" to the jury.

"All things considered, I'm happy with it," Lanier said that afternoon.

It was time for the jury to deliberate. For the rest of us, it was time to wait.

Lanier had hoped for a verdict by day's end. His weekend bag was stashed in the trunk of his rental car, ready for the short drive from the courthouse to the private airfield where his plane was parked. Hegar had packed a small bag too. Leone hadn't. Either he liked to travel light, or more likely, he didn't want to tempt fate.

As it happened, the jury left for the day without reaching a verdict, and Lanier, Hegar, and Leone returned to the Borgata after all.

CHAPTER 12

The Verdict

Atlantic City, March 2, 2007

BOB LEONE SOUNDED ALMOST petulant when he walked into Lanier's hotel room the next morning.

"I have some concerns, Mark," he grumbled. "I don't like the way this jury is deliberating." He said it looked bad for the trial's punitive phase.

Leone was already looking ahead to the next phase of the trial, when Lanier and Seeger would present the specifics of the Hermans and Humeston cases and be required to prove that Vioxx had caused the two men's heart attacks. The big money in the cases would come only if the jury slapped punitive damages on Merck (as the Texas jury had done in Lanier's first Vioxx case with a punitive award of $229 million). But this jury was taking so long to come back for the plaintiffs in the first phase that Leone was worried it wasn't angry enough to punish Merck in the trial's next phase.

Lanier was sanguine. Earlier that morning, he had told me he was confident the jury would find in favor of the plaintiffs on the first two questions, which asked, first, if Merck had failed to warn doctors of Vioxx's cardiovascular risks; and second, if Merck had misrepresented Vioxx's risks in its advertising to both doctors and consumers. Lanier was less sure the jury would go his way on the third question, which asked if Merck had *knowingly* omitted, suppressed, or concealed information about Vioxx's risks from its marketing. But he had done everything he could, Lanier said, and the outcome was now out of his hands.

When Lanier and his team got to court, they learned that one of their favorite jurors, a chef and restaurant owner named Mohamed Bahgat, had called in sick. A burly, bearded man of Egyptian origin, Bahgat had smiled and nodded vigorously as he followed testimony and had taken copious notes. The plaintiffs were sure he was theirs.

"I want to get the vocal jurors, the passionate ones," Lanier had said early in the trial. Those were the ones whom the less aggressive jurors would follow, he said, and he'd pegged Bahgat as a jury leader.

Now, Bahgat was gone.

Higbee summoned the other jurors to the courtroom to tell them Bahgat was sick and on his way to the doctor's.

"So, at this point, we're going to have to proceed without him." With eight jurors left, she said, it would take seven votes to get a verdict. "If you have voted on any issues, you should vote again," Higbee said, and sent the jury to deliberate.

"It is a shame," the judge said after the jury left the courtroom. "His chicken cacciatore was wonderful."

Bahgat's restaurant had supplied the jury's lunch the day before. Apparently the judge had partaken of it too.

IT WAS MID-MORNING WHEN Higbee got word that Mohamed Bahgat wished to speak to her. She took his call, in the presence of lawyers from both sides and the court reporter.

"Hello, Mohamed?" Higbee said.

"Hi. How are you?" Bahgat said.

"The attorneys are in here with me," the judge told him.

"Okay," Bahgat said. "I hate to do this, Judge, but I think," he began. "But it is best, and I am very…" Bahgat seemed to be searching for the right words. He tried again. "It is important to know a lot of what happened in the jury room, and I…"

"Wait a second. Wait. Wait. Wait. Wait. Mohammed, wait. Don't speak yet," Higbee said, and paused for the court reporter to stop transcribing the conversation. She continued it off the record.

The judge went back on the record when she got off the phone.

"Tell the jurors to stop deliberations for a few minutes," she said.

"Is something wrong?" Chris Seeger asked.

There was. Bahgat was upset about how the jury was deliberating, Higbee said. "He didn't say how they were voting," she told the lawyers, "but he said, 'it is making me sick.'"

"So he is not physically sick?" Seeger asked. He was not.

Higbee said she had asked Bahgat to come in to the courthouse to tell her about his concerns. She said she wasn't sure she should have taken Bahgat off the jury, and implied she may have to put him back on.

"How does he join back in when they have deliberated without him?" Lanier demanded. "I don't know New Jersey law. In Texas, once they deliberate and talk about the case in his absence, he wouldn't be allowed to join back in."

"It has been an hour or so. They can start all over again," said Freiwald.

Strain backed her up. "The Court will instruct the jury," he said.

"Well, I'm not saying I'm putting him back in the jury room," said the judge. "It's a question of whether we interrogate him about his problems, whether we poll the whole jury about the problems, whether we just leave them to continue."

Higbee was in a delicate situation. It was her job to protect the integrity of the trial and bring it to a successful conclusion. If there had been any irregularity in the jury deliberations she needed to know. But if her investigation disrupted the deliberations and prevented the jury from reaching a verdict, she would have defeated her purpose. Higbee told the lawyers she wanted to consult with other judges, and they left her office while she did that. For the moment, the trial was on hold.

Mohamed Bahgat was at the courthouse within the hour. As lawyers from both sides listened, Bahgat told the judge the bailiff had tried to sway the jury. If what Bahgat said was true, it sounded like someone had used the bailiff, a veteran court employee, to get to the jury. Jury tampering is a crime, and if it was proven to have been committed, the first casualty would be the trial, and the next, the bailiff's job. Twenty minutes after he got there, Bahgat was escorted out of the conference room by Higbee's law clerk. His visit left Higbee no choice but to question the bailiff and the jury.

FOR THE FIVE MEN and three women who remained on the jury, this day had begun like any other during the trial. They parked their cars in the nearby lot, crossed the broad expanse of Atlantic Avenue, and walked to the courthouse a block away. They were supposed to be in the small first-floor room overlooking the courthouse lobby by 8 o'clock, and each morning, they looked for each other and hoped no one was late. The entire group had to wait until the straggler arrived before being escorted to the fourth floor, where the trial was being held. Bahgat was missing that morning, but they were taken upstairs anyway.

After seven weeks together, the jurors had become like family in their cozy room behind the courtroom. They ate together. Each person sat at the same place every day around the large oval table in the room. They brought food for each other. When the lawyers' squabbling kept them out of the courtroom, they whiled away the hours playing cards. (Texas Hold-'em was a favorite.) And they shared the daily battle with the courtroom's frigid temperatures—all except for the juror who had worked in the ShopRite stocking shelves at night, when the heat was turned down and the lights were off. He said he was used to the cold. At least they could thaw out during breaks—their room was warm, it had its own coffeemaker and a bathroom.

Mohamed Bahgat's customary seat at the foot of the table was empty that morning. But the remaining eight jurors were hard at work when the judge sent word they were to stop deliberating. An hour went by, maybe more. Then, one by one they were taken from the jury room, without explanation. As their numbers dwindled, the ones still in the jury room grew more anxious. None of the jurors who'd left had returned.

Juror number 10, James Paxon, was the last to be escorted out, down a long corridor to a small room. Inside sat the judge and perhaps two others. The judge was cheery. Paxon felt the effort she was making to put him at ease.

"Has anything been said to you that would affect your decision?" she asked Paxon.

Paxon looked her in the eye and answered without hesitation. "No way," he said.

She asked him again, and he gave the same answer.

The interview lasted only a minute and a half. When it ended, Paxon was led to another room. His fellow jurors were already there. They compared notes and pieced together the story. From the judge's questions, they inferred she believed there had been an attempt to influence the jury. Someone had told her that, but who? Their suspicions fell on their fellow juror, Mohamed Bahgat, who after attending the trial faithfully for seven weeks, was absent that day. The judge had told them Bahgat was sick, but one of the court staff told the jurors he had been at the courthouse. Plus, a new bailiff had been assigned to sit outside their door, which suggested their own bailiff was somehow caught up in the morning's events. The jurors liked their bailiff. She had shepherded them in and out of the courtroom and looked out for their needs for almost two months. They concluded that Bahgat's absence, the judge's concerns, and the disappearance of their regular bailiff were related. (Their conclusion was later confirmed by a member of the court staff.) They were stunned and angry.

"He was a jerk. He led us on," Paxon would say of his fellow juror later. "Oh, come to my restaurant. We'll all get together after the trial," Paxon remembered Bahgat as saying.

He said Bahgat gave every appearance of being at ease in the group.

"He never gave us any indication that he was under duress," Paxon said. "Next thing you know, he said the bailiff was trying to sway us."

"She never said beans as far as I'm concerned," he said.

Juror number 8, Rita Ann Downs, agreed. The bailiff did not interact with jurors individually but as a group, and it would have been impossible for her to influence a juror without the others knowing, Downs said. The bailiff had not tried to sway the jury, she said.

The judge had apparently reached the same conclusion after speaking to all the jurors. But Merck's lawyers disagreed. They said they had serious concerns that the bailiff *had* tainted the jury, and moved for a mistrial. Higbee denied the motion and ordered the jurors to return to their deliberations. Bahgat would not rejoin the jury.

"It threw us off," James Paxon said later of the episode. But the jurors were a smooth-moving group, he said, and they did as the judge asked.

There was one final act to the drama stirred up by Bahgat's allegations. Merck's lawyers filed an emergency appeal of Higbee's decision to go on with the trial. Later that afternoon, New Jersey's appellate court responded—it declined to hear Merck's motion. Higbee ordered Merck's motion and related record sealed. The allegations against the bailiff, the judge's interrogation of the jurors, and the resulting mistrial motion by Merck would not be part of the public record.

In the end, one question remained unanswered. *Why* had Bahgat implicated the bailiff in jury tampering?

Was he an "oddball," as the other members of the jury thought? Had he cracked under the pressure of the trial?

For Merck's lawyers, who said they believed Bahgat's story, the answer to the questions was obvious. Bahgat was an honest man who had described what he saw.

For the plaintiffs' lawyers, it wasn't so simple. They had known the bailiff for many years and over many trials, and respected her professionalism and integrity. They had considered Bahgat's allegations far-fetched from the start.

David Buchanan, usually so even-keeled, said after Bahgat's meeting with the judge, "We're just in disbelief."

When the judge found Bahgat's allegations to be baseless and Merck pushed for a mistrial, their disbelief deepened. There were murmurs that the whole affair had been somehow orchestrated.

"It's going to be a long, hard weekend. Lots of whiskey," Jeff Grand, one of Seeger's associates, declared. "Just when I thought I couldn't be more cynical..."

After seven weeks of pitched battle, there was more than a hint of paranoia in the air, especially after an earlier incident involving Lanier's rental SUV, which was mysteriously removed from outside the local Italian restaurant where he frequently ate. Lanier had returned to the car after dinner to find it blocked in by a police car. The police said it was a stolen car, and it was towed away, as he waited, along with Leone and Hegar, for one of his staff to give them a ride back to the hotel. Lanier said the police later told his private investigator that the car hadn't been stolen but was impounded as a "practical joke" by two off-duty officers. Being from out of town, Lanier said, he thought it wiser not to press charges. But he couldn't shake the feeling that the incident was in some way connected to the trial, and he changed some of his routines.

He had stopped going out for a run in the evenings unless he was accompanied by the ex-Marines in his employ—one ran ahead of him and the other behind. When he went to the Italian restaurant, he traveled in a two-car convoy. The first car had Leone and Hegar, with Lanier at the wheel. The second car contained the ex-Marines, Juan Wilson and Jesse Alcorta. They kept watch over his car while Lanier had dinner and followed him back to the hotel when he was done.

"They're very, very loyal," Lanier said. "They would probably take a bullet for me. I would for them without a second thought."

WITH THE JURY BACK at work, several of the lawyers returned to the conference room to argue motions related to the trial's next phase. For everyone else, the verdict watch began in earnest. Lanier's team assembled in the courtroom. Leone sat in his usual spot in the courtroom well, only now his chair was half-turned towards the Humestons, who sat in the gallery's first row. Lanier's associates were present, as were Wilson and Alcorta.

"They should have Bingo or something like that when you're waiting for a jury verdict," Leone said to the Humestons.

It was a quintessential Leone comment, slightly absurd but presented matter-of-factly. Would Leone really have played Bingo if he could have at that moment, I wondered. I concluded that he may well have. He had waited for so many juries in his life that this ritual was old hat, and in his experience, it usually ended well.

"You know, I think I have now spent about five months of my life in this room," Leone said to the Humestons with a smile. "So have you."

After a while, Leone remarked to Wilson, "*Now* it's taking too long."

Lanier burst into the court room a few moments later. It was 3 P.M.

"You guys, we have a verdict," Lanier said. "We got to get our clients." He had been with the judge when the bailiff brought word to her.

"Remember what we said," Lanier told Kyle Hermans when he arrived. "Act composed. You don't want to brag. You have to go to Phase II with the same jury."

Hermans nodded obediently. He was alone at the trial except for his girlfriend. His mother had been there earlier in the week, but she was on her way back to Wisconsin, hoping to beat a winter storm. The Humestons had brought in reinforcements. Next to the couple sat their daughter and her husband.

The judge got to the point right away when the jury got to the courtroom.

"Will the foreperson please stand?" Higbee said. "Has the jury reached a verdict?"

"Yes, we have, Your Honor," said Else Vetter, juror number 1 and the jury's foreperson.

She was an older woman, perhaps in her 70s, who had left her native Norway in 1950 and lived in the United States ever since. Vetter delivered the verdict, starting with the Humestons, in a clear voice that sounded surprisingly young.

On question 1, whether Merck had failed to warn that Vioxx carried cardiovascular risks before Mike Humeston's heart attack in September 2001, the jury had voted, 8–0, yes, for the plaintiffs.

On question 2, whether Merck misrepresented Vioxx's cardio-vascular risks in its marketing to consumers and physicians, the jury voted yes, 8–0.

On question 3, whether Merck had intentionally suppressed, concealed, or omitted Vioxx's cardiovascular risks from its marketing to consumers and physicians, the jury's answer again was yes, 8–0. It was a clean sweep.

Mike Humeston's claim against Merck had cleared the first hurdle and would continue into the trial's second phase.

The judge asked next how the jury had voted on the Hermanses' claims. Brian Hermans's heart attack occurred a year after Humeston's, in September 2002, and the jury questions were identical to the Humestons' questions, except for the date.

Vetter read the jury's verdict on question 1. "No," she said, with a slight but unmistakable emphasis.

By a vote of 7–1, the jury had found that Merck's amended Vioxx label provided adequate warning of Vioxx's cardiovascular risks to Hermans's doctor. Kyle Hermans would not be returning in Phase II to ask for compensation for the loss of his father. Nor could he hope for the big-money punitive damages that Leone had been worrying about earlier in the day.

I noticed Jeff Grand of Seeger Weiss, who sat to my immediate right, mouthing the words, "It's not fair."

On questions 2 and 3, the jury found *for* the plaintiffs, 8–0. Merck's marketing had continued to misrepresent and intentionally suppress Vioxx's cardiovascular risks even after the amended label provided adequate warning of those risks. If Lanier could show Vioxx had caused his father's heart attack, Hermans would be entitled to recover the few hundred dollars that his father had paid for the Vioxx prescriptions, and Merck would pay Lanier's trial expenses.

"Because of the way you've voted, there will be a Phase II to the case," Higbee told the jury, and she asked them to report on Monday.

The jury stood up and filed out. Lanier kept his gaze fixed on the jury until they were gone. Only then did he turn around to face his young client.

At 20, Kyle Hermans was a little younger than Lanier's own son. Lanier held out his hand to Hermans. They shook hands. Lanier's face was flushed and for once, he was at a loss for words. Hermans looked like he was going to cry.

"I'm sorry," Lanier said to Hermans softly. "This is bad."

A minute later he disappeared into the plaintiffs' back room, with Hegar close behind. Seeger and Buchanan followed. The Humestons were left to comfort Hermans, and they hugged him, looking stricken at the difference in their fortunes. Seeger came back a few minutes later to say the lawyers had some ideas and all was not lost.

"We won't sleep," he promised Hermans and returned to the back.

I noticed Leone was still in his seat and wandered over to talk to him. I was sorry they'd lost, I told him. Leone didn't want my sympathy.

"Why are you sorry? This isn't so bad," he said, barely looking up from his BlackBerry. "I don't think the jury understands what they did."

In the courtroom next door, Freiwald was giving a mini press conference. Merck was "very heartened" by the jury's verdict in the Hermans case, Freiwald told reporters. Someone asked why she thought Merck had prevailed.

"We were able to show the jury, as we've shown other juries, that the questions of science were uncertain and remain uncertain," she said.

Freiwald was underestimating the jury, as Leone may have a few minutes earlier.

LANIER REGROUPED AND RETURNED to the courtroom a half hour later, and sat quietly at the counsel table, writing on a pad of paper. The other plaintiffs' lawyers sat in their seats, staring into their Black-Berries or talking in low tones.

"How's Mark doing?" I asked Hegar, who was standing near her usual first-row gallery seat.

"Fine," she replied. "He's working on something right now."

It was hard to believe that Lanier was "fine." It felt like a wake in there. But Hegar was doing what she did so well. She was projecting cool control.

Lanier broke the silence a few minutes later, calling out from where he sat. When was Brian Hermans's last Vioxx prescription phoned into the pharmacy, he asked? If it was before April 2002, it "will be a big help," Lanier said. April 2002 was when Merck amended the Vioxx label. If Hermans's last prescription had been called in before that, his doctor could not have seen the warning on the new label before writing that prescription. Two rows behind me, I heard Lanier's associates Meredith Gursky and Maura Kolb typing furiously into their laptops as they searched for a copy of the prescription. They found it. It was dated May 2002. Was it called in by a nurse, Lanier asked? It was not, he was told. The prescription bore the doctor's signature.

The courtroom filled up before long. A passel of Merck's lawyers arrived. I noticed some of the judge's senior staff in the gallery's back row. They had attended few of the trial's sessions thus far—it was clear this would be no ordinary hearing.

"Counsel have anything they want to say about the verdict before we move on?" the judge said when she was seated.

"Your Honor, Mark Lanier, on behalf of the Hermans," Lanier said, standing up. "It is my request that you enter a judgment, notwithstanding the verdict on question number 1, to allow the Hermans case to continue into Phase II."

Lanier was asking the judge to set aside the ground rules that the two sides had fought over so bitterly before the trial. Under those rules, the jury was to determine if Merck was liable, in principle, for the injuries of all the plaintiffs in Phase I of the trial, and resolve each plaintiff's specific claim against Merck in separate mini-trials in Phase II. Higbee had proposed the bifurcated structure as a way to try several cases simultaneously. The plaintiffs' lawyers had agreed, believing that the arrangement would increase pressure on Merck to settle, while Merck had strenuously opposed it. Now, Lanier was arguing that that the trial structure he earlier supported had prevented the jury from reaching "a valid verdict."

"Think about it this way. What does the jury not get to know because of the phasing and the way this is questioned?" Lanier said to the judge, and he reeled off a list.

The jury did not get to know that Brian Hermans had started taking the drug in February 2001, which was more than a year before Merck changed the label in April 2002, Lanier said. Nor did they know that Hermans's last visit to the prescribing doctor, in November 2001, had also been before the label change. The only specific fact the jury had about Hermans's Vioxx use, Lanier said, was the date of his heart attack—September 15, 2002—five months after Merck issued the amended Vioxx label that had provided an "adequate warning" of Vioxx's risks, according to the jury.

The jury also did not get to know that the amended label *could not* have alerted Hermans's doctor to the risks of prescribing Vioxx to Hermans, Lanier continued. That's because the label advised caution in prescribing Vioxx only to patients who had already had heart attacks or angina (instead of the far larger group the FDA had recommended—those *at risk* of heart disease). Brian Hermans had never had a heart attack before the one that killed him in September 2002.

Lanier proposed Higbee remedy the situation by allowing Hermans's claim to piggy-back on the jury's finding that Merck had not provided adequate warning of Vioxx's risks before *Humeston's* heart attack, on September 18, 2001. Brian Hermans had been taking Vioxx for six months by then, and Lanier suggested that the jury be asked if Merck's failure to provide an adequate warning as of September 18, 2001, had been a substantial factor in Brian Hermans's heart attack and death.

"Let's see whether or not they believe that it was, once they hear the factors surrounding Brian Hermans's death," he said.

Merck's lawyers responded with scorn. From the start, they said, they had opposed the notion that Merck's liability could be determined without specific information on each plaintiff.

"We objected at every turn," Paul Strain began. "We asked for the right to present additional information about Mr. Hermans and the other defendants *(sic)* during Phase I. Over and over again the plaintiff objected to our being able to do so, and over and over again the Court sustained and said, 'no, this is not a part of Phase I.' That was over our objection with the support and request of the plaintiffs."

Freiwald rose from her seat in the gallery and, walking past her colleagues at the counsel table, stood near the bench to address the judge.

"This is what [the plaintiffs] lobbied for, what they asked for, what they said was an appropriate and wonderful process for the Court," she said. "To suggest that there was something wrong with the way Your Honor posed these questions when they have…in fact, advocated that Your Honor do exactly [as] you did, is incredible."

What the plaintiffs were asking for, Freiwald said, was a "do-over."

Higbee said she understood Merck's arguments—that the plaintiffs had fought for the phased structure and got what they asked for, "and that they were in favor of it and you weren't."

"I fully understand that, and I really have to grapple with that," she said.

But she said she had to grapple with a second issue as well. Were the plaintiffs' lawyers right in arguing that Brian Hermans's case should be allowed to proceed to Phase II?

"Is there a logic to their argument that they should still be able to argue proximate cause?" Higbee asked, because the jury was given the "wrong date" when it considered Merck's potential liability for Hermans's heart attack (that is, only the date of the heart attack).

"You can't find that the system of trying cases in a vacuum doesn't work when the plaintiffs lose, and does work when the plaintiffs win," Freiwald responded.

"Counsel, you know, Hope, Miss Freiwald," Higbee said, "That's so far off from the mark."

Freiwald tried again a few minutes later.

"Your Honor, the point I was trying to make saying you can't say it is unfair if the plaintiffs lose, and it is fair if the defense loses is this. What I hear the plaintiffs arguing is that they were prejudiced by not being able to put the warning information in the context of Mr. Hermans," she said. "They said this could be decided in a vacuum, and that's how they wanted it decided, and they lobbied at every turn. Mr. Lanier did get to argue that the label didn't go to all users. He argued very vigorously that the label was limited, that it wasn't as broad a warning as it should have been. It appears from the verdict that the jury disagreed."

The trial had been an "experiment," Lanier countered.

"We're sitting here now looking at a result that I think was pretty unexpected in some regards," he said. "You have already got the jury. You have already got the opportunity. Let's let them hear this question and see if I can pull it in under the Humeston verdict sheet, because I reckon I can."

The judge brought the hearing to an end when the lawyers began repeating themselves.

"If any of you have any additional briefing on the subject you want to submit, send it to my home email," she said. "I cannot decide this tonight."

Lanier's case was still alive, albeit on life support.

Outside the courtroom, wire service and newspaper reporters surrounded Lanier and walked with him to the long, slightly grungy waiting area near the elevators. Why had he lost, they wanted to know. Lanier, who usually had to be pried away from reporters, stayed only for a few minutes.

"I have to speak to my client. He's my priority," Lanier said.

He walked to the other end of the waiting area, where Kyle Hermans sat on one of the brightly colored plastic chairs bolted to the floor. Hermans's face quivered with unshed tears. They spoke for a minute, then hugged in the way men do. The hug lasted a millisecond and ended in a slap on the back.

As Lanier stepped into the elevator to leave, I shook hands with him. I told him I looked forward to seeing him the following week.

"I may not be here much next week," Lanier said, with a rueful half-smile.

Then the elevator doors closed, and he was gone.

I walked to the judge's chambers to ask her secretary about calling a taxi to the train station. Higbee was in her office, and I could hear her talking about the day's events with her two law clerks. When she heard my voice, she asked one of them to shut the door. The bailiff, the secretary, and another member of the judge's staff, who were standing nearby, looked shell-shocked.

I don't remember if I ever got a cab, or if I dragged my suitcase over several long blocks to the train station. I remember doing that once, but it may have been a different time. On the train back to Washington, I wrote everything I remembered of the preceding hours. It was 8 or 9 when my train pulled into Union Station. My husband was waiting outside. We drove home and I went directly to bed. I wanted to be done with the day.

I had started this journey as an observer. As Lanier might have said, I had no dog in the fight. I was still an observer with nothing tangible to gain or lose. But after seven weeks of watching the plaintiffs' lawyers pour themselves into the fight, I wanted them to win. And I wasn't prepared for how bad I would feel if they lost.

David Egilman called the next morning to report that Lanier was taking the loss very hard. I told Egilman I didn't understand how the jury could have found for Merck. I had no historical perspective, Egilman said dismissively. The asbestos cases were lost many times before they were won. He predicted Higbee would grant Lanier's motion to continue into Phase II.

"I've thought about it all night," Higbee told the lawyers in a conference call later that morning. "I've decided to deny Mr. Lanier's motion."

Lanier would not be returning to Atlantic City.

SEEGER'S CREW DID RETURN, along with Mike and Mary Humeston, but the zip had gone out of the plaintiffs' camp.

"This feels like shit," Seeger's associate Moshe Horn said in court that Tuesday morning, when the trial resumed. It felt wrong to be there without Lanier, Leone, Hegar, and the rest, he said.

Horn and his collegues were still in shock. I smelled fear as well. Seeger had lost the Humestons' case once, and they were afraid he would lose it again. Seeger had asked Lanier to come back and help him try it, but Lanier turned him down. Leone returned for a day to prepare Mike Humeston to take the stand.

"I was wiped out and tired," Lanier would say later.

Seeger attributed darker motives. He thought Lanier *wanted* him to lose. And though Lanier denied it, the speed with which he was pulling up stakes could make you see why Seeger felt as he did. The ex-Marines, Juan Wilson and Jesse Alcorta, had already dismantled the war room and were loading up their trucks with computers and office equipment for the drive back to Houston. Seeger's lawyers still gathered in the war room. But without the infrastructure of a functioning office, and, perhaps even more important, without Lanier's steady hand at the helm, their meetings felt a little aimless.

Organization was not Seeger's strong suit. Earlier in the trial, I had attended a meeting in his suite. It was cluttered with dirty dishes, empty wine bottles, and clothes.

"It's the anti-Lanier room," Seeger had said, by way of explanation. "I smoke. I eat fattening food. I drink wine."

Lanier, who had had tried about a hundred cases in his career, had run the trial like a military campaign—with a battle plan and a well-honed system to execute it. This was Seeger's third trial and he was muddling through. The Humestons took note of Seeger's performance and looked pained.

"His documents are out of order. He's up there tap-dancing," Mike Humeston said. "We're going to lose this case like we did the first one."

Seeger had three associates in the courtroom and they, too, were worried. There was an unending stream of notes and looks and stage whispers between Moshe Horn, Larry Nassif, and Jeff Grand, as Seeger examined his witnesses.

Diane Sullivan and Paul Strain attacked Humeston's claim on multiple fronts. They said workplace stress was the real cause of his heart attack. They questioned if Humeston had even been taking Vioxx when he had the heart attack. In any case, they said, Humeston hadn't suffered much cardiac damage. Mike Humeston rebutted those arguments with his demeanor as much as his testimony, coming across as a stoic and an honest, honorable man.

"You don't have a statistic in the courtroom. You have real people," Seeger said, striking a stirring note in his closing argument.

Projected on the screen behind him was FDA scientist David Graham's estimate of Vioxx's toll in the United States, alone—over 100,000 heart attacks over five-and-a-half years.

"I keep thinking how good that close was. That was so good," Mike Humeston said afterwards, as they waited for the verdict in the plaintiffs' back room.

"It *was* good. So good it made me cry," Mary Humeston said.

Seeger was half-listening, with his eyes closed and his legs up on a chair. He hadn't slept much the night before. He said he kept waking up with "Diane's voice" in his head. It was like a "nightmare," he said.

The Humestons didn't lose. They won big. The jury awarded them compensatory and punitive damages of $47.5 million.

"I knew Chris wasn't going to have any trouble winning the case. The feast was cooked," Lanier said afterwards. "Someone just needed to stand around and collect the check."

Seeger responded tartly that Lanier had tried the easiest part of the Humeston case.

"The most difficult and the single biggest reason two-thirds of the cases lost was case-specific (proving the client had a heart attack caused by Vioxx as opposed to high cholesterol, high blood pressure, etc.)....Lanier was nowhere to be found for that phase or for the punitive damage phase, which we won, without him, resoundingly," Seeger wrote in an email.

And while they had not agreed beforehand that Lanier would stay to help, Seeger said, "that's what anyone else would have done. He picked up everything (computers, his staff, documents, etc.) and left."

The fragile peace between the two men was over.

LANIER AND I SPOKE a few times in the months after the trial ended. But we didn't discuss the verdict in Kyle Herman's case until December 2008, when I visited him at his office in Houston. It had been almost two years since the jury spurned him in Atlantic City, but Lanier was still reluctant to concede he'd lost Hermans's case.

"Well, we won his fraud case," Lanier said, "and I knew I would be able to leverage that to get something done." He said he had secured a "seven-figure award" for the Hermans family. "So we took care of that family."

Besides, he added, "It was the Merck lawyer who ran out of the room crying, not me."

Lanier was talking about Diane Sullivan. I hadn't seen her running out, but then I was watching Lanier's reactions to the verdict, not hers. I reminded Lanier gently that I had been in the courtroom with him and his team, and it had looked and felt like they'd lost.

"It was a blow," he finally acknowledged. "I often tell my clients, 'I try real hard to be a gracious winner. But I'm a very poor loser.' The jury comes back and you lose, I'm not real good at standing around and pretending nothing happened. You know you pour your heart and your soul into this...I mean, you were there, blood, sweat, and tears...I'm absolutely convinced I'm right, or I'm not up there doing it, it's not a show for me...So you want the justice system to work."

Lanier *had* poured his heart into the case. It was what I liked best about him. But his desire to win ran much deeper than just wanting the justice system to work. And that afternoon, as he sat amid the spare, mid-century leather, chrome and glass furnishings of his Houston office, Lanier reflected on how deep that trait runs in him.

"I've always been fiercely competitive," he said. "I can remember in fifth grade, we were having a school race. It was track and field day in Vollmer Elementary, in Rochester, NY, and my class had entered me in the distance run, and I didn't think I was going to win."

He said he "begged and pleaded" not to go to school.

"It never occurred to me," Lanier said, "that there should be peace in doing your best regardless of whether you win. If I was going to do it, I wanted to win."

"So, what happened?" I asked him.

"I went to school. I ran and didn't win. It crushed me, but I learned a valuable lesson," he said. It was the effort that mattered.

I pressed him, "Really? You learned that?"

"That's what I tell myself," Lanier said, with a laugh.

He didn't appear to believe it either.

Why *had* the jury found against him on the crucial first question in the Hermans case, I asked. Lanier said, as Leone had right after the verdict, that the jury hadn't understood their answer would effectively knock him and Hermans out of the game. They had wanted to throw a bone to Merck's lawyers, he said.

I tended to agree with Lanier that the jury had not realized the implications of their verdict, though I was skeptical that they were driven by the desire to "throw a bone" to Sullivan and Strain or, indeed, that they would have voted differently had they understood the consequences of their vote. At least one juror, James Paxon, juror number 10, suggested the jury knew exactly what it was doing when it voted 7–1 against Hermans on that first question.

"We sent [Lanier] away like a wet dog. We squashed him with our verdict," he told me.

Paxon compared the Vioxx label to insurance policies. Most people don't know what's in them. They never read them. That's how it was with the Vioxx label when it was changed, Paxon said. Its risks were "buried." But he said, the warning "was there in black and white. You couldn't get around it."

Leone had once told me, "Nothing in the world is too complicated to break down and explain to a jury." You can explain brain surgery, heart surgery, anything, he said. "The key is to break 'em down in a simple enough way," he said. "Then if the truth is on your side, you will win."

Lanier had managed to teach the jury so many complicated lessons. He had taught them how Vioxx is believed to cause heart attacks and why Merck's Vioxx studies were not to be trusted. He had persuaded them that Merck had knowingly misled doctors and patients with its marketing.

So why had he failed to make clear that the amended label did not so much warn that Vioxx could be risky, as reassure that it was not?

Egilman thought one reason was that Lanier hadn't explained the import of the Alzheimer's studies sufficiently to the jury. Those studies, which compared Vioxx to placebo, found ample evidence that Vioxx was risky, but their findings were blatantly misrepresented in the amended label. It was the "best piece of data" for the plaintiffs' lawyers, Egilman said, but they didn't embrace it.

"Mark never learned [the] Alzheimer's [information]," Egilman said. Lanier thought he had enough to win without it, Egilman said, and he blamed himself fot not pushing Lanier harder.

Harlan Krumholz, the Yale cardiologist who testified for the plaintiffs, agreed that the Alzheimer's studies were "the critical piece" of the Vioxx puzzle. Merck conducted a rigorous analysis of the cardiovascular events and deaths in two Alzheimer's studies, in April 2001. (One of the studies was complete, and the other was ongoing.) The analysis showed the risk to be three times higher on Vioxx than placebo, and it corroborated VIGOR's findings of Vioxx's risks.

"That evidence is at the center of everything. [Merck scientists] looked at it, they reviewed it, they understood it," he said, and they were "under an obligation to relay it to the FDA."

But Merck didn't tell the FDA, he said, not then, and not in the fall of 2001, when the FDA questioned the propriety of continuing to expose Alzheimer's patients to Vioxx's cardiovascular risks in the ongoing study. By then Merck scientists had amassed yet more definitive evidence of those risks. They also knew that Vioxx did not prevent or retard the course of Alzheimer's, but *hastened* it. Still, they insisted to the FDA that the study was safe.

"Why isn't this Tuskegee?" Krumholz demanded, comparing Merck's decision to keep testing Vioxx on Alzheimer's patients after it was known that Vioxx was hurting them to the infamous syphilis studies in Tuskegee, Alabama. (The U.S. Public Health Service withheld penicillin from the study's African American subjects long after penicillin had been proven to treat syphilis.)

Krumholz said he pushed Lanier to explain Merck's conduct more fully to the jury—I had seen him do that—but Lanier thought it was too complicated to explain to the jury.

"Mark can be the most charming person, but he can also be stubborn," Krumholz said. "It's his show. And everyone is telling me he wins all the time. I gave him a lot of advice, [but] I always felt sheepish."

Lanier bristled when he heard his experts believed he had erred in not presenting the Alzheimer's story more fully to the jury, and, further, that he had not understood its significance to his case.

"I learned [Alzheimer's] well enough," he said, to "figure out that there is *no* way a jury could understand it."

"If I have success as a trial lawyer, it's because I know there are limits [to what] the jury will be able to understand," Lanier continued. He repeated the precept he lived by at trials—a jury cannot take in more than two or three difficult concepts a day.

With the trial clock ticking, he said, he could not have done what Egilman and Krumholz thought he should have.

Besides, he said, "That's not what I lost on. Alzheimer's doesn't make a difference to the label."

The way to win the Hermans case, Lanier still thought, would have been to show that the amended label didn't apply to Brian Hermans because the old label was in force for most of the time he took it. That was the argument Lanier had made to Higbee *after* the verdict. So why hadn't he made it before? The answer, it seemed, was that neither Lanier nor anyone else on his team had anticipated that Merck's changes to its label could be a hurdle to winning, because they hadn't been an obstacle in Lanier's previous cases. It was an odd omission. As a general matter, it's harder to win product liability cases when the drug label contains any kind of warning, even an inadequate one.

"The juror is thinking, 'There's something there. It's blessed by the FDA,'" Jerry Kristal, the veteran plaintiffs' lawyer at Weitz & Luxenberg, explained, and "it becomes a little less sexy for jurors" to find against the company.

Seeger said he counseled Lanier many times to tell the jury that Brian Hermans had started taking Vioxx long before Merck added the VIGOR information to the Vioxx label. (Lanier could not recall Seeger giving him that advice. But Mike Humeston volunteered that he had overheard Seeger saying that to Lanier on the day of the closing argument.)

Seeger said Lanier always responded, "'I'm not fussing that. The label was bad in the beginning. It was bad in the end.' He just felt the case was going well."

"Mark is a broad-brush guy. He's not a particularly detail-oriented guy," said Kristal, who had tried a Vioxx case in Higbee's court with Lanier in 2006. "Sometimes it's good. Sometimes it's not. The reality is you have to do both."

Hindsight is, as they say, 20-20.

After pouring almost $2 million into the trial, and despite his fluid command of the Vioxx story and the courtroom, Lanier had fallen short of the mark in the Hermans case. Remarkably, the loss come as a shock to Lanier and those around him. Vioxx was a "monster" case, as Lanier said, but he had made trying it look so easy that even he may have lost sight of how hard it really was.

Lanier *had* won Mike Humeston's claim. Given the odds against winning, it was a spectacular outcome.

"Mark's a tremendous lawyer…a great lawyer. Even great lawyers who think they're winning can lose," Kristal said.

He laughed, as he added, "There's no such thing as a slam-dunk case."

EPILOGUE

IN THE END, MERCK did settle. The deal came just months after Mark Lanier and Chris Seeger tried the Hermans and Humeston cases in Atlantic City. Unbeknownst to Lanier, Judge Eldon E. Fallon, who was overseeing the federal multidistrict litigation (MDL), and Judge Carol Higbee, had summoned a small group of plaintiffs and defense lawyers to New Orleans before the Hermans-Humeston trial opened. Lanier's co-counsel was at the meeting, which occurred in December 2006.

"We were basically told that the judges collectively believed that the parties should start thinking about settlement," Seeger said.

A little over two years had elapsed since the withdrawal of Vioxx at that point, and the statute of limitations on personal injury claims, which varies by state, had run out almost everywhere. Merck could be assured that settlement talks would not cause the plaintiffs' ranks to swell. And so, the negotiations the plaintiffs had long sought began. As co-chair of the multidistrict litigation plaintiffs' steering committee, Seeger was in the thick of them even during the trial. Lanier had been Merck's chief nemesis in the courtroom, but he played no part.

"That was a party I wasn't invited to. I wasn't part of the MDL," Lanier said afterwards, adding, "I'm proud of the fact that Merck would not do the deal unless I signed on."

The deal, between a small committee of plaintiffs' lawyers and Merck, was announced on November 9, 2007. Under its terms, Merck would pay $4.85 billion to resolve some 50,000 Vioxx claims. Both sides claimed it as a victory. So did the deal's unofficial brokers, Judges Fallon, Higbee, and Victoria Chaney (of California). The three judges, along with Judge Randy Wilson of Texas, had jurisdiction over almost 95% of the Vioxx cases in the country.

"The system worked," said Higbee, who joined Fallon at the bench in his New Orleans courtroom for the announcement of the deal. "[It] is a fair resolution of this huge dispute. It's good for the plaintiffs. It's good for Merck."

The system had worked—for Merck and its lawyers, for the plaintiffs' lawyers, even for the judges. It enabled Merck to put a costly legal battle behind it. It allowed the mass tort judges to clear their dockets of thousands of cases. And it cleared the way for plaintiffs' lawyers to reap the returns on their investments in the Vioxx cases.

But many observers wondered if "the system" had done as well by the injured plaintiffs. Certainly, the deal offered plaintiffs a surer avenue for compensation than a court trial would have. And, unlike many other mass settlements, the money from the Vioxx deal was disbursed expeditiously, and according to a set of transparent rules. Payouts to heart-attack plaintiffs ranged, on average, from just under $100,000 to $375,000.

But legal fees and expenses, and payments to health insurers for medical care associated with the heart attacks, took a big bite. A plaintiff's $100,000 award, for example, could be reduced to half as much after those deductions.

There were also questions about the fairness of the formula used to calculate the payouts. The formula took into account the seriousness of the heart attack, the consistency and length of Vioxx use, and the extent to which factors other than Vioxx, such as high cholesterol, obesity, or smoking, made the plaintiff prone to the heart attack.

"Where's the logic or do they just think we're stupid?" wrote one plaintiff on the *Wall Street Journal*'s website, after her late husband's award was reduced because of a prior history of heart attacks. "Common sense tells you that anyone with his history of heart problems should never have been put on a drug that could cause heart attacks."

Indeed, according to the plaintiffs' own experts, there was no scientific rationale to award a Vioxx plaintiff with high cholesterol or high blood pressure less than someone without those risk factors.

"It's totally the wrong thing to do. It's crazy," said Harlan Krumholz, the Yale University professor who testified in the Hermans and Humeston trial.

Vioxx was most dangerous for those who were already at risk of heart attack, due to high cholesterol, diabetes, etc, Krumholz explained, because, as Merck's studies showed, Vioxx doubled the risk of heart attack, and doubling a high risk is clearly worse than doubling a low risk.

Andy Birchfield, co-lead counsel (with Seeger) of the MDL plaintiffs' steering committee, dismissed the criticism. "That's a very academic argument that really does not play out in the real world," Birchfield said. Merck had won case after case at trial by arguing that those other risk factors, not Vioxx, had accounted for the plaintiff's heart attack, he said.

Legal ethicists had their own concerns about the settlement. They worried about provisions which obligated lawyers who wanted *any* of their clients to participate to recommend the deal to *all* their clients, and further, to withdraw from representing clients who rejected their advice and declined to settle.

"This is a black-and-white issue... Clients are not inventory that lawyers can just shed when they become inconvenient. It's forbidden," New York University law professor Stephen Gillers told the *Los Angeles Times*.

The Connecticut Bar Association called the provisions unethical. The plaintiffs' lawyers had inserted them into the agreement to guarantee the "global peace," or end to all legal hostilities, that Merck so craved ("They wanted global peace or they wanted continued war," Seeger said). The provisions worked, and all but 50 of the 58,000 potentially eligible plaintiffs accepted the settlement.

As Fordham University's Howard Erichson wrote in the *Kansas Law Review,* "Any client who declined the settlement faced the prospect of losing a lawyer and finding that every other lawyer handling Vioxx claims was unavailable. Unsurprisingly, the overwhelming majority of eligible claimants decided to participate in the settlement."

Erichson called the settlement a "power grab" by the plaintiffs' lawyers and by Judge Eldon Fallon, who "unofficially" approved the settlement.

"We were confident that lawyers could evaluate the settlement and recommend it to all their claimants," Birchfield said, in defense.

For Birchfield personally, the Vioxx litigation had been an odyssey. He had filed his first Vioxx case just after Carlene Lewis and Shelly Sanford filed theirs, in 2001. He tried multiple cases before Fallon, and he had worked on the nitty-gritty of the settlement for the better part of a year.

"It was so important for the sake of the clients to persevere. It was the right thing to do, and we got a good result and I am thankful," Birchfield said. "By any reasonable reckoning, it is a phenomenal success."

Reasonable people might disagree. But there could be no dispute on another score—the deal's biggest winner was Merck. The company would put almost all the Vioxx personal injury cases behind it for just under $5 billion. Add in legal expenses of roughly $2 billion, and the total tab of $7 billion was still a far cry from the $25-50 billion in liability that investment analysts had predicted right after the Vioxx withdrawal. Merck's aggressive anti-settlement stance and deep pockets had paid off handsomely.

The plaintiffs' lawyers also fared well, receiving 32% of their clients' settlement awards or more than $1.55 billion in fees plus "reasonable" expenses. Not bad for a day's work.

The biggest losers, arguably, were the millions of Americans who rely on medicines, whether occasionally—to bring down a child's high fever, perhaps—or everyday—to manage chronic conditions, such as high cholesterol, high blood pressure, or high blood sugar. Each and every one of them uses medicines in the belief that the medicines will help, not hurt. The Vioxx lawsuits gave Americans, and the world, unprecedented insight into how the research and marketing machines of a drug company can be used to hide the potential risks of medicines. Many observers had hoped the lawsuits would serve to deter such behavior in the future. In the end, though, the Vioxx mass tort may have sent quite the opposite message to companies: "Dig in and fight. Merck weathered the storm, and so will you." The odds were very long, but the Vioxx mass tort *had* presented a unique opening to promote more honest medical research and drug marketing by giving plaintiffs' lawyers, juries and judges the chance to show that such practices do not pay. That opportunity was largely lost. It would take Merck less than a year to earn back the $4.85 billion it had agreed to pay Vioxx plaintiffs.

ONE POT OF SETTLEMENT money was still being contested as this book went to press. It was the $315 million (6.5% of the settlement fund) earmarked to compensate plaintiffs' lawyers who had done work deemed to have benefited *all* plaintiffs. (Every lawyer contributed a share of his or her fees from the settlement towards the "common benefit" fund.) Some 100 plaintiffs' lawyers submitted records of more than half a million hours of "common benefit" work (in depositions, trials, and settlement negotiations) to a nine-member plaintiffs' fee committee. (Lanier was among the nine. "If you sign on, we'll put you on the fee committee and we'll treat you fairly," he said he was promised.)

The process took three years, but in January 2011 the fee committee made its recommendations public. It had voted to award the largest slices of the pie—$40.9 million each—to the co-lead counsels of the MDL plaintiffs' steering committee, Chris Seeger and Andy Birchfield. (Seeger's firm—in particular, his partner, David Buchanan—had played a pivotal role in the New Jersey mass tort as well, and Birchfield and his partners had tried three cases in federal court.) Both Birchfield and Seeger were members of the fee committee, as was New Orleans lawyer Russ M. Herman. The committee voted to award Herman $32.5 million for his work as plaintiffs' liaison to MDL judge Eldon E. Fallon. Mark Lanier's award was $27.0 million.

"Did I fare as well as I should have? Absolutely not," Lanier said. "I was not even number 3."

Though Lanier did not choose to contest his award, it was clear that his exchanges with the fee committee had been contentious. I caught glimpses of the acrimony when I spoke with him or Seeger about their respective roles in the litigation.

Shortly before the fee committee's awards were made public, for example, in an email exchange about the trial in Atlantic City, Seeger asserted his lawyers had "spoon-fed the [Vioxx] case" to Lanier from the start.

"That's funny," Lanier responded. "I am not sure what Chris is thinking...Maybe Chris meant they spoon fed him."

Though Seeger backed down when Lanier confronted him ("I was wrong and shouldn't have said that," he wrote me), that comment was consistent with opinions Seeger had expressed in many other conversations—that Lanier's trial skills and victories had contributed less to the overall Vioxx litigation than Lanier claimed they had.

"Mark is an outstanding trial lawyer, [but] his client lost," Seeger had written in the earlier email, referring to the outcome of young Kyle Hermans' claim in 2007. "Moreover, his client also lost in Cona/McDarby [the two cases Lanier tried in Higbee's court in 2006]. I just point that out so as not to have a revisionist account of what actually happened. Lanier lost."

Lanier *had* lost one case in each of those trials, but he'd also won a case each time. I wondered how much larger the settlement might have been had other plaintiffs' lawyers presented such a consistent threat to Merck in court.

Several lawyers were contesting their awards, and Judge Fallon would have to resolve those disputes before the money could be distributed.

MIKE AND MARY HUMESTON had left Atlantic City in March 2007 feeling vindicated by the jury's $47.5 million award, and hopeful that the worst of their legal battles was behind them. Like other cases Merck had lost at trial and was appealing, the Humestons' claim was not part of the settlement agreement. But shortly after Merck and the MDL plaintiffs' lawyers announced their deal, the Humestons' lawyers called to say Merck had offered to settle with them as well, for a sum of $1 million, free of taxes, and urged them to accept the offer. The Humestons said they were shocked and angry that their lawyers were advising them to settle for a tiny fraction of the jury award. They began to worry that their case was "being sacrificed at the altar of the settlement," Mike Humeston said.

"We were offended," he said. Our victory in court had strengthened the bargaining position of all the plaintiffs, he said, and "we realized we were fighting our counsel the same way we were fighting Merck."

Mike and Mary Humeston rejected the settlement offer, but a year later, in November 2008, their lawyers reopened the subject. The

Supreme Court was set to decide a case that turned on whether plaintiffs had the right to bring personal injury lawsuits in state courts, if the
products that caused the injuries had previously been approved by the
Food and Drug Administration. The Humestons' lawyers, like many
plaintiffs' lawyers, were bracing for the Court to rule in favor of the
drug industry and bar such lawsuits. If the Court did that, they said,
the Humestons' jury verdict would likely be nullified. Once again, they
urged the Humestons to settle.

In March 2009, the Supreme Court ruled that meeting FDA regulatory standards could not shield companies from product liability suits
in state courts. But by then, the Humestons had already settled for a
sum they agreed to keep confidential.

"We ended up settling for something that was not reasonable. We
were not happy," Mary Humeston said. "It's really regrettable."

"I'm just a guy out here in Idaho. Mare and I were just pawns,"
Humeston said. "We're suckers to them."

"I stand behind every decision and advice I gave them including
the decision to settle their case," Seeger countered. "I have nothing
but great respect and good feelings for Mike and Mare Humeston...I
think the passage of time sometimes clouds decisions made and fact[s]
as they existed in 2007 and 2008.

Mike Humeston laughed bitterly when I read Seeger's statement
to him.

"When you seek justice at this level, it becomes less about the plaintiff and more about the money. Somebody won big....but it wasn't us,"
he said. "We've never had a kind word from Buchanan or anyone [since
we settled]. They're done with us."

ENDNOTES

MANY OF THE DOCUMENTS introduced into evidence at the Vioxx trials, including those cited in this book, can be found online at the Drug Industry Document Archive, University of California San Francisco, dida.library.ucsf.edu/.

CHAPTER I

page

9   *Mass Torts*

Richard A. Nagareda, *Mass Torts in a World of Settlement.* Chicago: University of Chicago Press, 2007.

10   *COX-2 drugs and coronary heart disease statistics*

David J Graham, David Campen, Rita Hui, Michele Spence, Craig Cheetham, Gerald Levy, Stanford Shoor and Wayne A Ray, "Risk of acute myocardial infarction and sudden cardiac death in patients treated with cyclo-oxygenase 2 selective and non-selective non-steroidal anti-inflammatory drugs: nested case-control study." *Lancet* 365 (2005): 475–81.

10–11   *Mass torts and multi-district litigation*

John C. Coffee, Jr., "Class Wars: The Dilemma of the Mass Tort Class Action." *Columbia Law Review* 95 (1995): 1343–1465.

Delaventura v. Columbia Acorn Trust, 417 F. Supp. 2d 147 (D. Mass. 2006)

Eldon E. Fallon, Jeremy T. Grabil and Robert Pitard Wynne, "Bellwether Trials in Multidistrict Litigation." *Tulane Law Review* 82 (2008): 2323–2367.

Deborah R. Hensler, "Revisiting the Monster: New Myths and Realities of Class Action and Other Large Scale Litigation." *Duke Journal of Comparative & International Law* 11 (2001): 179–213.

Deborah R. Hensler and Mark A. Peterson, "Understanding Mass Personal Injury Litigation: A Socio-Legal Analysis." *Brooklyn Law Review* 59 (1993): 961–1063.

Deborah R. Hensler, "Asbestos Litigation in the United States: Triumph and Failure of the Civil Justice System." *Connecticut Insurance Law Journal* 12 (2005): 255–280.

Alexandra D. Lahav, "Bellwether Trials." *The George Washington Law Review* 76 (2008): 576–638.

Richard A. Nagareda, *Mass Torts in a World of Settlement.* Chicago: University of Chicago Press, 2007.

Charles Silver and Geoffrey P. Miller, "The Quasi-Class Action Method of Managing Multi-District Litigations: Problems and a Proposal." *Vanderbilt Law Review* 63 (2010): 107–177.

13   *Big Tobacco and dinner at Antoine's*

Peter Pringle, *Cornered: Big Tobacco at the Bar of Justice.* New York: Henry Holt & Company, 1998, 3–8.

21   *Choice of trial venues*

Barbara Martinez, "Vioxx Plaintiffs Want to Fight on New Front." *Wall Street Journal,* October 24, 2005, B1.

34   *New England Journal of Medicine editorials*

Gregory D. Curfman, Stephen Morrissey and Jeffrey M. Drazen, "Expression of concern: Bombardier et al., "Comparison of Upper Gastrointestinal Toxicity of Rofecoxib and Naproxen in Patients with Rheumatoid Arthritis."" *New England Journal of Medicine* 353 (2005): 2813–2814.

Claire Bombardier, Loren Laine, Ruben Burgos-Vargas, Barry Davis, Richard Day, Marcos Bosi Ferraz, Christopher J. Hawkey, Marc C. Hochberg, Tore K. Kvien, Thomas J. Schnitzer and Arthur Weaver, "Response to Expression of Concern Regarding VIGOR Study." *New England Journal of Medicine* 354 (2006): 1196–1198.

Alise Reicin and Deborah Shapiro, "Response to Expression of Concern Regarding VIGOR Study." *New England Journal of Medicine* 354 (2006): 1198–1199.

Gregory D. Curfman, Stephen Morrissey and Jeffrey M. Drazen, "Expression of Concern Reaffirmed." *New England Journal of Medicine* 354 (2006): 1193.

CHAPTER 3

70, 73   *Merck's scientific advisors recommend additional safety testing*

Programmatic Review—Vioxx Program, May 1, 1998. Bates Numbers MRK-AEI0002734-2746, dida.library.ucsf.edu/tid/oxx15r10.

73   *Merck responds to the call for additional safety testing*

Alan S. Nies, handwritten memo to Barry J. Gertz et al, September 29, 1998. Bates Numbers MRK-ABK0311068, dida.library.ucsf.edu/tid/oxx08s10.

79   *VIGOR results*

Claire Bombardier, Loren Laine, Alise Reicin, Deborah Shapiro, Ruben Burgos-Vargas, Barry Davis, Richard Day, Marcos Bosi Ferraz, Christopher J. Hawkey, Marc C. Hochberg, Tore K. Kvien and Thomas J. Schnitzer, "Comparison of upper gastrointestinal toxicity of rofecoxib and naproxen in patients with rheumatoid arthritis." *New England Journal of Medicine* 343 (2000): 1520–28.

Gregory Curfman testimony

Deposition Testimony of Gregory D. Curfman, In Re. Vioxx Litigation in the U.S. District Court, Eastern District of Louisiana, Boston, January 24, 2006.

82   *APPROVe study*

Robert S. Bresalier, Robert S. Sandler, Hui Quan, James A. Bolognese, Bettina Oxenius, Kevin Horgan, Christopher Lines, Robert Riddell, Dion Morton, Angel Lanas, Marvin A. Konstam and John A. Baron, "Cardiovascular Events Associated with Rofecoxib in a Colorectal Adenoma Chemoprevention Trial." *New England Journal of Medicine* 352 (2005): 1092–1102.

CHAPTER 4

89   *Vioxx label*

Bates Number MRKLBL0000031-0034, dida.library.ucsf.edu/tid/oxx01d10.

90   *Second Vioxx label*

Vioxx label, April 1, 2002. Bates Number MRKLBL0000067-0070, dida.library.ucsf.edu/tid/oxx01m10.

96   *FDA approves Vioxx for pediatric use*

Brian E. Harvey, Letter to Michele R. Flicker, August 19, 2004. Bates Number MRK-AAF0017139-7168, dida.library.ucsf.edu/tid/oxx16p10.

97   *British Medical Journal article*

Harlan M. Krumholz, Joseph S. Ross, Amos H. Presler and David S. Egilman, "What have we learnt from Vioxx?" *British Medical Journal* 334 (2007): 120–123.

99   *James Fries correspondence*

James F. Fries, Letter to Raymond Gilmartin, January 9, 2001. Bates Number MRKGUE0058858-8861, dida.library.ucsf.edu/tid/oxx00n10.

CHAPTER 5

117   *2001 FDA warning letter*

Thomas W. Abrams, Letter to Raymond V. Gilmartin, September 17, 2001. Bates Number MRK-AAF0007777-7785, dida.library.ucsf.edu/tid/oxx10i10.

Merck responds to the FDA

David W. Anstice, Letter to Thomas W. Abrams, October 1, 2001. Bates Number MRKAAF0007803-7853, dida.library.ucsf.edu/tid/oxx01k10.

122   *MVX*

David W. Anstice, "MVX for Vioxx: DWA to USHH Sales Force." September 13, 2001. Bates Number MRKABW0000062-0063, dida.library.ucsf.edu/tid/oxx03h10.

David W. Anstice, "MVX for Vioxx: DWA to USHH Sales Force," October 1, 2001. Bates Number MRK-AAR0036887, dida.library.ucsf. edu/tid/oxx17r10.)

123 *"Be the Power" video*

"Be the Power." MRK-AAR00732358.

126 *Cardiovascular card*

"CV Card." Bates Number MRK-HER0000001-0006, dida.library. ucsf.edu/tid/oxx10r10.

"Bulletin for Vioxx: New Resource: Cardiovascular Card," 28 April, 2000. Bates Number MRK-AAR0007383-7388, dida.library.ucsf.edu/ tid/oxx10q10.

128 *Response to New York Times article*

"Bulletin for Vioxx: New Resource: Revised Response to New York Times Article," May 24, 2001. Bates Number MRK-H.3STM001207-1211, dida.library.ucsf.edu/tid/ckb00a10.

Congressional investigation of Vioxx marketing

Committee on Government Reform, Minority Office, U.S. House of Representatives, "Merck documents show aggressive marketing of Vioxx after studies indicated risk," May 5, 2005.

131 *Bloomberg news story*

David Voreacos, "Merck Lawyer Admonished for Arguments in Vioxx Trial," *Bloomberg News,* January 23, 2007. www.bloomberg.com/apps/ news?pid=newsarchive&sid=a8wZRTnGZ3eM&refer=home.

CHAPTER 6

136–139 *Merck corporate strategy*

Perry L. Fagan and Michael Beer, *Merck & Co, Inc.: Corporate, Strategy, Organization and Culture. (A)* Boston: Harvard Business School Publishing, 1999.

Merck under Raymond Gilmartin

Clark Gilbert and Ratna G. Sarkar, *Merck Conflict and Change.* Boston: Harvard Business School Publishing, 2005.

138   *Pfizer's marketing strategy*

Greg Critser, *Generation Rx: How Prescription Drugs Are Altering American Lives, Minds and Bodies*. New York: Houghton Mifflin, 2005.

139   *David Anstice remarks on the Vioxx launch*

David W. Anstice, "Vioxx Launch Meeting/Remarks of Mr. David Anstice," 24 May, 1999. Bates Number MRK-ABI0004488-4499, dida.library.ucsf.edu/tid/oxx05s10.

141   *Vioxx vs. Celebrex market share*

2001 Profit Plan for Vioxx, September 1, 2000. Bates Number MRK-AAO0000073-0145, dida.library.ucsf.edu/tid/oxx05b10.

Vioxx operating plan

U.S. Long Range Operating Plan—Franchise: Analgesic & Anti-Inflammatory Products: Vioxx, Etorocoxib, July 2001, July 12, 2001. Bates Number MRK-ABI0008659-8683, dida.library.ucsf.edu/tid/oxx10j10.

143   *FDA Vioxx label draft*

FDA Label Draft, October 15, 2001. Bates Number MRK-AAX0008561-8581, dida.library.ucsf.edu/tid/oxx11x10.

143–145 *Merck internal communication on FDA label draft*

Edward M. Scolnick, Email to David W. Anstice, October 15, 2001. Bates Number MRK-ABW0004799, dida.library.ucsf.edu/tid/oxx10w10.

David Anstice, Email to Edward M. Scolnick, October 15, 2001. Bates Number MRK-ABW0004799, dida.library.ucsf.edu/tid/oxx10w10.

Edward M. Scolnick, Email to David W. Anstice, October 15, 2001. Bates Number MRK-ABW0004799, dida.library.ucsf.edu/tid/oxx10w10.

145–146 *Revised Vioxx label*

Vioxx label, April 1, 2002. Bates Number MRKLBL0000067-0070, dida.library.ucsf.edu/tid/oxx01m10.

148   *Roy Vagelos and Merck*

P. Roy Vagelos and Louis Galambos, *The Moral Corporation: Merck Experiences*. Cambridge: Cambridge University Press, 2006.

151   *VIGOR cardiovascular results*

Edward M. Scolnick, Email to Deborah R. Shapiro, Alise S. Reicin, and Alan S. Nies, March 9, 2000. Bates Number MRK-ABH0016219, dida.library.ucsf.edu/tid/0xx00c10.

Vioxx ads

Index of Advertisements. Bates Number MRK-AMI000000-1097.

CHAPTER 7

157   *JAMA paper on cardiovascular safety of COX-2 selective inhibitors*

Debabrata Mukherjee, Steven E. Nissen and Eric J. Topol, "Risk of cardiovascular events associated with selective COX-2 inhibitors." *Journal of the American Medical Association* 286 (2001): 954–59.

Wall Street Journal on the JAMA paper

Thomas M. Burton and Gardiner Harris, "Note of Caution: Study Raises Specter Of Cardiovascular Risk For Hot Arthritis Pills—Vioxx and Celebrex Marketers Dispute the Research, Sought to Downplay It—A Spurned Appeal to JAMA," *The Wall Street Journal,* August 22, 2001, A1.

158   *Cardiovascular safety and Vioxx sales reports*

David W. Anstice, Email Raymond V. Gilmartin, September 11, 2001. Bates Number MRK-ABI0006489.

Return on investment of Vioxx ads

Thomas R. Cannell, Email to Jo C. Jerman, Paul R. Fonteyne et al, November 10, 2001. Bates Number MRK-ABW0003613-3614, dida. library.ucsf.edu/tid/0xx06d10.

163   *1998 FDA warning letter to Merck*

Minnie Baylor-Henry, FDA Warning Letter to David W. Anstice, June 16, 1998. Bates Number MRK-HER0000592-0596, dida.library. ucsf.edu/tid/0xx12q10.

164   *2001 FDA warning letter to Merck*

Laura Governale, Letter to Thomas M. Casola, January 2, 2002. Bates Number MRKACI0013248, dida.library.ucsf.edu/tid/0xx01t10.

167   *New Vioxx label*

Highlighted April 2002 label. Bates Number MRK-HER0000610-0631, dida.library.ucsf.edu/tid/oxx13b10.

Bulletin for VIOXX: Action Required: Label Change for Vioxx GI Outcomes Research Study and RA Indication, April 11, 2002. Bates Number MRK-AAR0021509-1555, dida.library.ucsf.edu/tid/oxx17d10.

Jo Jerman, MVX for VIOXX (to) USHH Field Sales Force, "Label Change," April 11, 2002. Bates Number MRKADW0086174-6177, dida.library.ucsf.edu/tid/oxx02010.

Adam H. Schechter, Email to Peter S. Kim, Edward M. Scolnick, et al, April 12, 2002. Bates Number MRKAAC0100438, dida.library.ucsf.edu/tid/oxx02m10.

168   *1998 FDA warning letter to Merck*

Minnie Baylor-Henry, FDA Warning Letter to David W. Anstice, June 16, 1998. Bates Number MRK-HER0000592-0596, dida.library.ucsf.edu/tid/oxx12q10.

169   *Merck's marketing response to VIGOR results*

Top Ten Obstacle Handlers Memo. Bates Number MRK-AAR0007638-7699, dida.library.ucsf.edu/tid/oxx17u10.

Press release: Vioxx® significantly reduced the risk of serious gastro-intestinal side effects by more than half compared to naproxen in a new study, May 24, 2000. Bates Number MRK-PRL0000124-0127, dida.library.ucsf.edu/tid/oxx13x10.

Bulletin for Vioxx New Obstacle Response, May 1, 2000. Bates Number MRK-AAR0068150-8151, dida.library.ucsf.edu/tid/oxx15z10.

Bulletin for Vioxx VIGOR and CLASS study, May 25, 2000. Bates Number MRK-AAR0007367-7373, dida.library.ucsf.edu/tid/oxx17t10.

170   *Merck response to public comments*

Susan Baumgartner, Email to Leonardo Mendez, April 29, 1999. Bates Number MRK-AFI0174637, dida.library.ucsf.edu/tid/oxx12g10.

Leonardo Mendez, Email to Susan Baumgartner, April 29, 1999. Bates Number MRK-AFI0174637, dida.library.ucsf.edu/tid/oxx12g10.

List of Doctors—Neutralize/Discredit. Bates Number MRKAFI 0201416-1442, dida.library.ucsf.edu/tid/oxxo2y10.

170–172 *Merck and Gurkipal Singh*

Snigdha Prakash, "Documents Suggest Merck Tried to Censor Vioxx Critics, Part 1" *NPR,* June 9, 2005. www.npr.org/templates/story/story.php?storyId=4696609.

Snigdha Prakash, "Did Merck Try to Censor Vioxx Critics? Part 2," *NPR,* June 9, 2005. www.npr.org/templates/story/story.php?storyId=4696711&ps=rs.

Louis M. Sherwood, Email to David Abrahamson, Linda D. Grissom, et al, November 7, 2000. Bates Number MRK-ABO0002864-2865, dida.library.ucsf.edu/tid/oxx13k10.

James F. Fries, Letter to Raymond Gilmartin, January 9, 2001. Bates Number MRKGUE0058858-8861, dida.library.ucsf.edu/tid/oxxoon10.

Louis M. Sherwood, Memo to David W. Anstice, January 23, 2001. Bates Number MRK-ABI0007170-7173, dida.library.ucsf.edu/tid/oxxo5w10.

173 *Edward M. Scolnick and the James Fries letter*

Edward M. Scolnick, Email to Eve Slater, January 28, 2001. Bates Number MRK-ABD0002346-2347, dida.library.ucsf.edu/tid/oxx12i10.

CHAPTER 8

177 *Dr. Alise Reicin background*

Barry J. Gertz, Performance Review Form for Alise S. Reicin, March 6, 2002. Bates Number MRK-AAD0800032.

181 *Dr. Alise Reicin background (continued)*

Alise S. Reicin, Year-End Employee Input Form, From 01/01/01 to 12/31/01. Bates Number MRK-AAD0800030.

Barry J. Gertz, 2003 Personal Performance Grid for Alise S. Reicin, February 2, 2004. Bates Number MRK-AAD0800057.

186 *Merck internal discussion on "efforts to defuse the CV risk issue for Vioxx" on Wall Street*

Margie McGlynn, Email to Alise S. Reicin, May 25, 2000. Bates Number MRK-NJ0320174-0177, dida.library.ucsf.edu/tid/oxx11h10.

188   *Merck internal discussion of VIGOR results*

Edward M. Scolnick, Email to Deborah R. Shapiro, Alise S. Reicin, and Alan S. Nies, March 9, 2000. Bates Number MRK-ABH0016219, dida.library.ucsf.edu/tid/oxx00c10.

188   *VIGOR press release*

Merck Informs Investigators of Preliminary Results of Gastrointestinal Outcomes Study with Vioxx, March 27, 2000. Bates Number MRKPRL0000114-0115, dida.library.ucsf.edu/tid/oxx04b10.

191   *NSAID cardiovascular effects*

Alise S. Reicin, Email to Edward M. Scolnick and Alan S. Nies, March 13, 2000. Bates Number MRK-ABH0017386, dida.library.ucsf.edu/tid/oxx05r10.

192   *Merck internal discussion of VIGOR (continued)*

David W. Blois, Email to Eve Slater, Alan S. Nies et al, March 14, 2000. Bates Number MRK-ABH0017398-7399, dida.library.ucsf.edu/tid/oxx14c10.

193   *Merck internal discussion of VIGOR (continued)*

Laurence J. Hirsch, Email to Alise S. Reicin and Brian F. Daniels, March 19, 2000. Bates number MRK-ABD0001756-1762, dida.library.ucsf.edu/tid/oxx13v10.

Standby Statement—Vioxx and Cardiovascular Events in VIGOR (Version 2). Bates Number MRK-NJ0362784-2790, dida.library.ucsf.edu/tid/oxx12c10.

197–199 *Merck internal discussion of VIGOR and the need for more cardiovascular safety testing of Vioxx*

Edward M. Scolnick, Email to Alise S. Reicin, April 12, 2000. Bates Number MRK-AAR00732358, dida.library.ucsf.edu/tid/oxx05k10.

Key Marketing Messages HHPAC, May 17, 2000. Bates Number MRK-ABI0001899-1915, dida.library.ucsf.edu/tid/oxx12x10.

Wendy L. Dixon, Email to Steven A. Nichtberger, September 17, 2001. Bates Number MRK-ABW0005623-5625, dida.library.ucsf.edu/tid/oxx06f10.

Steven A. Nichtberger, Email to Wendy L. Dixon, September 17, 2001. Bates Number MRK-ABW0005623-5625, dida.library.ucsf.edu/tid/oxxo6f10.

Edward M. Scolnick, Email to Douglas A. Greene, Peter S. Kim et al, November 21, 2001. Bates Number MRKNJ0326037-2638, dida.library.ucsf.edu/tid/oxxo4s10.

CHAPTER 9

206–208 Alzheimer's studies

Deborah R. Shapiro, Email to Eliav Barr, Alise S. Reicin, et al, January 29, 2001. Bates number MRK-ACF0004015-4017.

Merck Research Laboratories, FDA Advisory Committee Background Information, Presented to Arthritis Advisory Committee, February 8, 2001, 87–89. Bates Number MRK-AFX0019350-9352, dida.library.ucsf.edu/tid/oxx16t10.

Alan S. Nies, email to George W. Williams and David W. Blois, March 22, 2001, dida.library.ucsf.edu/tid/oxxo4k10

Joshua Chen, Memorandum to Raymond P. Bain, MK-0966 Combined Mortality Analysis, Protocol 091 + Protocol 078, April 8, 2001. Bates Number MRK-AAX0000752-0776.

Rofecoxib Safety Update Report, July 6, 2001. Bates Number MRK-01420145856-5961.

Bruce M. Psaty and Richard A. Kronmal, "Reporting Mortality Findings in Trials of Rofecoxib for Alzheimer Disease or Cognitive Impairment: A Case Study Based on Documents From Rofecoxib Litigation." *Journal of American Medical Association* 299 (2008): 1813–1817.

Joseph S. Ross, David Madigan, Kevin P. Hill, David S. Egilman, Yongfei Wang and Harlan M. Krumholz, "Pooled Analysis of Rofecoxib Placebo-Controlled Clinical Trial Data: Lessons for Postmarket Pharmaceutical Safety Surveillance." *Archives of Internal Medicine* 169 (2009): 1976–1984

211   Raymond Bain memo on the Alzheimer's study

Raymond P. Bain, Summary of Mortality Analyses: Vioxx Alzheimer's Disease, October 31, 2001.

For more on the correspondence on the Alzheimer's data

Barbara Gould, Fax to Robert Silverman, December 5, 2001. Bates Number MRK-ACK0089944.

Robert Silverman, Letter to Jonca Bull, Response to FDA Request for Information, December 18, 2001. Bates Number MRK-01420167265-7267.

215   *FDA memo on COX-2 hypothesis*

John K. Jenkins and Paul J. Seligman, Memorandum to NDA files 20-998, 21-156, 21-341, 21-042, April 6, 2005. Bates Number MRK-HER0001121-1139, dida.library.ucsf.edu/tid/0xx16r10.

CHAPTER 10

219   *2005 advisory committee on COX-2s*

Transcript of the Joint Meeting of the Arthritis Advisory Committee and the Drug Safety and Risk Management Advisory Committee, Volume 3, February 18, 2005. www.fda.gov/ohrms/dockets/ac/05/transcripts/2005-4090T3.htm

220   *FDA memo on COX-2s*

John K. Jenkins and Paul J. Seligman, Memorandum to NDA files 20-998, 21-156, 21-341, 21-042, April 6, 2005. Bates Number MRK-HER0001121-1139, dida.library.ucsf.edu/tid/0xx16r10.

223   *Labeling recommendations of lead FDA scientist*

Meeting Minutes, Regulatory Briefing Meeting, Safety Profile of COX-2 Drugs, September 21, 2001. Bates Number FDACDER 002157-2160.

Maria Lourdes Villaba, Medical Officer Review, Vioxx, NDA 21-042 (capsules) and NDA 21-052 (oral solution) S 007 (Gastrointestinal Safety), March 30, 2001. Bates Number MRKEXH13470001-0007, dida.library.ucsf.edu/tid/0xx04d10.

224   *Legal background for FDA label approval*

Wyeth v. Levine, No. 06-1249, March 4, 2009. supreme.justia.com/us/555/06-1249/opinion.html.

230   *List of Vioxx studies submitted to the FDA*

Plaintiff's Exhibit 471, Bates Number MRK-AAD0492743-2812.

233   *FDA drug safety review process*

Committee on the Assessment of the US Drug Safety System Board on Population Health and Public Health Practice, Institute of Medicine, "The Future of Drug Safety: Promoting and Protecting the Health of the Public," September 26, 2006. www.nap.edu/catalog/11750.html

The Future of Drug Safety—FDA's Response to the Institute of Medicine's 2006 Report, January 1, 2007. Bates Number MRK-HER0001077-1114, dida.library.ucsf.edu/tid/oxx15h10.

233   *Edward M. Scolnick on the FDA*

Edward M. Scolnick, Email to Douglas A. Greene, Alise S. Reicin et al, February 8, 2001. Bates Number MRK-ACT0018064, dida.library.ucsf.edu/tid/oxx11p10.

Edward M. Scolnick, Email to Douglas A. Greene, David W. Blois and Bonnie J. Goldmann, April 6, 2001. Bates Number MRKACR0009151-9152, dida.library.ucsf.edu/tid/oxx03l10.

CHAPTER II

244   *Previous Merck response to potential safety risks of other drugs*

P. Roy Vagelos and Louis Galambos, *Medicine, Science and Merck.* Cambridge: Cambridge University Press, 2004, 145.

250   *Edward M. Scolnick on the FDA*

Edward M. Scolnick, Email to David W. Anstice, October 15, 2001. Bates Number MRK-ABW0004799, dida.library.ucsf.edu/tid/oxx10w10.

Edward M. Scolnick, Email to David W. Blois, Bonnie J. Goldmann et al, May 14, 1999. Bates Number MRK-ABH0015578, dida.library.ucsf.edu/tid/oxx05p10.

251   *COX-2 drugs and FDA coronary heart disease statistics*

David J Graham, David Campen, Rita Hui, Michele Spence, Craig Cheetham, Gerald Levy, Stanford Shoor and Wayne A Ray, "Risk of acute myocardial infarction and sudden cardiac death in patients treated with cyclo-oxygenase 2 selective and non-selective non-steroidal anti-inflammatory drugs: nested case-control study." *Lancet* 365 (2005): 475–81.

EPILOGUE

281   *Stephen Gillers on the settlement provisions*

Daniel Costello, "Vioxx Deal May Cause Pain," *Los Angeles Times,* November 15, 2007.

282   *Claimant participation in the Vioxx settlement*

Howard M. Erichson, "The Trouble with All-or-Nothing Settlements." *Kansas Law Review* 58 (2010): 979–1025.

See also:

Howard M. Erichson, "Public and Private Law Perspectives: Transcript of Professor Howard Erichson." *Southwestern University Law Review* 37 (2008): 665–669.

Howard M. Erichson and Benjamin C. Zipursky, "Consent versus Closure." *Cornell Law Review* 96 (2010): 265–321.

ADDITIONAL RESOURCES

Report of The Honorable John S. Martin, Jr. to the Special Committee of the Board of Directors of Merck & Co., Inc. Concerning the Conduct of Senior Management in the

Development and Marketing of Vioxx, September 5, 2006. www.merck.com/newsroom/vioxx/martin_report.html

Vioxx's potential cardiovascular risks

Francesca Catella-Lawson, Brendan McAdam, Briggs W. Morrison, Shiv Kapoor, Dean Kujubu, Lisa Antes, Kenneth C. Lasseter, Hui Quan, Barry J. Gertz and Garret A. Fitzgerald, "Effects of Specific Inhibition of Cyclooxygenase-2 on Sodium

Balance, Hemodynamics, and Vasoactive Eicosanoids." *The Journal of Pharmacology and Experimental Therapeutics* 289 (1999): 735–741

The VIGOR study

Claire Bombardier, Loren Laine, Alise Reicin, Deborah Shapiro, Ruben Burgos-Vargas, Barry Davis, Richard Day, Marcos Bosi Ferraz, Christopher J. Hawkey, Marc C. Hochberg, Tore K. Kvien and Thomas J. Schnitzer, "Comparison of upper gastrointestinal toxicity of rofecoxib and naproxen in patients with rheumatoid arthritis." *New England Journal of Medicine* 343 (2000): 1520–28.

Garret A. Fitzgerald and Carlo Patrono, "The Coxibs, Selective Inhibitors of Cyclooxygenase-2." *New England Journal of Medicine* 345 (2001): 433–442.

Questioning VIGOR

Debabrata Mukherjee, Steven E. Nissen and Eric J. Topol, "Risk of cardiovascular events associated with selective COX-2 inhibitors." *Journal of the American Medical Association* 286 (2001): 954–59.

Wayne A Ray, C Michael Stein, Kathi Hall, James R Daugherty and Marie R Griffin, "Non-steroidal anti-inflammatory drugs and risk of serious coronary heart disease: an observational cohort study." *Lancet* 359 (2002): 118–23.

Wayne A Ray, C Michael Stein, James R Daugherty, Kathi Hall, Patrick G Arbogast and Marie R Griffin, "COX-2 selective non-steroidal anti-inflammatory drugs and risk of serious coronary heart disease." *Lancet* 360 (2002): 1071–73.

Daniel H. Solomon, Robert J. Glynn, Raisa Levin, Jerry Avorn, "Nonsteroidal anti-inflammatory drug use and acute myocardial infarction." *Archives of Internal Medicine* 162 (2002): 1099–104.

Daniel H. Solomon, Sebastian Schneeweiss, Robert J. Glynn, Yuka Kiyota, Raisa Levin, Helen Mogun and Jerry Avorn, "Relationship Between Selective Cyclooxygenase-2 Inhibitors and Acute Myocardial Infarction in Older Adults." *Circulation* 109 (2004): 2068–2073.

Merck defends Vioxx

Marvin A. Konstam, Matthew R. Weir, Alise Reicin, Deborah Shapiro, Rhoda S. Sperling, Eliav Barr and Barry J. Gertz, "Cardiovascular thrombotic events in controlled, clinical trials of rofecoxib." *Circulation* 104 (2001): 2280–88.

Alise S. Reicin, Deborah Shapiro, Rhoda S. Sperling, Eliav Barr and Qinfen Yu, "Comparison of Cardiovascular Thrombotic Events in Patients with Osteoarthritis Treated with Rofecoxib Versus Nonselective Nonsteroidal Anti-inflammatory Drugs (Ibuprofen, Diclofenac, and Nabumetone)." *The American Journal of Cardiology* 89 (2002): 204–209.

S. A. Reines, G. A. Block, J. C. Morris, G. Liu, M. L. Nessly, C. R. Lines, PhD, B. A. Norman, C. C. Baranak, and on behalf of the Rofecoxib Protocol 091 Study Group. "Rofecoxib: no effect on Alzheimer's disease in a 1-year, randomized, blinded, controlled study." *Neurology* 62 (2004): 66–71.

Leon J. Thal, Steven H. Ferris, Louis Kirby, Gilbert A Block, Christopher R Lines, Eric Yuen, Christopher Assaid, Michael L Nessly, Barbara A Norman, Christine C Baranak and Scott A Reines on behalf of the Rofecoxib Protocol 078 study group, "Rofecoxib Protocol 078 Study Group: A randomized double-blind, study of rofecoxib in patients with mild cognitive impairment." *Neuropsychopharmacology* 30 (2005): 1204–1215.

Matthew R. Weir, Rhoda S. Sperling, Alise Reicin and Barry J. Gertz, "Selective COX-2 inhibition and cardiovascular effects: a review of the rofecoxib development program." *Am Heart J* 146 (2003): 591–604.

Response to the VIGOR study

Claire Bombardier, Loren Laine, Ruben Burgos-Vargas, Barry Davis, Richard Day, Marcos Bosi Ferraz, Christopher J. Hawkey, Marc C. Hochberg, Tore K. Kvien, Thomas J. Schnitzer and Arthur Weaver, "Response to Expression of Concern Regarding VIGOR Study." *New England Journal of Medicine* 354 (2006): 1196–1198.

Gregory D. Curfman, Stephen Morrissey and Jeffrey M. Drazen, "Expression of concern: Bombardier et al., "Comparison of Upper Gastrointestinal Toxicity of Rofecoxib and Naproxen in Patients with Rheumatoid Arthritis." *New England Journal of Medicine* 353 (2005): 2813–2814.

Gregory D. Curfman, Stephen Morrissey and Jeffrey M. Drazen, "Expression of Concern Reaffirmed." *New England Journal of Medicine* 354 (2006): 1193.

Alise Reicin and Deborah Shapiro, "Response to Expression of Concern Regarding VIGOR Study." *New England Journal of Medicine* 354 (2006): 1198–1199.

The APPROVe Study

Robert S. Bresalier and John A. Baron, "Adverse cardiovascular effects of rofecoxib." *New England Journal of Medicine* 355 (2006): 204–205.

Robert S. Bresalier, Robert S. Sandler, Hui Quan, James A. Bolognese, Bettina Oxenius, Kevin Horgan, Christopher Lines, Robert Riddell, Dion Morton, Angel Lanas, Marvin A. Konstam and John A. Baron, "Cardiovascular Events Associated with Rofecoxib in a Colorectal Adenoma Chemoprevention Trial." *New England Journal of Medicine* 352 (2005): 1092–1102.

"Correction to: Cardiovascular Events Associated with Rofecoxib in a Colorectal Adenoma Chemoprevention Trial." *New England Journal of Medicine* 355 (2006): 221.

How did this happen?

Curt D. Furberg, "Adverse cardiovascular effects of rofecoxib." *New England Journal of Medicine* 355 (2006): 204.

Steven E. Nissen, "Adverse cardiovascular effects of rofecoxib." *New England Journal of Medicine* 355 (2006): 203–204.

Joseph S. Ross, Kevin P. Hill, David S. Egilman and Harlan M. Krumholz, "Guest Authorship and Ghostwriting in Publications Related to Rofecoxib: A Case Study of Industry Documents From Rofecoxib Litigation." *Journal of American Medical Association* 299 (2008): 1800–1812.

Eric J. Topol, "Failing the public health—rofecoxib, Merck and the FDA." *New England Journal of Medicine* 351 (2004): 1707–09.

The continuing re-evaluation of Vioxx

American Heart Association. "Use of nonsteroidal antiinflammatory drugs: an update for clinicians: a scientific statement from the American Heart Association." *Circulation* 115 (2007): 1634–1642.

David J Graham, David Campen, Rita Hui, Michele Spence, Craig Cheetham, Gerald Levy, Stanford Shoor and Wayne A Ray, "Risk of acute myocardial infarction and sudden cardiac death in patients treated with cyclo-oxygenase 2 selective and non-selective non-steroidal anti-inflammatory drugs: nested case-control study." *Lancet* 365 (2005): 475–81.

Peter Jüni, Linda Nartey, Stephan Reichenbach, Rebekka Sterchi, Paul A Dieppe and Matthias Egger, "Risk of cardiovascular events and rofecoxib: cumulative meta-analysis." *Lancet* 364 (2004): 2021–29.

Bruce M. Psaty and Richard A. Kronmal, "Reporting Mortality Findings in Trials of Rofecoxib for Alzheimer Disease or Cognitive Impairment: A Case Study Based on Documents From Rofecoxib Litigation." *Journal of American Medical Association* 299 (2008): 1813–1817.

Joseph S. Ross, David Madigan, Kevin P. Hill, David S. Egilman, Yongfei Wang and Harlan M. Krumholz, "Pooled Analysis of Rofecoxib Placebo-Controlled Clinical Trial Data: Lessons for Post-market Pharmaceutical Safety Surveillance." *Archives of Internal Medicine* 169 (2009): 1976–1984

FDA evaluation of Vioxx's risks and benefits

Food and Drug Administration, Arthritis & Drug Safety and Risk Management Advisory Committee Briefing Package, February 16–18, 2005. www.fda.gov/ohrms/dockets/ac/05/briefing/2005-4090b1-01.htm

Shari L. Targum, Cardiovascular Safety Review, Rofecoxib, Consultation NDA 21-042, S-007, February 1, 2001. Bates Number MRKA05640001-0044, dida.library.ucsf.edu/tid/oxx02a10.

Maria Lourdes Villaba, Medical Officer Review, Vioxx, NDA 21-042 (capsules) and NDA 21-052 (oral solution), May 20, 1999. Bates Number MRK-PUBLIC0000156-0283, dida.library.ucsf.edu/tid/oxx17e10.

Maria Lourdes Villaba, Medical Officer Review, Vioxx, NDA 21-042 (capsules) and NDA 21-052 (oral solution) S 007 (Gastrointestinal Safety), March 30, 2001. Bates Number MRKEXH13470001-0007, dida.library.ucsf.edu/tid/oxx04d10.

Maria Lourdes Villaba, Memo to file re. Cardiovascular Data in Alzheimer's Studies, March 12, 2002. Bates Number MRKA02680001-0006, dida.library.ucsf.edu/tid/oxx01l10.

ABOUT THE AUTHOR

SNIGDHA PRAKASH HAS BEEN a print and broadcast journalist for almost twenty years. Most recently, she was a reporter for National Public Radio, from 1998 to 2007, where she documented several important chapters in Vioxx's history for NPR's flagship newsmagazines "All Things Considered" and "Morning Edition." In 2009, she was awarded the Gene Roberts Book Award by the Fund for Investigative Journalism. This is her first book.

ACKNOWLEDGMENTS

THE BOOK BEGAN AS a series of reports on the history of the pain-killer Vioxx that aired on NPR's news magazines in 2005 and 2006. I am grateful to Marcia Angell, Paul Armstrong, Lisa Bero, Catherine DeAngelis, Kay Dickerson, Curt Furberg, Steve Nissen, Drummond Rennie, David Rothman, and Eric Topol for their patient and insightful tutelage. I am also grateful to Bill Marimow, managing editor and later vice president of NPR News, for his editorial advice and backing.

I am grateful to the plaintiffs' lawyers in the Atlantic City trial for the helpfulness and (mostly) good-humored tolerance they extended to the intruder in their midst. The group consisted of Mark Lanier and his team—Jesse Alcorta, Cliff Atkinson, David Egilman, Meredith Gursky, Dara Hegar, Maura Kolb, Bob Leone, Rick Meadow and Juan Wilson; as well as Chris Seeger, David Buchanan, Jeff Grand and Moshe Horn of Seeger Weiss. I thank them also for the many professional courtesies they have extended since. I am humbled by Mary and Mike Humeston's decision to share the harrowing story of Mike's heart attack and of their struggles since, and I thank them for their trust.

Thanks also to Shelly Sanford for the many long hours she spent reconstructing the early history of the Vioxx lawsuits and the roles she and her law partner Carlene Lewis played. I am grateful for my brief and memorable acquaintance with Carlene Lewis, for Shelly Sanford's willingness to plumb the painful memories of her friend's death, and for the cooperation of Alene Rhodes and Greg Lewis.

Thanks also to Jerry Kristal of Weitz & Luxenberg for the Friday afternoon rides from Atlantic City to Philadelphia during the trial and for his unstinting and expert help throughout the writing process. Thanks to Ellen Relkin of Weitz & Luxenberg, who explained the workings of the Vioxx mass tort in New Jersey, and Deborah Savours, who assisted with related research. Thanks also to Andy Birchfield and Genie Pruett of Beasley, Allen, Crow, Methvin, Portis & Miles, for their gracious help over the years.

Thanks to David Graham, Harlan Krumholz, Wayne Ray and Alastair Wood for lending their expertise to this project. Howard Erichson and Carl Elliott read portions of this book, and I am grateful for their comments and encouragement.

Thanks to Sara Taber at the Bethesda Writer's Center for her support at a time when the book was literally a sentence long, and to fellow-students in Sara's writing workshops for their enthusiasm for the early chapters.

I am grateful to Howard Yoon for "seeing" what the book had become and shaping the book proposal, to Gail Ross for selling the book, and to the book's first editor, Don Fehr at Kaplan, for buying it. Thanks to Cullen Stanley at Janklow Nesbitt for her previous efforts on my behalf. Thanks also to Gail Ross and Howard Yoon for putting me in touch with Tom Shroder, who edited this book in its final stretch even as he wrote his own. I thank him for his generous and wise counsel. I only wish I'd met him sooner.

Thanks to the Fund for Investigative Journalism for the Gene Roberts Book Award and a generous grant.

Thanks to Dan Grosse and Vivian Cavalieri for hundreds of delicious meals, to Ariella Grosse for her interest in "Deathly Secrets," and to Julia French, Mary Lou Rife, Craig Sechler, Scott Swenson, Mary Jo Vrem, Judy Warner, Julie Waterman, Lisa Watson, Liz Wickhart and everyone else in the Friday-morning yoga class for cheering me on. Thanks to Deborah George, Jon Hamilton, Anne Hawke, Rachael Jones, Lynn Neary, Peter Overby, Marisa Penaloza, Kathleen Schalch, Tracy Wahl, and John Ydstie at NPR for providing succor when I needed it most. Thanks to Roslyn Brumfield for her fierce belief in the book and in me. I am grateful to Rosalie Begun for working her magic on a frozen shoulder and to Eric Shaw for working his on everything else.

Thanks to the crew at Broad Branch Market—Betty, Yobanni, John, Janie, Kyle, Rose, and Tracy—for supplying caffeine, baguettes, and good cheer. Thanks to the Modern Times Café for providing refuge and superb cappuccinos, and to Barbara Meade and Mark LaFramboise at Politics & Prose for support and encouragement. I am sorry Carla Cohen is not here to see the great bookstore she and Barbara built spawn yet another neighborhood author. Thank you, Carla.

There are two people without whom this book would not have been written, and to them I owe the deepest gratitude. Riki Schneyer taught me to listen for my own voice and to strive to trust it. I thank her for her stubborn perseverance and love over the years.

And, I have the great good fortune to be married to Jonathan Green, my best friend and staunchest ally. His deep kindness, razor-sharp wit and abiding love are as vital to me as the air I breathe. In so many ways, this book is as much his as it is mine.

Snigdha Prakash
March 2011

INDEX

DATE DUE

~~NOT RENEWABLE~~	
SEP 3 0 2011	
OCT 0 6 2011	
OCT 2 0 2011	
NOV 0 3 2011	
NOV 1 7 2011	
DEC 0 9 2011	
JAN 0 7 2012	
JAN 1 8 2012	
FEB 1 8 2012	
MAR 1 9 2012	
APR 1 0 2012	
29	

GAYLORD   PRINTED IN U.S.A.